Sexual Scripts

The Social
Construction of
Female Sexuality

Sexual Scripts

The Social Construction of Female Sexuality

Judith Long Laws
Cornell University

Pepper Schwartz
University of Washington

The Dryden Press
Hinsdale, Illinois

Excerpts on pages 58 and 66 are copyright © 1974 by Shere Hite excerpted from *Sexual Honesty by Women for Women,* published by Warner
Books, Inc.

Introduction, Chapters 2 and 4 were contributed by Judith Long Laws

Chapter 5 was contributed by Pepper Schwartz

Chapter 7 was co-authored by Judith Long Laws and Pepper Schwartz

Chapter 3 was contributed by Dr. Mary B. Parlee

Chapter 6 was contributed by Dr. Jennifer James

To Our Parents

Preface

The end of the sixties marked the most recent reincarnation of the feminist movement in America. One of its first targets was Freudian theory on female sexuality, according to which orgasm through coitus is the only mature form of female sexual experience. The feminist critique of Freudian theory focused on two distinct levels: the way women are controlled in sexual relationships and the power that researchers and theorists have in defining female sexuality. Another decisive challenge to the Freudian paradigm came at about the same time in the form of the influential study *Human Sexual Response*, published in 1966 and authored by Masters and Johnson. It is the coincidence of research such as Masters and Johnson's and the growth of the contemporary feminist movement that has inspired the present book.

Human Sexual Response was important in two ways: it provided some very important information about the subject matter of female sexuality, and it represented a methodological breakthrough in sex research. By bringing sexual behavior into the laboratory for study, Masters and Johnson set a new standard for evidence in theories about sex. This was a departure from the research tradition that until that time had relied only on uncorroborated reports of past events obtained from sources such as interviews or questionnaires. In the laboratory, stimulation could be controlled and responses measured objectively; findings could be replicated. Though findings based on traditional clinical methodology are still reported in the sex research literature, the unsupported inferences and grand theories of a nonempirical nature are on the wane. Masters and Johnson moved sex research out of the armchair and into the laboratory.

Masters and Johnson's findings about the female orgasm have had particular impact. Their research established the importance of the clitoris for orgasm and thus irreversibly undermined the Freudian doctrine of the vaginal orgasm. The implications of this finding for power relationships between the sexes were immediately recognized by feminists. A first wave of feminist scholarship produced many important critiques of Freudian and nonempirical theories about sexuality. Writers like Friedan, Greer, Millett, Seaman, and Shelley combined analysis with personal testimony. They put sexuality into the context of women's lives. However, feminist perspectives, however, have had little impact on the research community.

Like Kinsey before them, Masters and Johnson were pioneers in the study of sexual *behavior.* Kinsey's (1953) work is still regarded as the standard, and his findings continue to be used as a yardstick to measure change. However, with the emphasis on measuring sexual behavior, the study of its *meanings* for the actor had been neglected. This absence of a social perspective has been a longstanding problem in sex research. We have accumulated a good deal of data about who does what, with whom, where, and when. But we still know very little about the ways in which people learn to be sexual and how their sexuality reflects this learning.

The most important alternative approach to sex research began with the work of Gagnon and Simon (1973) who introduced the notion of *sexual scripts.* In a series of articles, they challenged Freudian theory and opposed the reduction of sexuality to biological explanations. They argued that we are like actors with parts in scripts, which exist for sexual life just as they do for other areas of life. Rehearsal precedes performance, and others may coach us in our parts, but it is the scripts that give us preparation for situations we have not yet encountered. We expect our lives to follow certain scripts, and we make an effort to follow them, too. We also try to make our experiences accord with these scripts, sometimes even reinterpreting reality so as to make it fit them better.

These scripts are usually recognizable to us: "the good mother and wife," the "first date," or "the happy marriage." There are gaps, of course; the "first night" is not fully scripted, nor are many other areas. Nonetheless, we have a general idea of what is supposed to happen. There are, on the other hand, situations that are totally unscripted or scripted only within subcultures. How does a woman proposition a woman? No woman learns this script in the course of her early socialization in our society. It is unthinkable and therefore untaught. It is only with entry into the homosexual community that some such scripts become available. Even then, it takes a long time to learn them and some—like that for the management of a same-sex household—may still be unwritten and left up to individual innovation.

Gagnon and Simon's social perspective is a useful contribution to the tradition of sex research we have been discussing. Yet insofar as it fails to transcend the limitations of traditional thinking about women, it is inadequate. A feminist perspective is needed.

As feminist analysis of female sexuality continues to develop, the masculine biases in sex research become more apparent. Gross stereotyping, which is more the product of cultural than scientific training, is evident even in the professional literature. The selectivity of those who work and write in this area is striking. Newton (1955) has observed that aspects of female sexuality in which men have direct involvement are studied and those which do not involve men are not. The degree and kind of emphasis given to female sexuality in most sourcebooks is also revealing: women are still too often treated in footnotes or as an afterthought to the main focus.

In this book, women are the focus. We examine the social construction of female sexuality from a feminist perspective. We develop a distinctive approach to female sexuality. Our view of human sexuality is developmental and dynamic rather than static. Change is normal, and choice has a part in change. Our sexual self-knowledge is patterned by sexual scripts, but we can develop our own personal attitudes and concepts which differ from the traditionally approved ones. Because of this process, female sexuality can never be definitively described. We continually learn more about the possibilities in female sexuality, but we will never pin down its "nature." Female sexuality will always be relative to some set of scripts, and these change over time. At present we live in a pluralistic sexual world; there are a number of available sexual scripts, and individuals can examine and choose among them.

In this book, each selection is self-contained and does not depend on the others. Yet a convergence in perspective is apparent. Each author answers these questions: What are the available social scripts? How are they enforced? What competing constructions exist? What research does not exist and why? These questions underlie the five areas examined in the book: (1) the nature of *sexual identity* and its development in the life cycle; (2) the *biological processes* of women and their impact on female functioning; (3) the arena and expectations for *sexual interaction;* (4) *life-styles—* marriage and its alternatives; and (5) *sexual offenses* and *institutional responses* to female sexuality.

These areas are central to women's lives. There are many additional topics that might be considered. But it is not our aim to be encyclopedic. We have designed this book to be scholarly, but not weighted down with endless citations and footnotes. Each author has organized a broad range of material around a limited focus. The popular literature provides a context, but not the content, for the book. In many places research is lacking and we can only point out directions for future research. Nevertheless, each selection is grounded in the research literature. In taking a critical stance toward the existing research, we hope to provoke imaginative new inquiry on the part of our readers, whether they be well versed in the popular feminist literature and seeking to discover what research can tell us or professionals who, though familiar with the research literature, will be confronting questions they have never before asked.

In short, we want to bridge the separation between the popular interest in sexual behavior, the research literature, and feminist concerns. Our book is intended as a forum for the discussion of female sexuality within this perspective. We want to understand the sexual scripts that have guided our lives, to present the "lost" data that these scripts did not allow us to see, and to stimulate new questions. At the close, we will engage in creative speculation about sexual options and scripts for the future.

References

Friedan, B. (1963). The Feminine Mystique. New York: Dell.

Gagnon, J., and W. Simon (1973). Sexual Conduct: The Social Sources of Human Sexuality. Chicago: Aldine.

Greer, G. (1970). The Female Eunuch. New York: McGraw-Hill.

Kinsey, A.C., et al. (1953). Sexual Behavior in the Human Female. Philadelphia: Saunders.

Masters, W., and V. Johnson (1966). Human Sexual Response. Boston: Little, Brown.

Millett, K. (1970). Sexual Politics. Garden City, N.Y.: Doubleday.

Newton, N. (1955). Maternal Emotions. New York: Harper & Row.

Seaman, B. (1972). Free and Female: The Sex Life of the Contemporary Woman. New York: Coward, McCann, and Geoghegan.

Shelley, M. (1970). Notes of a Radical Lesbian. *In* Sisterhood Is Powerful. R. Morgan, ed. New York: Vintage Books.

Contents

Sexual Scripts

The Social Construction of Female Sexuality

Chapter One

Introduction

Now more than ever the world of human sexuality is the subject of many competing definitions. Different institutions in society—the family, the law, and the church—have traditionally held views of sex that fit their own purposes. The divergence in these views is even more apparent in the present than it was in the past. The scientific domain of sex research is based upon a few identifiable paradigms which bear little resemblance to most people's experience: a Freudian paradigm, a social accounting model, and a behavior-modification paradigm.

Attitudes toward sex vary as well. Many Americans are comparatively traditional in their views on sex. Mothers and daughters have different sexual standards; women and men have different standards. Individuals located in different economic strata and ethnic traditions accept different versions of sexual reality. Strong taboos against talking about sexuality still exist, while at the same time the media portray a wide range of sexual practices. Most young people feel that their sex education has been inadequate, even though they are increasingly sexually experienced. Many individuals experience radical redefinitions of sexual identity in the course of their sexual history, while for others sexual options appear fixed. These confusing contradictions exist at the same moment in time but, in a very real sense, in different worlds.

Female sexuality has been defined in a number of ways. In this book we attempt no absolute definition, but our focus does include many aspects of female sexuality which other accounts omit. We include the biological substratum of female sexuality and take a closer look at physiological functioning than do many others. When we examine the micro-events of female sexuality, however, we do not divorce them from the way women experience them. Female experience is central to female sexuality, in our view. The personal side of that experience forms sexual identity. The social side is formed, in large part, by sexual scripts and by the individual's sexual experience with others. *By sexual scripts we mean a repertoire of acts and statuses that are recognized by a social group, together with the rules, expectations, and sanctions governing these acts and statuses.* In this book we identify the dominant sexual script that defines women's sexuality in our society, and we also examine variant scripts that are espoused by subgroups in society. Although we take a close look at all of these influences on female sexuality, we doubt that we have mapped all of its dimensions or adequately estimated its potential. We are limited by the forms of existing knowledge and research.

One of our purposes here is to report the present state of knowledge concerning female sexuality. Our sources include medical reports, recent and classic research findings in sociology and psychology, and feminist writings. These focus on different aspects and represent widely divergent views of female sexuality, a lack of agreement characteristic among differing fields of investigation and interest.

The Social Construction of Female Sexuality

What we consider knowledge is rooted in our way of seeing the world. When we accept a given item as known, we are also accepting the validity of many rules for establishing the reality or truth of something that exists outside ourselves. Ordinarily we are unaware of these rules, or the particular "world" to which they belong. And we generally do not think about the means by which these worlds become established and can be challenged and overturned.

The dissection of such social constructions—definitions of reality under which humans operate—is one purpose of this analysis. A second purpose is to analyze the various current constructions of female sexuality and relate them to the social worlds in which they are anchored. Social facts are no more context-free than they are value-free, and the same holds true for knowledge based on social facts. Social facts have reality, just like physical facts; but social facts are created through human agency. Social facts also have explanations, just like physical facts, and in both instances these explanations are part of the social construction of reality.

When we are examining the explanation of the nuclear family, social forces may be more apparent to us than they are in the explanation of rain. In analyzing the "functions" the family performs for the society— regularizing inheritance, channeling sexuality, and providing new citizens for the state—it is not difficult to see the family as an instrumentality, as being "for" something. We view rain in a similar way. While in many cultures rain may appear as a kind of reality that "just is" and cannot be influenced, we have already begun to tamper with the seeming naturalness and immutability of the "natural fact" of rain: we routinely seed clouds and "make" rain. Further thought reminds us that in other cultures rain has different explanations, which we might reject as "primitive" and unscientific, while members of those cultures equally reject our explanation.

Clearly, our explanations are not only created by human agency but modifiable in the same way. If we were to discover that rain, like ozone, is not the inexhaustible natural resource we had thought it to be but is in fact in danger of extinction, we would develop new explanations of it and attitudes toward it. And the "knowledge" about rain of the next generation would then differ from that with which we grew up. Thus to us it seems a false dichotomy to regard the social as artificial and the physical as natural or real. To the extent that we relate to social or physical events in terms of meanings for us—for example, what to do about them—we are acting on the basis of social constructions, of knowledge received through socialization.

This false dichotomy in thinking can be particularly misleading in the analysis of human sexuality. Biological events, or "facts," do not have a direct effect on sexual experience in humans. With infrahuman species researchers have been able to demonstrate rather direct connections between hormones and behavior, but for humans sexual behavior is mediated by meanings. Willingness to engage in coitus has repeatedly been shown, for women, to be a function of the state of the social relationship between the individual and her potential partner. Even the effect of nonsocial or micro-events in the female sexual cycle (like menstruation) depends on social meanings that are attached to them. Menstruation may be dreaded every month by the woman who views it in terms of discomfort, the possibility of staining, or the disruption of her normal sexual relationship. Menstruation may be positively evaluated by the woman who views it as proof of her female potency, or evidence that she has avoided conception in the past month. The very occurrence of events such as menstruation, orgasm, and false pregnancy can be determined by psychological and cultural factors.

The meanings that sexual events and behaviors have for an individual woman are determined by her social position and cultural indoctrination. Her culture (or subculture) thus equips her with ways of understanding and judging many aspects of sexuality, from the functions of her body to morals. These ways of making sense of her experiences are embedded in a world view which is accepted as reality by all those around her and in the sexual scripts that are a part of the world view.

Many of the insights into the nature of social reality in the discussion to follow are derived from the work of Berger and Luckmann (1966). They describe the human origin of social realities very simply as a process by which individuals who repeatedly confront a task or situation relevant to their lives develop habitual ways of dealing with it. When people recognize a situation as one that recurs, they have identified a type. A situation, once typified in this way, may lead to the development of roles, or functions which cooperating partners perform in connection with the task involved. For example, suppose Friday is payday, and a group of regulars assembles at a neighborhood bar every Friday night. One of them always needs help getting home when the bar closes. Once the group has developed a way of telling when their drunk has had enough, as well as routines for separating him from his stool and delivering him home, the situation already resembles a mini–social structure. The routines are capable of being generalized beyond the first two partners, and thus others can solve the problem in the same way.

Though we could call this arrangement a form of social structure, this does not imply that such a social form will last forever, or even tell us how long it will survive. At this rudimentary stage of social organization, social routines such as the management of a drunken buddy are heuristic. Routinization is a small step away from the establishment of a problem-solving process in which all possibilities are considered. A routine is a problem solution that is available and on call. Over time and with repeated usage, other elements of institutionalization develop. When we speak of full-fledged social constructions, we imply all the apparatus of institutionalization: consensual recognition of the realness and rightness of the constructed reality, plus socialization processes by which people acquire this definition of reality.

Just as a routine is one step removed from spontaneous problem-solving, the establishment of roles is one step away from a way of relating to a total person. A role focuses attention on some highlighted function or attribute of the person. To a degree, once roles are established, all persons who can fulfill the role expectations are interchangeable. They can be identified according to their functions in the division of labor, rather than as total persons. If they perform these functions effectively, the need for communication, accommodation, and negotiation is reduced.

The institutionalization of interaction poses a dilemma for intimate relationships which is particularly apparent in the case of sexual love. In our society, romantic love is viewed neither as an aberration nor a frivolous interlude, but as the basis for some of the most solemnly regarded functions of the society: marriage and family formation. The self is experienced as the most vividly real aspect of reality (Berger and Luckmann), and being in love involves a desire to know and appreciate another as keenly as one appreciates oneself. Similarly, in love the individual seeks to disclose herself—or her own subjective reality—fully. Love implies a way of relating that is different from the usual role-governed way. The feeling tone is intense, and the interaction is absorbing and time consuming. Inevitably, however, as lovers develop commitment, they enlarge their social sphere and are confronted with the task of presenting themselves as a pair (i.e., two persons) or a couple (one unit) and making the bond between them intelligible to others. Whatever their private definition of that bond, most will fall back on the scripts for marital roles. As they move through a socially recognized sequence of statuses—pinned, engaged, married—conforming to these roles becomes less optional and more obligatory.

Much has been written about the feelings of women who have become submerged in marital and familial roles, and we will examine these dilemmas in more detail in Chapter 5. In many personal relationships, the transition to routinized interaction in terms of roles is experienced as a dilemma. Sometimes individuals seek to transcend the sexual scripts, and sometimes they merely adjust their experience to fit them, as do lovers, who move from the stages of courtship into marriage and the institutionalized statuses of wife and husband. The dialectical relationship between personal realities and social constructions is a recurring focus in this book. Often the individual woman brings her personal reality into line with the social construction. Sometimes, however, the personal reality becomes a basis for attacking or rejecting the social construction.

Sexual Scripts as Social Institutions

Social arrangements which have survived over time and become standard are called institutions. It is easy to forget that institutions have a history: they arise under specific material and historical conditions—a famine, a war, a given technology—to which they are exactly the kind of heuristic solutions we have been discussing. They are products of human agencies, not impersonal forces. Once they are reified, we lose sight of their origins and the related possibility that they may change. We also forget that responses to social problems can vary and carelessly slip into thinking that the form in which we observe a social institution is its only, its normal, or its natural form. Thus in scholarly writing in the U.S., as in the popular media, the assumption is often made that the nuclear family, with father as breadwinner and children and wife as economic dependents, is the normal and best form of family life. All others are suspect. And if problems appear to be associated with aspects of family life, the solution proposed is often to reinforce the dominant family form, rather than seeking new forms which might be more effective.

Highly institutionalized sectors of a society such as the family, the military, or the economy do have great complexity. They provide formulas for routine action, scripts for the actors, backed up by ideology which stresses their *rightness* as much as their efficiency. They include means for educating people not only into these routines, or scripts, but into the system and thus affect the individual's self-concept and personal identity. And they include language, which externalizes subjective reality and, to the extent that it is used and shared, reinforces a *social* reality. By its very nature, institutionalization exercises social control, not only over behavior but over feelings, reducing the potential variability in both by means of positive channeling and reward far more than by the use of negative sanctions.

In this book we are arguing that not only routines and structures but also meanings can be institutionalized and exhibit the features just discussed. Social constructions are such institutionalized meaning structures. In applying the idea of social construction to the area of sexuality, we are saying that sexuality is scripted. Sexual scripting governs both sexual behavior and sexual identity. A social construction which is fully developed includes not only the routines and the mechanisms for educating, or socializing, newcomers into the system, but also means for maintaining the definition of reality on which it is based and the subjective loyalty of individuals. A community and a language by which the community reaffirms its dominant reality and discredits competing social constructions are the two basic mechanisms that function to maintain the subjective reality of a social construction. Contact with both the community and its language must be consistent (Berger and Luckmann, 1966: 117, 127; see also Chapter 3). Above all, there must be face to face contact which repeatedly affirms the desired identity of individuals within the context of the social construction in order for the subjective reality to be maintained. Moreover, competing constructions, even the awareness of them, must be kept at the periphery of each individual's life and identity. As we examine sexual scripts, we will see that alternative scripts are denigrated or denied. This has the function of maintaining the dominance of the dominant or institutionalized script and preventing others from appearing as options.

If we think about the prototypical situation of the homemaker living in a single-family dwelling in a suburb, it is easy to see some of the mechanisms which help reinforce the social construction of traditional marital roles and insulate the woman against alternative constructions. Physical isolation is one factor. The social homogeneity of most suburbs makes it improbable that the homemaker will be exposed to alternative sexual life-styles frequently or in depth. She is isolated from women whose occupation is a primary component of their identity. Indeed, many have claimed that the housewife is cut off from contact with *any* other adults. Her competences in tasks other than homemaking wither away—or at least her confidence in them does. Her lover, the person who most validated her individual attributes before marriage, has now become her husband. His stake in her attributes as *wife, mother, and housekeeper* now serves to further reinforce these traditional roles. Interactions with neighbors also take the sexual life-style of monogamous marriage as given, so even where its rules are circumvented, they are not challenged.*

Emergence of Social Constructions

When we look at social arrangements in small scale or as new inventions, it is easy to see that they involve processes of reciprocal accommodation and negotiations. Indeed, in these situations individuals make more frequent attempts to disclose their own subjective reality and grasp each other's than when social institutions are well developed. At this stage of preinstitutionalization, the routines that two partners work out are fluid and flexible. They are heuristic (Berger and Luckmann, 1966: Chapter 2). They are adopted because they seem to work, and changing them requires no more than setting them up did: merely communication between the partners.

When the partners seek to extend their social system, however, whether by including more contemporaries or by bringing in a new generation, much of the fluidity is lost. A new person who is to take part in the system must be taught the routines the partners have worked out. Rules must be made explicit. The system becomes frozen in the explanations of it, and the newcomers perceive its features as absolutes—"the way things are." The social structure they have inherited is "opaque" (Berger and Luckmann, 1966: 55). The ways in which it was constructed are invisible to them, as are the elements which compose it; and so they do not see the possibilities for combining these elements in different ways.

As the goldfish is unaware that its medium is water and without conscious knowledge of its characteristics, so human individuals are unconscious of the existence and characteristics of the social environment. Although social arrangements are invented with conscious intent, that intent is neither perceived nor questioned by those who inherit them. Although they are designed as instrumentalities, they are accepted as ends in themselves, rather than as means to ends.

---

*Nevertheless, our society does not fit the simple model proposed by Berger and Luckmann. It is a pluralistic society, in which multiple options exist and vie for plausibility. Berger and Luckmann concede that the "problem of identity" can arise only where there are options, not where a dominant social construction remains unchallenged. With respect to sexuality, the "problem of identity" is of particular interest to us throughout this book.

Subjective Reality and Socialization

There is only one "reality" for the individual (Berger and Luckmann, 1966: 124). It is maintained by the kinds of social arrangements discussed above and by a developing personal identity which is congruent with those social constructions. We have discussed the ways in which social constructions develop and crystallize to the point of becoming the focus of socialization for the young. Now we would like to look at the other side of the transaction: the development and shaping of subjective reality, the individual's personal construction of reality.

For each of us, the social world we are born into has the experienced characteristic of utter and sole reality. To the young child for example, the family is the world. His or her mother is not simply *a* mother (i.e., one of many; one of a class); she is Mother (Berger and Luckmann, 1966: 124). The routines and arrangements of the world we are born into are nonproblematic: they require no explanation, and they are neither challenged nor doubted. Not only is this suspension of doubt handy for the society, it simplifies daily life for the individual. Of course, any challenge to the reality of the dominant social constructions immediately complicates life for the individual and for the society. But various mechanisms are mobilized by society to maintain the subjective plausibility of the dominant reality.

Socialization is the group of processes by which subjective realities and social constructions are brought into congruence. Though socialization continues throughout the life cycle, it is *primary socialization* to which we must ascribe the greatest impact (Berger and Luckmann, 1966: Chapter 3). Through socialization, social constructions are internalized, and as experience is filtered and understood through meaningful symbols, the kernel of individual identity is formed.

The "absoluteness" of subjective reality resulting from primary socialization appears to be a function of two factors: the cognitive immaturity of the young child and the affective quality of the teaching and learning that take place at this stage of development. Socialization by parents begins in infancy. Within the family, in the preschool years, the young child learns many "facts of life": about femaleness, maleness, nudity, modesty, the physical expression of affection, bodily functions, and the bodily appearance of adults and children, to mention a few. Note that at this stage of development the child does not have the kind of cognitive framework that includes notions like "fact" or "knowledge"; rather, what is learned at this stage is, for the child, reality, pure and simple.

These socializing agents (most often parents) control important outcomes for the child; the child's reliance on them in this respect is termed *effect dependence*. They also determine what reality the child is exposed to and what conceptual tools he or she has for solving problems; from the viewpoint of the child, this is *information dependence*. Both effect dependence and information dependence contribute to the power of the socializing agents and the probability of internalization (Jones and Gerard, 1967). Relative to the agents of primary socialization, those involved in subsequent socialization (teachers, media) have less power, and less monopolistic power, simply because the child is no longer so completely dependent on them.

The other factor in the forcefulness of primary socialization is the *emotional investment* of the elders in the child and in what they are teaching the child. This affective quality of primary socialization is not to be found in subsequent socialization, including formal education. The latter is deliberately affect-free, "objective," and impersonal. The reality claimed by such learning is "fugitive" and more easily bracketed (Berger and Luckmann, 1966: 131). College students, for example, read Freud and learn to think of the nuclear family in terms of incest taboo and oedipal conflicts. When they are spending Christmas vacation with their own families, however, they are more likely to be acting on the original reality of their family learned through primary socialization than upon Freud's. They have bracketed or compartmentalized the Freudian view, leaving it behind in the classroom.

Identity and Sexual Identity

One of the earliest attributes individuals identify in themselves is that of femaleness or maleness. Gender identity, as this is called, appears to crystallize at about age two to two and a half and is considered to be irreversible (see Stoller, 1968; and Green and Money, 1969). Traditional sexual scripts specify much "feminine" sex role behavior that "goes with" basic femaleness. Yet the individual can deviate from these scripts without seriously questioning her gender identity. Gender identity thus seems to illustrate the potency of primary socialization. *What is internalized through primary socialization retains much of its subjective reality, even when later learning overlays and contradicts it.* Most gay persons retain their primary gender identity even when they depart from the heterosexual script in their sexual preferences and behavior at a later age.

Sexual identity is built upon the foundation of gender identity. The basic mechanism is the same for the construction of all identity: young children learn to use verbal labels for themselves and their behavior, as well as for others and their behavior (Long, 1969). These labels come to have the same meaning for the learners as they do for the "old hands." Social constructions thus embodied in the language shared within a group come to be embedded in the foundation of individual identity by means of language. Gender identity is a neat illustration of this: our system of labels recognizes only male and female, no "third sex," no androgynous orientation, no bisexuality, no mixed cases. Consequently, gender identity appears (to researchers from our culture) to occur in two dichotomous forms: female and male.

It is perhaps not surprising that the first component of sexual identity rests upon sex role categories, which constitute a basic division in society. The female and male sex role scripts, to be sure, contain many elements which are not sexual. Female sex role scripts might be thought of as a collection of prescriptions for femininity—including, for example, the expectation that women shall be passive rather than aggressive, reactive rather than agentic. Such prescriptions, of course, carry over into the realm of sexual behavior. Identity is formed through the individual's perceiving herself in roles and recognizing the continuity of her behavior in those roles across situations and time (Berger and Luckmann, 1966: 121 ff.). In other words, the individual observes her own behavior and judges it, as she does the behavior of others. In making such judgments, of course, she uses scripts provided by society. The meanings of behaviors and the judgments that attach to them are part of these scripts. Identity arises through self-consciousness: roles permit us to see others as types, and in fact, to see ourselves in the same way.

The evolution of sexual identity thus involves the individual's attempt to match her own experience with the available sexual scripts. She learns not only the language that is applied to sexual feelings and events, but also society's expectations for a person of her age and sex. She learns the reciprocal behaviors, attitudes, and demeanors expected of someone of the "opposite" sex, as well. In this way she becomes prepared to enact the sexual scripts which are acceptable in her culture.

The problem of transition between sexual scripts has not been examined until now. In a sense there is a script for each stage of the sexual life cycle described in Chapter 2. In addition, the sequence of stages is scripted, and the transitions are scripted, within the dominant script. It is not apparent to most individuals, however, that there are alternative scripts at each stage. Our sexual socialization makes areas outside the spotlight *appear* unscripted. This appearance functions to maintain adherence to the dominant script. Yet it is a fact of the pluralistic sexual world we inhabit today that many individuals will be making unscripted transitions in the course of their sexual histories. To find, experience, and articulate sexual options outside the dominant script is more costly and involves more risk than to follow the dominant script.

The match between personal experience and social constructions or scripts is never perfect. Many areas of experience remain unscripted, and there is neither widespread comprehension of these nor a common language to facilitate comprehension. Many individuals find the accepted sexual scripts adequate guidelines for making sense of their own experience, and thus form coherent sexual identities essentially in line with the scripts. For others, available scripts do not fit their experience. The development of sexual identity is for these individuals more problematic. The social nature of constructed reality makes it extremely difficult for the individual to achieve and maintain identity in social isolation. Communities where these alternative sexual life-styles are sustained are often sought out or created by such individuals. These communities facilitate *resocialization*—a process which matches primary socialization in intensity and includes mechanisms for displacing or discrediting the reality of the dominant sexual script. Accounts of ''coming out,'' publicly indicating homosexuality, particularly through transvestism, show that a powerful process of personal change and social influence lies behind assuming a gay identity and joining the gay community. The emergence of the idea of the gay community is a recent enough phenomenon that the memoirs of gay individuals record a terrible struggle to make sense of and to validate sexual feelings at variance with the heterosexual script (Miller, 1971; Johnston, 1973; and Millett, 1974).

The sexual identity that deviates from the dominant script suffers from an absence of validation as well as from invalidation, or negative sanctions imposed by those who assume roles in the dominant script. There is no standard language to describe or express experiences and identities which are not socially recognized. Consequently, it is difficult for individuals to communicate about such phenomena. But without such communication, the validation of these experiences by others is impossible, and their reality, for lack of verbal recognition, becomes shaky (Berger and Luckmann, 1966: 141).

There is a nightmarish quality about having an identity which is not socially validated. This appears to be true whether what is not validated is a major component of sexual identity like sexual orientation or a small item of behavior. The history of masturbation is an example. For generations, the existence of masturbation was seldom acknowledged. Those who engaged in this unscripted behavior felt guilty and imagined dire consequences. The social construction of masturbation that developed was entirely negative: it was defined as a sin and its potential dire consequences—if not in this life, then in the hereafter—were thus confirmed.

More recently, social constructions have developed which define masturbation as normal and innocuous—for males. Females are omitted from these constructions, and by default female masturbation remains, for many people, nonexistent or unacceptable. In this area, as with others, the feminist movement has attempted to create new social constructions. It has promoted the acceptability of female masturbation as an inherent aspect of women's right to control their bodies, to enjoy sexual satisfaction, and to freedom of choice. These constructions, however, are not universally accepted. In the population at large, female masturbation is still linked with constructions according to which masturbation is believed to make women ''unfit'' for heterosexual coitus or is considered disloyal to a male partner (Schaefer, 1973). In other words, female masturbation is incongruent with the dominant sexual script for women: women are heterosexual/monogamous/married—permanently.

While we have emphasized the pluralistic nature of the contemporary American sexual climate, it is important to note that not every woman is equally aware of the existence of a variety of sexual life-styles. The individual's cognizance of divergent life-styles is a function of her location in the social structure. While some know about the gay community, others do not. Some are convinced that humankind is inherently bisexual, while others are sure that there are only two possible sexual roles—those modeled after Adam and Eve. By the nature of the social construction of reality, the received reality is the only reality; hence, what is different is not merely lacking in validity, but is hard to imagine—unthinkable. If the pattern set before us is reality, then deviation appears to be an aberration counter to reality, or ''crazy.'' In Chapter 5 we will discuss the dilemma of the individual whose experience does not fit a script.

The "Problem" of Sexual Identity

The problem of identity is, however, relevant to many people in a pluralistic society. Although some persons follow the sexual scripts provided, the achievement of masculinity and femininity is not an automatic process like skeletal growth. It is not a maturational process, but a social one. Even the majority, for whom inner reality and social reality are in agreement, sooner or later encounter claims for the validity of alternative scripts. Any challenge to the accepted social construction of reality presents a problem. Even when the individual conforms to the dominant sexual script, awareness of alternatives brings awareness of choice. And where choice is present, the automatic and unquestioned acceptance of social constructions is disrupted. Hence for all individuals, not just those who are following variant sexual scripts, achievement of sexual identity is problematic. In many cases, the subjective reality of the dominant scripts (with the force of primary socialization behind it) remains unshaken. Through education and hearsay, individuals learn of other sexual life-styles, but unless these have personal relevance they will not be adopted.

Constructions of reality are not only distributed differently over the social structure but have also varied substantially over time (as the example of masturbation demonstrates). Female sexual identity is problematic for an additional reason. Living in contemporary America, we are heirs to a number of different social constructions of female sexuality, which have been dominant in different periods. Virtually all of these have been promulgated by men rather than women, and it is only in our own time that women have begun to define their own sexuality. Some of these new constructions differ radically from the traditional ones. Thus women are confronted with choice between old and new, and between male-perspective and feminist social constructions of female sexuality.

Constructions of Female Sexuality

The contemporary social climate in America offers a great number of simultaneous constructions of female sexuality which are by no means consistent with each other. The double standard that is discussed in Chapter 4 appears to be a relic of Victorian morality, which provided dichotomized constructions of the Good Woman (wife) and the Bad Woman (whore). What made Good Women good was a set of moral virtues which included the absence of sexual feeling. In this construction the Bad Woman was aberrant, for she appeared to like, seek, and appreciate sex. The Good Woman of Victorian times was as appalled to detect sexual feelings in herself as the heterosexual woman of today is when she feels attraction to other women. From the feminist perspective, the double standard reflects the differential between the sexes in power and privilege which is found in all sectors of social life. Under the double standard, the sexual scope permitted men is broader, and the sanctions against their sexuality fewer.

Social constructions of pre-Victorian eras, for example, the Restoration and Elizabethan periods, portrayed appetitive and lusty women, without embodying a double standard. These social constructions are not, however, part of the American heritage.

The Judeo-Christian cultural tradition has contained, since the accounts in Genesis, two social constructions of womankind, as exemplified by Eve on the one hand and the Virgin Mary on the other. Within the patristic tradition of a celibate male clergy, these two constructions were fostered in the history of Catholicism and have been little altered by Protestantism. Sexuality is part of each of these constructions and appears in quite a different light in each. Sexuality as exemplified by Eve is a constant temptation to man, which must be distanced and disdained. Carnality has no part in man's "better" nature, which yearns for union with God. In fact, according to tradition, it was Eve's intervention that ruptured the harmonious relationship between man and God and caused the expulsion of humankind from paradise. Paradise can only be regained because of the witness of Jesus, the faultless man of virgin birth.

The Christian tradition's other image of the female is the Virgin Mary, also known as the Mother of God. She is holy precisely because she is sexless. Totally free of the taint of carnality, she herself was conceived without coitus (Daly, 1973: 82) and remains virginal in perpetuity. The sexual construction we know as the Virgin Mary is instrumental to *men's* well-being in two ways: first, she was the medium for the birth of Jesus, the redeemer; and second, she has served as an efficacious mediator between sinful man and forgiving God through the centuries of the Christian tradition. She also serves as a model for Catholic women, who are approved insofar as they are self-effacing, devoted to others' service, and absent from the economic and political spheres (Daly, 1973: 76–77).

In neither of these traditional constructions does female sexuality appear in a positive light. In Eve, female carnality is held responsible for bad outcomes for men. In Mary, the absence of female carnality is held to have good outcomes for men. Outcomes *for women* do not appear in the calculus. Present-day attitudes appear to inherit much from these constructions, which represent men's fantasies about the character and sexuality of women, with very little input from women. In theology, as in the study of sexuality, new perspectives are now being contributed by women (Daly, 1973).

Perhaps the most influential social construction (or paradigm) of female sexuality in our time is the Freudian. While in many ways Freud was radical, as in postulating infantile sexuality and studying the unconscious, the study of women was neither a major interest of Freud's nor his best work. Yet so powerful has Freud's impact been that the thinking of succeeding generations embodies his basic assumptions. Freud constructed a theory of female sexuality and a parallel theory of female personality which are based upon stigma. In Freud's view, women are mutilated, and in an area, the genitalia, in which men are particularly narcissistic. Shame, pain, and even horror are the feelings Freud associated with the female genitalia and the normal processes involving them: menstruation, intercourse, and birth. These are, of course, Freud's reactions, not those of women. It is easy to see these images as a male projection. Until recently, however, the validity of Freud's constructions on female sexuality went largely unquestioned. Consequently, Freudian psychology has exercised powerful and often destructive control over the personal experiences of generations of women.

Freud is responsible for the social construction that defined adequate female sexuality (and personality) in terms of vaginal orgasm during coitus. Other forms of sexual pleasure, according to this construction, *detracted* from adequate femininity. In the Freudian view, the "true woman" experienced orgasm only through penile stimulation of the vagina; the woman who experienced orgasm through clitoral stimulation was "immature" and possibly "masculine"—very powerful negative judgments. Moreover, when a woman did not experience orgasm through penile penetration, she was a "failure."

For generations after Freud, women found that both their husbands and their therapists were sure to reinforce the "rightness" of the Freudian social construction and the "wrongness" of their own subjective reality . The social construction was essentially a projection of male psychology— the still prevalent assumption that the same activities which produce male climax simultaneously and necessarily produce female orgasm (Moulton, 1973). The goal of simultaneous orgasm—now waning in popularity, but much stressed in the marriage manuals of a decade ago—is clearly a part of the same social construction. With its emphasis on sexual phenomena like the vaginal orgasm and simultaneous orgasm, this social construction exposed women to social pressures to conform to invented norms. Therapists and husbands could berate women for failing to have vaginal orgasms (an event for which males had no corresponding subjective reality) on the strength of a social construction they had read about in books. To the sexually liberated women of today the spectacle of women's being held accountable to the "Emperor's new orgasm" may seem laughable, but it was no joke twenty years ago. In addition to condemnation from others, the woman whose subjective reality did not conform to the social construction had to deal with the uncanny feelings and self-doubts that arose from being "different."

The epic controversy of our time, vaginal versus clitoral orgasm, can be seen as a conflict between Freud's construction of female sexuality and a competing construction developed by feminists (and supported by the findings of Masters and Johnson, 1966). Women who wanted to assert the truth of their own experience—that they did not experience orgasm from penile stimulation but did experience orgasm through stimulation of the clitoris—had to contend with the devastating judgments of Freudian authorities that they were "frigid." *It is evidence of the power of social constructions over subjective reality that the experience of women was set aside, decade after decade, in favor of the authoritative pronouncements of Freud, who was of course physically incapable of experiencing a vaginal or clitoral orgasm much less discriminating one from the other or judging one as superior to the other on the basis of his own subjective experience.*

In Chapter 3 we will find that many of the attitudes and assumptions based on the Freudian construction of female sexuality and personality are still very much in evidence. Extremely conservative constructions of female sexuality still appear, regrettably, to be prevalent among physicians and therapists. Scully and Bart (1973) have observed that the authors of gynecology textbooks even today seem to portray the female as a cranky child (her psychology) bearing a uterus (her physiology). Even observations on ostensibly objective and palpable "facts" of biology are often influenced by identifiable social constructions of reality. Also, as the reader will see in Chapter 3, certain research questions are investigated, while others are overlooked: current researchers have thought of some issues but not of others. *The unthought of issues are probably "unthinkable" within the paradigms or social constructions* prevalent today. Similarly, questions that go unasked in contemporary research are probably "unaskable," not because respondents' experiences do not provide material, but because researchers cannot formulate questions outside their own constructions of reality.

Scientific Paradigms in Sex Research

Berger and Luckmann (1966) have suggested that legitimating ideologies and the different social constructions they match may have developed through a sequence involving mythology, then theology, then (secular) philosophy, and finally science. This observation seems to fit the area of sexuality. As we have mentioned, the "scientific era" in the study of sexuality dates from the monumental empirical works of Kinsey and his associates. Since that time, sex research has been a recognized enterprise, associated with research techniques borrowed from survey research. Increasingly, sexual *behavior* rather than more subjective aspects of sexuality has been the focus of sex researchers. Masters and Johnson (1966) broke many traditional taboos by studying female orgasm in the laboratory, and introduced a newer paradigm.

Much recent sex research utilizes laboratory settings and many techniques borrowed from behaviorist psychology. A good deal of this research has therapeutic goals; its aims are to further individual adjustment rather than to explore basic issues in sexuality. Hence it does not receive a great deal of emphasis in this book. Yet it is worthwhile to note that, in the same historical period when most young people still feel that they do not receive an adequate sex education and most sexual topics are still taboo in conversation between parents and children, subjects are participating in laboratory experiments where their physical responses to sexually arousing stimuli are measured.

The advent of scientific sex research overshadowed the preempirical paradigms of Freud and weakened the plausibility of arguments from clinical evidence. However, although the methods have changed, many of the dominant concepts in current sex research still resemble Freud's. This has resulted in a focus on "Mom and Pop" sexuality (Laws, 1973) and psychology which is naive, taking the heterosexual script as the only reality, with a consequent neglect of variant sexual orientations and social arrangements. Chapter 5 attempts to correct for this monistic focus by examining the array of sexual life-styles currently available in the U.S. This is only a partial correction, however, for the material presented in Chapter 5 is necessarily based on contemporary research data, and sex researchers still tend to ignore the effects of their own location in the social system on the questions they ask and the "knowledge" they accept. Sex research is largely a male preserve, and the prevailing types of studies undertaken reflect male preoccupations and male constructions of sexual reality (Laws, 1973).

In this book it is our aim to criticize the prevailing constructions of female sexuality, as well as to give an account of current understandings of them. In each area of the discussion to follow, gaps in current knowledge that require new research will become evident. In our conclusions we hope to summarize existing and emerging trends and point to new ways of understanding female sexuality. Chapter 2 adopts a social psychological approach to the development of female sexuality. Each major stage can be seen as involving a personal organization of a biological event for which there is a dominant social construction available. Processes of socialization are given great emphasis in forming subjective reality, through communication between the individual and significant others who are particularly relevant to the events of each stage. The model of sexual development reflects the complexity of sexual learning in contemporary America, for the individual orients toward different publics, and their evaluation, at different developmental stages. The development of variant sexual identities and life-styles follows the same rules as the development of the dominant sexual orientation and life-style. "Successful" socialization is generally thought to produce congruence between subjective and social "realities." Subjective possibilities are more numerous and raw experience more complex than the social constructions toward which they are shaped by socialization.

In Chapter 3 the mechanisms of the biological substratum of femaleness are examined, and it becomes apparent that social constructions overlaid upon them have an element of arbitrariness. Research has revealed cultural variations in (for example) the meanings attributed to menstruation and the behavioral concomitants of these. We are still in the process of discovering the contribution biological events make to sexual functioning in humans. It is apparent that there is no direct mapping of endocrinological events into behavior, as is the case with some species. Although treating newborn or fetal rats with hormones has been shown to affect mating behaviors and nest building, it is hard to point to direct analogues of these relationships in humans. Human sexual behavior is so diverse and subtle that there are few types which are universally characteristic of either females or males. What Chapter 3 does demonstrate, however, is the carryover of *social attitudes* toward females into the "objective" practice of medicine and research.

Chapter 4 focuses on some of the most familiar sexual scripts, or elements of social constructions which define female sexuality. The prevalence and power of such constructions is illustrated by the fact that they underlie other situations besides those in which they appear most "natural." Thus we find parallels between heterosexual courtship routines, homosexual "cruising," and wife-swapping.

Chapter 5 inventories the variety of sexual life-styles available in contemporary America. These vary greatly in the social meanings attached to them. Individuals may vary, as well, in which options they elect at various points in their own sexual history. Chapter 5 illustrates how malleable and complex female sexuality is, especially in comparison with the restricted sexual scripts.

In Chapter 6, a particular sexual institution (prostitution) is examined. The social construction of female sexuality as evil and responsible for evil consequences (Eve) appears powerful in this situation. Where social institutions dominated by males (the police, the courts) confront women—as prostitutes, victims and juveniles—the social construction of female sexuality as an evil power (Eve) appears starkly.

In our conclusion, Chapter 7, we draw connections among the issues raised in different chapters. The emphasis on process and change is underscored. Aspects of female sexuality which need future research are reviewed. Basic theoretical issues—e.g., sexual object choice, sexual identity—are viewed through a feminist perspective. The contribution of the feminist perspective is spelled out in detail. Major blind spots in the traditional literature are identified. Existing sexual scripts are analyzed, and inverted.

References

Berger, P., and T. Luckmann (1966). The Social Construction of Reality. Garden City, N.Y.: Doubleday.

Daly, M. (1973). Beyond God the Father. Boston: Beacon Press.

Green, R., and J. Money (1969). Transsexualism and Sex Reassignment. Baltimore: The Johns Hopkins Press.

Johnston, J. (1973). Lesbian Nation: The Feminist Solution. New York: Touchstone.

Jones, E., and H. Gerard (1967). Foundations of Social Psychology. New York: Wiley.

Laws, J.L. (1973). Exotica≠Erotica: A Plea for Continuities in the Study of Human Behavior and Sexual Behavior. Paper presented at the convention of the American Psychological Association, Montreal.

Long, J. (1969). Self-Identity Theory. Unpublished, Chicago.

Masters, W., and V. Johnson (1966). Human Sexual Response. Boston: Little, Brown.

Miller, M. (1971). On Being Different: What It Means to Be a Homosexual. New York: Random House.

Millett, K. (1974). Flying. New York: Ballantine Books.

Moulton, J. (1973). Philosophical Confusions in Descriptions of Sexual Behavior. Unpublished, Philadelphia.

Schaefer, L. (1973). Women and Sex. New York: Pantheon Books.

Scully, D., and P. Bart (1973). A Funny Thing Happened on the Way to the Orifice: Women in Gynecology Textbooks. American Journal of Sociology 78(4):1045–1050.

Stoller, R. (1968). Sex and Gender. New York: Science House.

Chapter Two

Female Sexual Identity

In this chapter we focus on what is peculiarly human about female sexuality: the meanings that are attributed to sexuality, and the ways in which meanings are acquired and modified. In the next chapter the focus is the biological substratum for female sexuality, and the sexual events which stem directly from it. Most sexual events, however, are triggered in a social context and follow a sexual script. This is true for events that involve only one individual (for example, menstruation or masturbation) as well as those that involve more than one. In this chapter we will examine the ways in which female sexuality is scripted through a developmental history. We will also look at the processes by which individual women make sense of their sexual experience. In order to do so, we will make use of the concept of sexual identity.

Sexual Identity

We might think of a woman's *sexual identity* as her individual awareness of herself as a female and of the attributes that make up her femaleness. These include knowledge she has of her body and bodily functions, images of femininity, and her own sexual preferences and sexual history. The earliest component of sexual identity is *gender identity*, the basic sense of oneself as a female (or male). Acquired very early, it is thought by many authorities to be irreversible (Stoller, 1968). Other components of sexual identity build upon this basic sense of femaleness (or maleness).

Sexual identity is not one thing but a related set of self-attributes. It is not inborn, but develops through experience. This experience carries social meanings and is subjected to social construction. The individual's sexual identity is influenced by a sequence of sexual scripts which are loosely tied to a biological timetable. We view the female life cycle as a sequence of stages, each of which is marked by a biological event and the social meanings attached to it (see Table 1). Each column in Table 1 represents a distinct stage in the development of sexual identity. Biological events act as markers for the transition from one stage to the next. The primary significance of these biological events is not that they occur, but that they are marked by others. They have social significance; terms exist to refer to them, and communication occurs about them. Much of this communication is directed toward the developing person and socializes the individual about her sexuality. For each scene in the sexual script, certain significant others are the designated partners. Their performance is geared to that of the developing person, and vice versa. They are especially significant for that phase of sexual identity development. For each stage in Table 1, therefore, we have listed biological events of significance, the social events that they cue, and the significant others who are most involved in the scripted interactions of the period. Each of these stages is discussed at length in this chapter. Processes of socialization accompany each stage that is socially defined. The transition from one stage to another is thus scripted.*

If self-identity is thought of as a system, sexual identity may be thought of as a major subsystem. As with any identity, sexual identity is constructed from internalized social constructions which provide a map for "reading" experience. The individual need not be conscious of the social constructions, or of the ways in which her personal identity corresponds to social constructions. She can experience her sexual history as simple reality.

The primary characteristics of identity are also true of sexual identity. The term *identity* means recognizable as the same, but it does not imply that the entity which is "the same" does not vary over situations and time. Through reflection, the individual recognizes that it is the same person who experiences a variety of sexual events, over a variety of situations. The continuity does not rely on absolute consistency, however, nor is it static. Rather, it is continuously revised and updated. The capacity for dynamic change and development is the second defining characteristic of

---

*This holds true for the development of the basic awareness of gender identity. The current literature on sex research reflects the social constructions which are prevalent in the society at large. Gender identity is conceptualized as female *or* male. If there are individuals with an androgynous or bisexual gender identity, we do not (yet) recognize them. An intriguing question for the future is whether researchers will be able to identify the socialization experiences which produce a bisexual gender identity, as contrasted with a male or female one.

Table 1
Developmental Model for Sexual Identity

	Stage 1 *Prenatal*	*Stage 2* *Birth and* *Childhood*	*Stage 3* *Puberty*	*Stage 4* *Sexual* *Intimacy*	*Stage 5* *Fertility/* *Parenthood*	*Stage 6* *Loss of* *Sexual Powers*
Biological events	*Biological events*	*Biological events*	*Biological events*	*Biological events*	*Biological events*	*Biological events*

	Conception
	Fetal development
		Birth
		Normal sexual
		  morphology
			Development of
			  secondary sex
			  characteristics
			Menarche
				Sexual initiation
				Frigidity/impo-
				  tence
					Conception
					Pregnancy
					Parturition
					Lactation
						Menopause
						Surgical loss
						Aging

Social events	*Social events*	*Social events*	*Social events*	*Social events*	*Social events*	*Social events*

	None	Sex assignment
		Sex-role
		  socialization
		Sex rearing
		Sexual exploration
			Dating
			Popularity
			Sexual experimen-
			  tation
			Sexual morality
				Role conflict
				Assumption of
				  marital role
				Resocialization
				  regarding sex-
				  ual behavior
					Marital role
					Parental role
						Freedom from
						  fertility
						Wound to self-
						  esteem
						Change in sex
						  identity

Significant others	*Significant others*	*Significant others*	*Significant others*	*Significant others*	*Significant others*	*Significant others*
	None	Parents Peers Physician	Peers	Partner(s) Peers	Spouse Parents Peers Community	Spouse

identity. *Identity has aspects of both continuity and change;* it is not static but dynamic.

The awareness of oneself as a sexual being provides continuity through time. This identity can be added to and modified, without being changed radically. Thus in the individual's sexual history, the events of pregnancy and motherhood may be added onto previous experiences. Likewise, new components are added onto sexual identity, which is the abiding awareness. Depending on the individual, sexual identity development can follow existing sexual scripts closely or diverge from them. The exceptional individual's experience may follow the sexual script for the most part and deviate only slightly, or it may be different from the beginning.

One issue involved with identity is the degree of awareness of the forces which mold identity. A related issue is the question of choice. For one of the characteristics of the self-awareness we call identity is that the individual can influence its further development through conscious choice. She can choose behaviors and definitions which seem to her consistent with her identity, or she can choose to change it. Thus we can imagine an individual who is completely unaware of sexual scripts, but who acts them out predictably. We can also imagine an individual who is aware of the social constructions of female sexuality, and who finds them consistent with her self image, and *chooses* to match her experiences to the script.

We might predict that to the extent that the individual's sexual development and history correspond to the social scripts, sexual identity will be unproblematic. Conversely, exposure to experiences which are not in the script or which are out of sequence or out of synchrony with age mates will make sexual identity problematic. This will tend to make the individual aware of the relationship between herself and the sexual script. In seeking to make sense of her experience, the exceptional individual may discover alternative constructions of reality. For some women, an alternative construction of sexuality may fit the subjective experience better than the standard script does. For these individuals, a transformation of identity occurs. Even this, however, may be radical (involving change in all the components of sexual identity established to that point) or partial. Thus for example, an individual comes to recognize that her sexual preferences are for partners of her own gender. This may change many aspects of her sexual identity, but not, ordinarily, gender identity. A partial transformation requires the reinterpretation of many events in the sexual history (e.g., heterosexual involvements) but at the same time attempts to maintain or recreate consistency among them. The radical transformation does not attempt to maintain consistency between the old and new constructions of reality.

Of course, sexual identities do not originate in a social vacuum. The social constructions available determine what sense the individual can make of her own inner experience. Sexual identities, like other identities, can only be maintained in a social context where they are accepted as real, and where others share this reality. The situation of the isolated gay person, struggling with the lack of congruency between her own sexuality and the social constructions, is very different from that of the individual who is part of a gay community. *Sexual life-styles, then, imply not only alternative social constructions of reality but the community that supports and reinforces them.*

Pluralism and the "Problem" of Sexual Identity

For many of the reasons discussed in Chapter 1, the dominant sexual script is probably the most salient for the majority of women. In an era of sexual pluralism, however, other sexual life-styles are visible and make explicit claims of validity. Of the variant sexual life-styles, some are more aggressive in challenging the dominant sexual construction than others. Gay activists, in seeking their rights, make themselves available as public speakers, give press conferences and engage in demonstrations. Couples engaged in swinging, another variant life-style, advertise in special media for new participants, but engage in no public recruiting or persuasion. The media, however, have a way of making public the existence and the claims of uncommon life-styles, including sexual life-styles.

The practical consequence of this is that for most women—perhaps especially young women—a variety of sexual options appear as possibilities. The analysis of sex roles and of sexual institutions by feminists has made the premises of the dominant script explicit and open to challenge, evaluation, and choice. It has become apparent that one can be nonheterosexual and married, married and nonmonogamous, heterosexual and unmarried, monogamous and unmarried, monogamous but not permanently committed, married but not permanently. Unless these options are completely discredited (and the element of choice thereby minimized), their reality competes with that of the dominant script. In this case, the "problem of identity" is endemic to sexual life in our time. Many women, in the course of a lengthening sexual lifetime, will be experimenting with a variety of sexual life-styles and reflecting on their experience with awareness of its consequences for sexual identity. If in a more traditional past only one sexual script ever had any reality for most women, now choices are almost unavoidable. Libby and Whitehurst (1977) make a distinction between choices which the individual can theoretically make and the actual options available for her own personal behavior. The distinction would seem to be tied to the individual's contact with a community embodying variant sexual life-styles or with partners who provide such a link. In other words, the media can make us aware that transvestites or lesbian communes exist, but without personal contact these possibilities do not really affect the individual. Conversely, personal contacts and experiences can involve individuals in sexual life-styles which they never anticipated. This is the case with many persons with bisexual experience, according to Blumstein and Schwartz (1974). Many of their respondents reported that, with no thought of abandoning the heterosexual script, they simply fell in love with someone of their own sex.

Social Constructions of Female Sexuality

Our model of the development of sexual identity takes account of social expectations and biological events which are associated with a related series of social constructions concerning female sexuality. We assume that virtually all individuals in the culture are exposed to the scripts founded on these constructions, although not all will be internalized by each person. As we take up the stages in the development of sexual identity in sequence, we will find exceptions. Some individuals are exceptions in terms of biology (anatomy or hormones). Other exceptions are social: individuals choose not to marry or not to bear children. Some are exceptions by choice, some as a result of conditions outside their control. While some individuals attempt to repair or compensate for their exceptionalness, and ''rejoin'' the script, others build a variant sexual identity around their exceptionalness.

Every woman's history is a unique constellation. Nevertheless, women in our culture have some events and meanings in common. Humans are socialized for sexuality, just as we are socialized to use language and silverware. Indeed, the culture contains norms for appropriate sexuality that are age-graded and sex-typed—that is, certain behaviors or attributes are considered appropriate for young women but not older ones; certain behaviors are considered appropriate for men but not women. Sexual scripts are even differentiated by social class, and behavior which is considered normal in one class is sometimes considered perverse in another.

In this chapter we will be concerned with the succession of expectations that females are exposed to as they pass through the stages of the female life cycle. These expectations are held by others with whom the individual comes into contact: mother, sisters, brothers, father, teachers, friends and peers of both sexes, doctor, other adults. When the contact is slight or fleeting, the expectations may not be explicitly communicated, and the other person's expectation has only a minor effect. When the individual is in frequent contact with the other, however, chances are that there will be communication. Role expectations are communicated: those behaviors and attributes which are appropriate to a female of a particular age. These role expectations are a blueprint for a successful (adequate, proper) woman. The individual is compared with these expectations, and the evaluation of her adequacy is communicated to her. The significant others with whom this communication is exchanged have great influence over the development of the individual's sexual identity.

Thus sexual identity is in part acquired through learning from others. Only in most cases these others are not passive onlookers as the individual's sexuality innocently unfolds. On the contrary, they take an active role in directing the acquisition of sexual identity. They push the approved or "normal" sexual script; they reward certain aspects and punish others. The child's feeling that she is an "OK" person depends on her being treated as such by the caretaking adults. In the same way, the individual's conviction of her sexual adequacy is based in the acceptance and approval of her significant others. Her ideas of right and wrong in sexuality trace back to these sources. Not only her values about sex but what "facts of life" she learns and does not learn depend on those who are in control of her sexual education.

The significant others who affect the development of an individual's sexual identity do not remain the same over the entire life cycle. Early in life the individual has no choice in the matter, but as she grows older, she can exercise selectivity. Who the partners or reference groups are is critically important for maintaining or changing sexual orientations.

Sexual identity is largely forged by meanings attached to experience. Yet there is a biological substratum for sexuality; many of the events and attributes to which meaning gets attached are biological. The understanding of sexual identity requires an appreciation of both biological givens and the social realities. A common error of oversimplification is to assume that biological facts determine social realities. In fact, quite different social realities are constructed from the same "facts," for interpretation always has a context. Because this is so, even the seemingly simple "facts" of biology become complicated. A good example of this is provided by the components of sexual identity which antedate awareness of the sexual self.

Stage 1: Prenatal Events

When we refer to the biological fact of male or female anatomy, we are talking about *gender*. Gender differences include not only the external genitalia but the internal sexual organs as well. Ordinarily gender is thought of as unambiguous, but it is more complex than we sometimes suppose.

The basic fact of gender is determined at conception, when the egg unites with a female-producing or a male-producing sperm to form a chromosomal pattern that is normally 44+XX (female) or 44+XY (male). However, this is only the normal pattern. There are others, although they are statistically very rare. (For a thorough review of biologically based sexual abnormalities, see Money, 1968). These produce individuals who are physically abnormal in ways that affect the development of sexual identity. Individuals with Turner's Syndrome, which is caused by a genetic abnormality, have an incomplete female genetic pattern (44+XO) and lack ovaries. Other abnormalities (short stature, subnormal intelligence, webbed neck) are commonly found along with the genetic abnormality.

While the fertilized ovum develops in the womb, it is exposed to two other sets of influences which can determine its sexual development: the mother's hormonal environment and the functioning of the gonads in the fetus itself. Since the mother's blood feeds the fetus, she communicates to it not only food but drugs she ingests. Ordinarily, the hormones produced by the mother do not affect sexual differentiation of the fetus, but hormones she ingests as medicine can do so. In the womb external genitalia become differentiated at about the third month. Before that there is a general purpose genital tubercle which can develop either into clitoris and labia or into scrotum and penis. The chromosomes carry the blueprint for this differentiation. However, hormones to which the fetus is exposed during pregnancy can impinge on the fetus in such a powerful way that the blueprint is overruled. This is what happens, apparently, when mothers take male hormones at the critical period in pregnancy. Recent research indicates that drugs which many women took to correct infertility produced anomalies in the pregnancies so induced. Thus, for example, progestin-induced hermaphroditism has been discovered in genetically normal (44+XX) female children whose mothers took this hormone during pregnancy.

As the fetal gonads mature, they begin to secrete sex hormones which direct further development. A failure in this function can also produce problems. Some fetuses exhibit the androgen-insensitivity syndrome: although the chromosomally male fetus secretes androgen, its system does not absorb it, and the development of male genitalia is consequently inhibited. The androgen-insensitive boy will neither experience puberty nor develop the secondary sex characteristics appropriate to his gender.

Anomalies of sexual development do not affect sexual identity directly. Indeed, the problems originating during fetal development are unobserved. The individual cannot be said to have a sexual identity before birth. Sexual anomalies raise problems after birth and in later life *when the individual is seen to be different* from what is expected of her or his sex and age. As we have seen, adequate sexual identity depends on fitting the age-graded and sex-typed norms. For example, neither the Turner's Syndrome (44+XO) girl nor the androgen-insensitive boy will develop secondary sex characteristics when their peers do. For her there will be no breast development, no pubic hair, no menstruation, no ovulation—and, of course, no pregnancy, childbirth, or lactation. For him there will be no change of voice, no growth of body hair; his genitals will not mature; he will not acquire ejaculatory capacity; he will be sterile.

Nevertheless, normalization of individuals with sexual anomalies is not only possible but is standard procedure. Treatment may involve surgical correction, hormone-supportive therapy, counseling, or a combination of all three. The key to "normalization" is to make the individual fit into the social script society provides for sexuality. While not all physical anomalies can be completely reversed, it is possible to achieve an outcome in which the individual is perceived by others and by herself or himself to be adequate. Normalcy, to a great degree, is in the eye of the beholder. It is easy to see that this is the case when we think about the unusual instances we have been discussing. When there are gender anomalies, the development of sexual identity is problematical. Individuals need a rather decisive intervention to "get them back on the track." We have not yet examined, however, what the "track" consists of. When we do that, we discover that sexual identity is problematical for everyone, not only for those who are different.

The transition between Stage 1 and Stage 2 in Table 1 is marked by an important biological event—birth—and an important social event—sex assignment.

Thus far we have been discussing processes and attributes that are unseen. The normality or abnormalities of conception and fetal development are not known until birth. At birth a very significant person, usually the attending physician, starts the infant on a social career as a female or a male by authoritatively labeling it. Others—nurses, relatives, parents, siblings—immediately pick up on this cue and begin to build a sex-appropriate identity. A name is picked; in most cases this too is a sex-signifying label. Very early, persons in the immediate environment start thinking about the child's future identity, and these expectations differ by sex.

Sex assignment is thus the starting point for the construction of sexual identity. The consequences of being labeled girl or boy are so many and so inclusive that in cases where a mistake has been made, anatomy is usually corrected to conform to the social identity, rather than the other way around. The reasoning behind this is that personal and social identity have been based upon sex assignment and continue to develop throughout the life cycle. Eliminating physical ambiguity is comparatively simpler, and produces less disruption, than trying to reverse the individual's whole history and unseat his or her personal identity. In the case of the true hermaphrodite, who has gonads of both sexes, the initial sex assignment may be to the male gender. Subsequently, the development of breasts may reveal that the so-called boy has ovaries and a uterus. If the individual has an established sexual identity as a male, the female organs will be removed, thus providing continuity in the (male) sexual identity.

Even more dramatic is the case of the transsexual. Transsexuals are persons whose sexual identity is at variance with their anatomy. The male transsexual has the anatomy and gonads of a normal male; genetically too he is a normal male—but his subjective sexual identity is that of a woman. The male transsexual believes fervently that he *is* a woman, imprisoned in a male body by mistake. He wants desperately to undo the mistake, and he seeks sex reassignment surgery which will remove his male gonads and substitute female organs. Sex reassignment is effected by a combination of corrective surgery and supportive hormones which permit the development of the secondary sex characteristics. Those who make the change have often lived and "passed" as persons of the chosen sex. (For a recent account of a transsexual's life and transformation, see Morris, 1974.)

Normally, gender identity is consistent with sexual morphology, not inconsistent. Gender identity develops during Stage 2 (Table 1), following sex assignment and many subsequent acts of labeling. To this basic sense of femaleness or maleness are added many specifics as the individual passes through succeeding stages of development. Each stage in the model of sexual identity development involves a different "task" by which the adequacy of the individual is judged and a different set of others who make that judgment.

It is relatively difficult for an individual to maintain a given identity if all significant others emphatically deny and interdict it. This is as true for sexual identity as for any other aspect of identity. If a young girl announces, for example, that she wants to become a performer, the reaction of her significant others may determine whether she persists or not. In one family she may be given lessons to develop her talents; the parents may take the role of theatrical agent and try to get her jobs; they may provide opportunities for her to perform and applaud enthusiastically; they may provide financial support while she gets a start in her chosen career. In another family a young girl with the same amount of talent may be laughed at and squelched in her ambition. If she does not find another sponsor, someone to facilitate and encourage her, she may abandon her claim to be a performer.

Parents and other agents of socialization play a somewhat similar role in shaping sexual identity, by responding differentially to the behaviors children exhibit. Ordinarily their effect will be to encourage the traditional sex-appropriate behaviors and discourage other behaviors. The dominant script in our society is a heterosexual one. The roles provided for females and males are different, but they are orchestrated into a whole. Mothers and fathers (who each have their own roles in the same script) are delighted with their children's attempts to play their roles. They provide them with the appropriate props and costumes, coach and applaud them, and, of course, provide models of how to do it. By the time children are four years old, they are well rehearsed in their sex roles. A great deal of developing sexual identity in childhood involves sex *role* learning, as distinct from sexual behavior and gender identity.

Stage 2: Childhood

We have seen that sex assignment, a form of labeling that is constantly reinforced throughout the life cycle, sets the child on a well-marked path. Among the developmental tasks of Stage 2 are the formation of gender identity—a subjective reality—and recognition of the social identity of the child. In addition, Stage 2 contains experimentation with sexual behaviors, alone and with others, and the beginnings of socialization with regard to sexual object choice.

Sex assignment is reinforced by expectations about what activities, preferences, and attributes are appropriate to girls and boys. These influence the formation of the cognition we have called gender identity. Gender identity appears to crystallize early in life, perhaps before the child becomes proficient at speech. Stoller (1968) places this event at about age two; Kohlberg (1966) finds that gender concepts are reversible in children until sometime between two and four. Between two and four they begin to realize that cats cannot change into dogs nor girls into boys.

Gender identity is not merely a personal construct but is tied to the perception of sex categories. Thus by age four children have learned to tell the genders apart. They know what to expect of each. Children of this age assert that "Mommies can't be doctors" as well as "Daddies can't have babies." They have learned that gender is a very important basis for differentiating among things. This appears to be a social distinction rather than (as Freud thought) anatomical. Kohlberg finds that children learn these judgments before they know about genitals (or any other biological "facts of life"). In one study children were asked who were ladies and who were men, who were boys and who were girls. They discriminated quite accurately, and when asked how they did it, they revealed that they had studied the grown-ups' shoes.

Sex Role Learning in Childhood

A part of the learning that goes into the child's sexual identity at this stage concerns sex roles. Children learn what goes with what and where they fit in. As part of normal socialization, they learn what is expected of boys and of girls. In some respects, these expectations are highly sex differentiated, and in some respects they are similar for boys and girls. At the same time they are exposed to age-specific expectations, however, children are exposed to adult models of both sexes. Even when the children's world is unisex, activities and attributes of the adults in their lives tend to be sharply differentiated. On TV, to which most children are massively exposed, the differentiation between the sexes is very sharp.

Pleck (1973) has suggested that children adhere to sex role standards much more rigidly when they are young and still learning the standard than when they are older. Young children do not make the distinction we are making here between gender identity and the cultural manifestations expected of females and males. To be a girl is to *be* feminine, to behave and react in certain ways, have certain preferences, and feel gratified when this identity is confirmed. As they grow in experience and cognitive complexity, children's ideas about girls and boys, femininity and masculinity may be less gross. Block (1973), too, has suggested that children's sex role attitudes are more rigid or strict at younger ages.

In early childhood, cognitive dichotimization of the genders has behavioral consequences as well. When female and male are defined as polarities, becoming and remaining feminine entails being not-masculine. Consequently, repudiating or avoiding what is masculine helps confirm femininity. Of course the obverse is true for boys. Interestingly, both behavioral and attitudinal avoidance is more pronounced in boys (Ross, 1971).

A major task of this developmental stage is to establish gender-appropriate *social* identity. Playing with same-sex friends, in sex-typed activities, with sex-typed accessories, reinforces this social identity. Preferences for sex-appropriate friends and toys are expected. Cross-sex preferences are not expected and may be discouraged. Observational studies show that parents and nursery school teachers try to lead girls to the doll corner and lead boys away from it; they attempt to substitute sex-appropriate toys for sex-"inappropriate" toys (Fagot and Patterson, 1969). Like son, like father: fathers appear more concerned to establish sex typing in their children than mothers (Kohn and Carroll, 1960), and boys show greater avoidance of girls' toys and tasks than girls show with regard to boys. The habits of avoidance established in this stage have consequences for the behavior of young adults. Bem and Lewis (1975) have found that college students with the most strictly sex typed feminine and masculine identities experience the strongest discomfort when induced to engage in sex-atypical behavior. It seems that people are trained to condition themselves, so that in adulthood a whole range of "opposite" sex typed activities are distasteful.

Given the socialization forces to which young children are normally exposed, the development of a feminine social identity in girls seems over-determined. However, experiences during Stage 2 can result in variant social identities which affect the way the individual fits into the dominant sexual script in subsequent stages. Let us suppose that the individual has an appropriate gender identity. The corresponding social identity for a female is that of girl. If, however, a girl prefers to play with boys or prefers ''boy things,'' her social behavior will not be consistent with the sugar and spice script. It may happen that she prefers girls, but is rejected by the girl children in her neighborhood or school. Or perhaps there are no girls for her to play with. Perhaps the toys and activities to which she is exposed are not sex typed. Then she simply does not learn the sex role script appropriate to this developmental stage. Any experience which cuts her off from ordinary interactions—a childhood illness, for example—can potentially weaken the force of sex role socialization specific to Stage 2.

Another kind of atypical experience, early physical maturation, can affect the development of sexual identity in a different way. The girl who matures early is separated from the normal experience of girl children during Stage 2. She is out of step with her age-mates and must cope with the tasks of nubility when she is much younger than her partners and other female ''peers.'' Table 2 lists some of the complications which may ensue. The developmental tasks of the later stages may be telescoped into Stage 2. However, the individual has not had the advantages of the scripted transition between these stages.

Although there is a dominant script for Stage 2, a number of variant social identities are clearly possible. Having a variant experience in Stage 2 does not preordain a variant sexual identity in adulthood, or even in the next stage. It may, however, open up the possibility for the development of a variant personal identity, depending upon the reactions of others.

The Electra/Oedipus Drama as Role Rehearsal

Very little is known about factors that determine *sexual object choice,* the categories or signs that we find attractive or arousing in our adult sexual lives. Many authors have sought the explanation to homosexuality in decisive early experiences by which sexual feelings are linked to a person of the same gender. However, no universal etiology for homosexuality can be discerned. It should not surprise the reader to find that we know as little about heterosexual object choice as about homosexual object choice. It is easy to see how socialization scripts the choice of an appropriate sexual object, but we do not yet know how sexual feeling is made to conform to the heterosexual script.

Part of the puzzle may lie in a phenomenon studied by Freud, to which

Table 2
Effects on Sexual Identity of Sexual Experience Which Diverges from the Dominant Script

	Stage 1 *Prenatal*	Stage 2 *Birth and Childhood*	Stage 3 *Puberty*	Stage 4 *Sexual Intimacy*	Stage 5 *Fertility/ Parenthood*	Stage 6 *Loss of Sexual Powers*
Biological events	Conception Fetal development	*Normal events* Birth, sex assignment Normal anatomy Sex role socialization Sexual exploration	*Biological events* Development of secondary sex characteristics Menarche	*Biological events* Sexual initiation Frigidity/impotence	*Biological events* Conception Pregnancy Parturition Lactation	*Biological events* Menopause Surgical loss Aging
Social events	None	*Atypical events* Puberty: development of secondary sex characteristics Sexual attention from older males Flirting, dating? Seduction? Menarche Sexual initiation? Pregnancy? Motherhood?	*Social events* Dating Popularity Sexual experimentation Sexual morality	*Social events* Role conflict Assumption of marital role Resocialization regarding sexual behavior	*Social events* Marital role Parental role	*Social events* Wound to self-esteem Change in sex identity
Significant others	None	*Significant others* None	*Significant others* Peers	*Significant others* Partner	*Significant others* Spouse Parents Peers Community	*Significant others* Spouse

we give a different interpretation. In the attachment of very young children to their parents, Freud discerned a pattern which has come to be called the Electra/Oedipus complex. Freud thought that little children fall in love with their opposite sex parent and fasten their immature feelings upon this adult. He believed that these feelings were sexual in nature, although given the state of children's sexual knowledge, the end goal might be less than clear-cut. Because the sexual script has age-graded norms, the child's sexual ambitions toward the opposite sex parent are discouraged through socialization. However, the sexual script is also sex-typed, and the sexual object choice (opposite sex parent) is considered appropriate and normal.

Parents insist that the child cannot marry (later) or have sex with the opposite sex parent. Nevertheless, research has shown that little girls and boys are encouraged in sex role–appropriate behavior and particularly by the opposite sex parent. A father encourages girlishness, cuteness, flirtatiousness, and other evidence of "femininity" in his daughter. To a lesser extent mothers encourage behaviors in their sons that mimic the adult roles of protector, breadwinner, and even domestic tyrant.

Psychoanalytic literature has sometimes emphasized the traumatic aspect of the Electra/Oedipus conflict and its resolution. But we must emphasize its positive function in the learning of "normal" sexual identity. It, like much of the play activity of young children, provides an opportunity to rehearse the dominant patterns in the roles of woman and man. Specifically, it is a rehearsal for appropriate sexual object choice. The child fastens on the nearest and dearest of the "opposite" sex and tries to win acceptance as a sex role partner. The parent guides and reinforces these efforts rather than categorically interdicting them. The general direction is approved, although the immediate aim of the child may be denied.

Freud's formulation of this drama does not deal with possible feelings of love and sexualization for the same sex parent. Many psychoanalytic treatments of male homosexuality have emphasized the relationship of young boys with their mothers but ignore those boys whose gender identity is male and whose sexual object choice is homosexual. More recent treatments have directed attention to mother-daughter relationships, but do not posit a simple deterministic relationship between feelings of love and sexual object choice.

Questions regarding the genesis of sexual object choice suggest the need for additional research. One focus for such research might be to map the directions of children's sexual overtures and experimentation *coordinate with the social responses of punishment or encouragement.* According to the above reinterpretation of the Electra/Oedipus situation, we might predict that the child who reaches out to one of the same gender will be in violation of both age norms and sex norms and will be disapproved on both accounts. The child whose contact is with one of the other gender, however, violates only the age norm, and the response may contain some degree of tolerance or even encouragement.

Sexual Experimentation in Childhood

Freud thought that after the resolution of the Electra/Oedipus dilemma the child entered a latency stage in which sexuality was not a preoccupation. We now know, however, that sexuality is anything but latent in many children of elementary school age. Recent studies have found women apparently more willing to talk about masturbation, and we have learned that for many masturbation has been a source of pleasure since early childhood. One in-depth study of women's sexual development (Schaefer, 1973) challenges many traditional myths about female sexuality. Schaefer's sample consisted of women whom she had seen in therapy over a period of years. Although the number of respondents is small and no claim is made that they represent a statistically adequate reflection of the U.S. population as a whole, the study is nonetheless revealing.

Schaefer's respondents were neither asexual nor passive. As children they were exposed to sexual instigation from others (adults as well as peers, and relatives as much as strangers), but they often actively sought sexual contact. Though in some research (Simon, Berger, and Gagnon, 1972) college women have reported that they never masturbated until after experiencing orgasm through coitus, Schaefer's respondents engaged vigorously in masturbation. A certain amount of inventiveness appears in these accounts:

> I was still in a crib—they kept me in a crib until very late . . . I remember masturbating or at least touching myself. When I was in the crib, I used to tell my mother to put blankets over the side because the light bothered me. But it wasn't that. It didn't occur to me that anybody could look over the edge, but actually I didn't want them to know what I was doing there. It was a very definite and very strong sexual feeling. (Schaefer, 1973: 30)

If Schaefer's respondents are at all typical, many little girls have masturbated regularly since an early age (sometimes before the age of three), and some have experienced orgasm from masturbation long before puberty.

Some young girls escaped feelings of guilt and wrongdoing in these experiences and only later learned the names and the social evaluation of their experiences. Others learned that what they were doing was forbidden, and the guilt and fear of retribution warred with the pleasure of the sensations they experienced. *This pleasure seems to be polymorphous, and from Schaefer's data there is no indication that children make a strong distinction between peers who are their own gender and the other.*

Me and two other girls who lived next door were under a blanket. I was four, maybe going on five. One little girl had wanted to explore and so we were under this blanket and we all had our pants down and a little boy looked into this hole in the blanket. Then he ran off to tell my mother, or his mother—actually, I'm not sure whose mother he told. And it seems to me she had warned me about this before, because I seem to recall going under the blanket with some mild—maybe not protest, but some kind of expiation of her warning, saying, "You know we aren't supposed to do this," and the girl says, "Come on, come ahead, do it anyway." (Schaefer, 1973: 28)

According to other accounts, mutual exploration or exposure ("doctor games") were severely punished and remembered as traumatic events. Responses of parents loomed large in most respondents' recollections. Parents seemed to disapprove of sexual activity of any sort and to try to put an end to it.

Parents as Sex Educators

It seems clear that in retrospective reports women can remember quite distinctly their sexual behavior when very young, their feelings about it, and the reactions of adults. The attitudes of adults, both explicit, as in explanations of pregnancy and menstruation, and implicit, as when the child was discovered in some sexual behavior, were very important.

Parents are important in early sex education in at least three ways. First, they give children explicit information about sex and bodily processes. This may be the smallest part of children's sex education, due to the taboos governing talking about sex and acknowledging children's sexuality. Children learn a great deal about sex, besides what is directly taught.

A second, and probably more important part of the learning children acquire from their parents is not taught explicitly. It is the feeling tone surrounding sexual matters which children pick up. A common feeling about the early sexual memories Schaefer's respondents reported included the need for secrecy, feelings of wrongness, fear of discovery and punishment, and, above all, guilt. Associations with nudity were non-specific but negative. A youngster at age four saw her friend's father nude and thought: "It was wrong of me to see a man undressed because I had never seen my parents naked, and bedroom and bathroom doors were always shut in our house. Somehow I just *knew* I wasn't supposed to see a man naked" (Schaefer, 1973: 34). Other recollections reflect parental shock and outrage at an accidental viewing of their nakedness by their child.

Third, parents perpetuate a myth that children are asexual and the complementary myth that parents are too. This learning has consequences beyond those of misinformation about the "facts of life" (which can be unlearned in later years). This communication is about the persons involved, not merely where babies come from. The seeds of a psychological conflict are planted by the parents' denial of their own and the child's sexuality. The message conveyed to the child is that she is a good (loved, worthy) person and that the parent is too. Simultaneously, the child gets the message that sex is dirty, undignified, painful, shameful—something to be ignored and not spoken of (and, probably, avoided). Schaefer describes *the effect of the "Big Lie" when the child is forced to relate the badness of sex with the goodness of the self: guilt.* When the child relates the badness of sex to the goodness of the parent, the result is sometimes anger at the parent's hypocrisy or repudiation of the parent as bad. Against the background of early learning of the parent as asexual, the common conflicts of adolescence can be exacerbated. Many writers have noted that as young people develop physically at puberty and move into the social patterns of courtship, parents try to control their sexual behavior. The resultant conflicts become even more severe when both parents and children violate the Big Lie. When adults blossom out into new sexual life-styles—when they engage in swinging, courtship, or sexual experimentation—they violate the child's image of the parent as sexless.

The Big Lie is damaging to rational sex education and to rational sexuality in several ways. It seems likely that the effects are greater for girls than for boys. Kinsey, Pomeroy, and Martin (1948) have shown that the male peer group assumes a major role in the development of a socially-validated sexual identity for boys. Kinsey found no such source of social support for sexual behavior for females, at least at the time of his research on women (Kinsey et al., 1953). A great deal of ignorance and misinformation abound. A number of studies have found that young people of both sexes evaluate their sex education as very inadequate.

Parents shy away from discussing any but the mechanical aspects of sexuality with their children. This seems to be true even in this "permissive" era when some parents sponsor their daughter's provision with contraception by the family doctor. Even these parents may avoid discussing the human issues involved in intercourse and contraception.

The earliest topics women learn about are gestation and menstruation, not intercourse, and these from their mothers. There seems to be a long hiatus between this early instruction and the sex education girls get from their peers in school. Sometime around the fifth grade individuals get a lot of information—dubious to be sure—from dirty jokes. Then, somewhat later, the source is "my own experience."* Male arousal, female arousal,

---

*These observations are based on the author's ongoing study of sexual identity in college women. In the interviews, respondents are asked about when they learned the "facts of life," and how and what they learned, from earliest to current learning.

fertility, and intercourse are the aspects of sexuality which parents shun and which are of greatest concern to adolescents. Insofar as sexual exchanges are initiated and controlled by males, the sexual learning that takes place by this means is in male terms. Thus females are receiving socialization with respect to *male* constructions of female sexuality.

The Big Lie has particular relevance to young girls. Parents, more than youth, believe in premarital chastity. The Big Lie appears as a support to virginity. The underlying parental thinking seems to be: (1) if I do not tell my daughter about sex, she will remain sexually innocent, and (2) if I do tell her, it will seem an invitation to become promiscuous. The facts do not bear out these fantasies: sexual ignorance does not prevent coitus, nor does sex information foster promiscuity. Parents are not the major source of most young people's sex information. The major effect of parents' Big Lie on their daughter is that she receives no validation or guidance for her sexuality from them.

Social Constructions of Prepubertal Sexuality   If Freud's theory about a latency stage was not literally true, it was at least metaphorically true in the sense that in the social script, children are asexual. A forbidding atmosphere is associated with parents' responses to children's sexuality. Yet as we have seen, sexual experimentation with others, and certainly masturbation, are prevalent among young children in Stage 2. Lacking a social construction to render these experiences intelligible and "speakable," how do children incorporate them into sexual identity?

The answer is that *many elements of sexual experience are not incorporated into the developing sexual identity.* Social constructions of female sexuality become available only at puberty, when the sex role script picks up momentum. The curtain rises on female sexuality only when others begin to respond to the girl child as a sexual being, and she picks up the script for Stage 3. That script is emphatically heterosexual and oriented toward marriage. Courtship routines which precede marriage underscore the importance of the male partner. It should not be surprising that elements of sexual experience that do not fit the emerging script are suppressed or "forgotten." This is the fate of sexual play with same sex peers, and of masturbation. The fate of masturbation illustrates two points about prepubertal sexuality: (1) what happens to the sexual behavior itself and (2) the meaning of the behavior, and where it fits into sexual identity. Parents tend to be disapproving of sexual activity of any sort and try to put an end to it. The evidence seems to indicate that children persist in a sexual activity that affords pleasure if the sanctions are not too severe and interrupt it if they are. The behavior may be discontinued either as a result of punishment or as a result of internalization of negative labels which make it unacceptable to the individual herself.

A child's masturbation can be kept a secret, but its secret status seems to prevent integration into ongoing sexual identity. Thus Schaefer (1973) finds that adult women report feeling "disloyal" to their sexual partners if they masturbate as adults. A male partner (particularly one legitimated by marriage) can give a woman permission to be sexual, but only with him and only in prescribed ways. Masturbation is, for many women, excluded from the category of permitted sexual behaviors. Schaefer's findings are substantiated by Hite's findings that, in part, the presence of a partner is felt to legitimate sex, but masturbation is felt to demean it. Guilt also appears when women ask their partners to provide the clitoral stimulation they prefer (Hite, 1976: 5, 213–218).

Girl children whose sexual explorations were interrupted by parental disapproval may find at least tacit encouragement for their sexuality at a later age. Approval will ordinarily extend, however, only to behaviors which fit the heterosexual courtship script and are instrumental to achieving marriage. Later in life, elements of sexual experience discarded at this stage may be rediscovered and incorporated into a changing sexual identity. Thus in defining a lesbian identity, writer Rita Mae Brown resurrects her early homoerotic contacts, which occurred simultaneously with the scripted heterosexual contacts of adolescence (Brown, 1973). Just as the sexual identity of the heterosexual woman prompted her to deny the significance of these relationships in adolescence, so the sexual identity of the adult lesbian causes her to dismiss the heterosexual history. *The lesson that we learn from Stage 2 is that most individuals have a rather polymorphous sexual history during early development.* In the selection that occurs among various possibilities both social forces and self identity can play a part. The effect of the dominant sexual script is to shape behavior and choice toward the narrow range permitted the adult woman in America: heterosexual/monogamous/married—permanently. At the point of puberty, socialization presumes reinforcement of this script.

Stage 3: Sexual Identity during Puberty

The period during which the secondary sex characteristics develop and the body becomes fertile is known as puberty. Although puberty involves many gradual changes, we have chosen the beginning of menstruation, the menarche, to mark the transition from the stage of childhood to that of adolescence.

While *puberty* refers to physical changes, *adolescence* refers to a social status. The adolescent is an immature person who is not yet an adult but no longer a child. *Teenager* is a social construction for the adolescent.

Connotations of this term include the idea of a strong peer culture, active social life, and little responsibility. Being an adolescent or teenager is a social status rather than a chronological period. Some individuals retain the social status of adolescent into their thirties (for example, the unmarried graduate student). Others, who are parents and full-time workers during their teenage years, do not assume the cultural role of teenager. The adolescent is ordinarily attending school full-time, and some adolescents hold paid jobs, but the primary identity is not derived from either of these activities. Rather, the emphasis in this period is on rehearsal for adult roles, sex roles in particular.

Additions to sexual identity during this period of puberty and before sexual intercourse is begun are organized around two focuses. The first includes body changes, experiences based on the facts of physical femaleness, and body image. The second includes expectations and images of the nubile woman. Many social constructions concerning women are based on the physical signs of puberty. It is these social definitions, more than the physical events, which are the focus of Stage 3.

The sex role expectations appropriate to the status of child give way to those of the adolescent, oftentimes as gradually as the physical signs of sexual maturity develop. The secondary sex characteristics are particularly noticeable as they emerge in females, and they elicit a social reaction. The appearance of breasts, hips, and body hair serves as a signal for the transition from the status of girl child to the status of nubile woman. While puberty refers to physical maturation, nubility refers to the marriageability of the individual. A female is considered nubile in many cultures as soon as she is capable of bearing children—after menarche. Similarly, a female is considered an adult as soon as she is married. In the United States, legal majority was until recently tied to attaining the age of twenty-one. However, in many states a woman younger than twenty-one was considered an adult if she was married. For women, adulthood is conferred by marrying and enhanced by bearing children. Adulthood is attained through rather specific channeling of a female's sexuality: through licensed intercourse and childbearing. Adulthood for the male is less closely tied to physical maturity or to sexual functioning. Rather, he assumes the status of adult when he can support himself and a family. His major identity as an adult is the occupational one, while the major adult female identity is expected to be the familial one. The man's adequacy is proved in the economic sphere, while the woman's remains within the sexual sphere.

Consequently, the social scripting for females and males diverges in this period of preparation for the assumption of adult roles. Study of aspirations and achievement among adolescents shows a tendency for women to focus on marriage at a period when men are orienting themselves toward long-term occupational commitments and ambitions.

The social function of Stages 3 and 4 is courtship and appropriate mate selection. Sex roles dictate that the males do the choosing; consequently, the female's role is to make herself as choosable as possible. Adequacy of sexual identity in Stage 3 is based on the female's ability to attract males (and males high in market value at that). Because of the great social importance placed on these transactions, we have devoted a large part of Chapter 4 to the marriage market. In this section we will focus on the scripting for the physical self of a woman, which comes into play during puberty.

Sexualized Parts of the Female Body

If marriage is the destination intended for women, then marriageability is the criterion for success in this adolescent stage of development. Marriage is also the destination intended for female sexuality, and the link between marriage and female sexuality is strongly underlined during this stage. The appearance and care of the body, particularly those aspects of it which are sexualized in our culture, assume great importance.

Those parts of the body which are sexualized in our culture—legs, face, breasts, and to a lesser extent, buttocks—are subjected to special routines of display and enhancement. Other body parts and functions are subjected to routines of concealment and sometimes taboo.

A socialization of the young woman for the role of sex object takes place during puberty. A great deal of attention is focused on the way she looks, and she receives a lot of feedback on her "good points" and "figure faults." She becomes an object to be noticed and appreciated by others and, in fact, learns to appreciate and observe herself in the same way. She acquires an awareness of the image others have of her in a new way; she learns the potency of her female beauty for others; and she learns the techniques of enhancement, display, and artifice. For each of the sexualized body zones there is an array of techniques of beautification and enhancement and an array of implements and products to aid in these transformations.

Before the braless era, a girl's first bra was a momentous event, and the progression from size 28 AAA to her adult size was closely monitored not only by the young woman herself but by her friends as well. Padded bras, push-up bras, and the infamous Playboy Bunny costume all reflect a cultural image of *the* desirable female breast and the readiness of women to transform themselves to fit the image. The current trend is toward more display of the natural breast and less concealment or remodeling. See-through attire and topless styles are, however, only the new look in an old cultural institution, the display and sexualization of the female breast.

Enhancement of face and hair is, of course, a multimillion dollar business. More women than ever before are coloring their hair, with constantly improving technology. Eyebrows may now be dyed as well as or instead of being tweezed. Makeup may now be used to contour and "redesign" the face, rather than merely coloring it in specific spots. And surgery is employed to change faces: cosmetic dentistry, facelifting, and "nose jobs," once the prerogative of professionals whose looks are their livelihood, are now the concern of ordinary folks who write to Ann Landers. In some segments of society, the nose job has replaced the Sweet Sixteen party for girls. This rather extreme (and expensive) means of self-enhancement has become a routine procedure, like orthodontics.

In the pantheon of American pin-up beauty, legs have enjoyed a fluctuating status. The display of legs was once the point of girlie calendars, and Betty Grable was the number one American pin-up girl during the Second World War. The sexualization of legs, however, had precisely defined limits. Ankles, calves and even thigh could be displayed, made up, adorned in black stockings—but not the crotch or buttocks. The pubis has always been tabooed and is the focus of much protocol whose purpose is to preserve modesty.

The rules of propriety and modesty are so complex that they might baffle the proverbial man from Mars, yet they are known and enforced. The dialectic between display and concealment, or permissible flaunting and taboo, can be seen clearly in the conventions of dress. In our culture, marriageability involves a carefully calibrated degree of display and concealment, neatly expressed through dress. A woman may dress in such a way as to express no desire to attract. The traditional habits of nuns, or the utilitarian overalls now worn by many women, signal unavailability for mating by avoiding the culturally permissible degree of display which is expected of nubile girls. If nuns' and feminists' dress is at one end of the spectrum, the dress of chorus girls, some prostitutes, and Playboy Bunnies is designed for display. Their dress communicates a preponderance of exposure over concealment, rather than a mixture of respectability and concealment with desire to attract. Concealment of sexual attributes (achieved through dress) is the hallmark of the respectable woman, virgin or matron.

Limits of Female Sexual Display

For each sexualized body zone, there are specific limits of display. Traditionally, degrees of accentuation and exposure of the breasts were permissible (depending very much on the situation and the social status of the object), but exposure of the nipples was taboo. Exposure of legs was also a matter of degree: longer skirts and stockinged legs were considered more modest than bare legs and miniskirts. The whole question of skirts versus pants is interesting to analyze from the perspective of the demands of display and concealment, freedom and modesty.

Only very recently did pants come to be an acceptable costume for occasions that require "good clothes." Before this, pants were reserved for gardening or camping, and skirts were expected whenever there was company or an audience. Children had more leeway in wearing pants (or shorts or overalls) than adults, and puberty often marked a transition between jeans and skirts for the young woman. Given the taboo on the genital area, it can be seen that the wearing of skirts imposes greater modesty requirements than the wearing of pants. In order to keep the pubis from view, the skirt-wearer must restrict her posture and actions (as illustrated by the rules that a proper woman crosses her legs at the ankle, never at the knee, when sitting on a platform; and that she must stoop rather than bend). Pants are more practical and less restrictive—but they conceal the legs and thus thwart the *permitted peeping* (by men) which is a central feature of this portion of the sexual script.

Another example of the dialectic between display and concealment is the saga of body hair. Body hair is taboo, and hence the procedure has been, for every part of the body that is sexualized and displayed, to portray it as hairless and to promote the use of depilatories so that the image can become the reality. *Playboy,* which pioneered the artistic (as contrasted with the pornographic) nude, had until quite recently air-brushed the pubic hair out of its frontal photographs. The psychology is simple: if certain aspects of the beautiful object *detract* from its appeal, we *subtract* them to enhance it.

The feminist movement has taken a principled stand against the tyranny of the "ideal" beauty and the dependence on cosmetics which results from the need to approximate the ideal. Every item in the arsenal of enhancement has come under the attack of feminists. In rejecting the use of artifice to achieve "femininity," many feminists have developed a competing social construction, in which the unadorned woman is the only true woman. Femininity, in this view, is like a garment one puts on in order to create false impressions. Given the influence of social constructions on identity, it is easy to see that the feminist construction could threaten and invalidate the sexual identity of the "feminine" woman in much the same way as being ignored by a man invalidates the sexual identity of the woman who is overweight.

Many feminists have disentangled themselves from the cultural institutions of display and concealment. They wear their body hair proudly, along with their natural faces and favorite clothes. In this they provide a more differentiated image of femaleness, challenging the idea of a single standard of womanly beauty. The feminist emphasis may have lessened the constraints felt by individual women, but it does not seem to have had much real impact on cultural standards of beauty and the industries which feed on these. A degree of cooptation is apparent: the "natural look" (but still, sans body hair) is very popular, and requires new cosmetics and new procedures to achieve. Advertisers (and presumably consumers) have simply substituted one image of the sex object for another. The feminist rejection of the status of sex object does not appear to have affected the sex-sell business.

Practices with respect to body secretions comprise a final example of body protocol. Fortunes have been made exploiting the image of nasty breath, perspiration and "feminine odor," and the consumer's guilt or fear of "offending." Body secretions, like body hair, must be done away with or suppressed. The ideal is permanent depilation or deodorization, or at the very least, "dependable protection." Some of the most distasteful euphemisms in the vernacular relate to body functions—menstruation, perspiration, excretion—and the products by means of which we dispose of them. A review of advertising for tampons and sanitary napkins makes the point. Euphemism abounds, coupled with images of women at their most pristine and glamorous.

Taboos: Personal Reality versus Social Constructions

There is a disjuncture between image and reality when it comes to the sexual attributes and sexual functioning of women. Although the mystification dates back to childhood, it is intensified in puberty. There are new aspects of the physical and sexual self which become salient in this period, and, because of the emphasis on marriageability, "correctness" is more consequential than before.

The disjuncture between the social and the personal is illustrated by menstruation. The social status of menstruation is as taboo: the feeling tone is of shame, secrecy, and even guilt. Even today, many young women are unprepared for the menarche because others observe the taboo and do not talk to the young girl about it. Even when it is happening, the event is kept secret, and fears of unintended exposure or detection are fanned by advertising. Girls are trained to fear not only the "telltale stain," or bulge, but also a telltale odor which may give them away. For generations, menstruation has been referred to as "the curse," and many young women learn to anticipate pain, discomfort, and restricted activity during "those days."

The personal reaction of the young woman to the menarche may diverge from this doleful script. The menarche may be something that she has looked forward to, as a sign of womanhood. In Schaefer's (1973) study, those who knew about the menarche before it happened reported feelings of joy and triumph when it happened: "at last I belong to the company of women." For those who had received no explanation, the bleeding was, understandably enough, alarming; and for many of them, there was the feeling that they must have done something wrong, a feeling of panic, coupled with a felt need to keep the whole disaster a secret. Here, as with many elements of sexual identity, the meanings attached to the event seem to have greater force than the mere physical reality of the event.

Menstruation may continue to have positive meanings for a woman throughout her adult years. Some associate the monthly flow (particularly if it is heavy) with female potency and a feeling that their reproductive system is working properly. Many women have a peak in sexual desire during their period, and enjoy sexual relations more frequently. And for those practicing contraception, the monthly flow is good news that they have not conceived. Culturally, however, menstruation continues to carry the aura of disability and taboo. It is not a topic for mixed company.

A feeling of taboo extends to many female functions, in addition to menstruation. Although there are many normal vaginal secretions which women encounter every month of their lives, they are not discussed. Women do not have a vocabulary for these, nor do physicians. Women, unlike men, do not have a literature that celebrates and affirms these aspects of femaleness. It is hard to imagine a female Mailer. Only very recently have some in the graphic arts begun to work with specifically female forms and experience. Judy Chicago (1975), who started the first feminist art studio, records in her book the refusal of the art world to recognize what her paintings were about, and the outrage and rejection expressed when recognition did dawn.

As a legacy of the Big Lie, girls enter puberty with comparatively little knowledge about sexuality. They are equally ignorant about their own sexuality and about sexual relationships. If our analysis of socialization for sexuality in childhood is correct, the girl child has essentially no self image as a sexual being. Her sexual experiences, being unacknowledged, have a fugitive quality. Personal or subjective constructions of reality (what we call sexual identity) include a good deal about femininity, but little about sexuality per se. In addition, the social script offers no constructions of sexuality for the prepubertal girl.

Both these elements—the social and the personal constructions of sexuality—change with puberty/nubility. The transition to the social constructions of nubility may be sudden. Puberty is the ticket of admission to a world where everything is sexualized, and the nubile female is part of it. Sexual significance winks from every advertisement and sexual price tags stick to all transactions. The young girl is subjected to continual influence with regard to the shaping and presentation of her body. After the information blackout of childhood, she is now surrounded by messages about sexuality. Although each message is blatant, it is not clear. It is impersonal and generalized; it does not focus on her personally. Moreover, sex is instrumental (as in advertising) or incidental; it is not the explicit focus of direct communication.

A more focused interpersonal context is required to bring together the social constructions with personal experience in such a way as to develop sexual identity. The nubile girl does receive direction (if not clarification) in Stage 3. Her sexuality is shaped in the direction of courtship and marriage. Peers provide a critical social context for these transactions (see Chapter 4). Male peers are particularly important, for they constitute the pool from which partners are selected. The social constructions of female sexuality which the girl inherits at puberty require a partner. The partner is especially critical for confirming the nubile girl as a sexual woman. According to the social construction, she is just starting to be sexual (nothing before "counts"). And according to the social script, she must be heterosexual and, soon enough, monogamous and permanently married.

Given the weak social support for earlier or other sexual identities, however, the partner does more than confirm sexual identity. More than any other social source through the stages of development, he has the power to define and form sexual identity, insofar as it involves genital sexuality. This relationship is thus the focus of Stage 4.

Stage 4: Sexual Initiation and Active Genital Sexuality

In discussing puberty we emphasized the gradual physical development of the nubile woman, and the beautification routines which are connected with a changing body. These routines are not the natural accompaniment of sexual development, but originate in the cultural expectation of marriage and the emphasis on marriageability. During this same development, the nubile woman becomes involved in another sequence of behaviors which derives its meaning from a connection with marriage.

Courtship is highly institutionalized, as are the social constructions that fit this stage of the dominant life script for women (see Chapter 4). However, the development of sexual identity, from Stage 4 on, can follow diverse paths. This reflects in part the availability of alternate social constructions of female sexuality and alternate sexual life-styles. It also reflects the increasing role of individual choice in one's sexual history and the awareness of one's sexual identity as the individual grows older.

Stage 4 involves four aspects of female sexuality: the postpubertal woman, a genital focus to sexual activity, the vicissitudes of orgasm, and an active sex life. These four elements appear in sexual scripts for variant sexual identities as well as for the dominant one: homosexuality, bisexuality, celibacy (if it includes autoerotic activity), and heterosexuality. After puberty, the individual is assigned the status of a sexual person; though sexual involvements need not be continuous, they are not unexpected or unscripted. Genital sexuality and orgasm need not involve a partner or penile penetration, but they are a focus of adult women's sexuality.

Initiation: Shaping Images of the Sexual Self

In our model, Stage 4 begins with sexual initiation. In most individuals' experience, a history of increasing degrees of sexual intimacy leads up to this event. In the dominant (heterosexual) scripts dating and courtship provide a context for the sexual relationship and also a script for its development. Although a sexual relationship may seem private, personal, and individual, it develops according to a script. Research has shown that heterosexual relationships follow a sequence from hand holding and necking to light and heavy petting and coitus (Gagnon, Simon, and Berger, 1970). Norms and expectations have been verified that specify what sexual contacts are acceptable between what persons. These norms are called sexual standards or sexual scripts. Reiss (1960) holds that a number of sexual standards operate simultaneously in contemporary America. These are alternative constructions of sexuality, female and male, and they are socially distributed—that is, individuals in certain social locations are more likely to accept one construction than another. Thus, parents tend to adhere to a sexual standard which differs from that of their college-going offspring. Females and males also tend to hold differing standards.

The social history of our culture includes two major versions of the dominant sexual standard: a single standard of abstinence, and the famous double standard. The single standard of abstinence permits sexual intercourse only between spouses. Reiss (1960) says that this is still the preferred and official standard. However, another has come to be widely accepted: the double standard. While the standard of abstinence is still applied to females, the double standard permits men to have sexual intercourse with others than their spouse. In particular, it allows the unmarried male an active sex life, while forbidding it to the single female.

The sexual standard which emerged during the sixties has been called *permissiveness with affection* (Reiss, 1960). This single standard holds that coitus is acceptable for both sexes when the partners are in love. But *when is love present?* A certain ambiguity appears in the judgment of this, and predictably enough (given the traditional double standard), research shows that males tend to interpret love differently from the way females do. The permissive standard of the sixties has undergone modification, and at the end of this section we will return to the question of current constructions of female sexuality that derive from this standard.

It is probably safe to say that most young women today have been exposed to these three sexual standards by the time they enter Stage 4. The three standards are contradictory: the single standard of abstinence says sexual intimacy must wait until marriage. This standard has been bent to tolerate "everything but" intercourse, leading to a distorted emphasis on technical virginity in a physically intact but far from innocent young woman. The double standard creates other paradoxes: if men may not have sexual contacts with "nice" (marriageable) women, with whom may they have intercourse? And if "nice" girls may not have sexual relationships, what happens to their sexual needs? According to the permissive standard, coitus is acceptable under the condition of love but does not define love. It is a single standard, meaning that both partners should love in order for sex to be acceptable. But this standard provides no way to tell if your partner feels the same way you do.

Being exposed to three competing definitions of reality is confusing at best. The difficulty is heightened by the fact that each standard is associated with specific social others whose expectations are brought to bear on the nubile female. If her parents are like most, they support the single standard of abstinence (although they do not discuss it fully with her). Violating their expectations may cause guilt in the young woman and serious reactions from her parents if they find out. Yet she has the freedom of dating: she can choose her partners, and spend long periods of unchaperoned time with them. This fact leads to many of the dilemmas of dating discussed in Chapter 4. Although sexual standards may be preached by parents, the day-to-day responsibility for the sexual behavior is largely left to the young people themselves.

The young woman is even more vulnerable under the double standard. Since sexual activity is acceptable for the male under this standard, the total responsibility for resisting coitus falls to the female. Under the double standard, she is subject to pressure from her male partner to engage in sexual behavior which will be disapproved by both her parents and her peers, insofar as they believe in either the double standard or the abstinent standard. Her partner may be her ally (if he keeps her secret), or her nemesis (if, believing in the double standard, he assigns her to the nonmarriageable category once she has had intercourse with him).

The permissive standard does not brand the sexually active woman as a bad woman, but it has its pitfalls. Though virginity is no longer the ideal for many young people, marriage is still the model. Love and sex are still seen within the context of marriage, and the premarital relationship follows a monogamous pattern. Schwartz (1973) found that though Yale undergraduates reported they would not lose respect for a woman who was sexually experienced, their respect did in fact decline when faced with a woman who had ten or more lovers. Some experience is expected, but "too much" can still blight a woman's "value."

The permissive standard affords women more sexual rights than the other standards, but does not protect them from exploitation. It is easy enough to pretend to care, if that is the ticket to sexual intimacy. A deception of this type can be very cruel, for in the ulterior transaction communication focuses on the self rather than on sex. And it is thus the self which is rejected and feels betrayed when deception is exposed.

In some sense the more traditional standards offer more protection to the female than does the permissive standard. Under the permissive standard, the only assurance that a young woman has comes from her partner. Though peers may share the permissive standard (and hence will not be a source of negative sanctions for nonmarital sexual activity), they may have doubts about the particular partner. Moreover, as friends are not party to the sexual contact, they are not in a position to give feedback and definitions regarding the woman's characteristics as a sexual partner. Once again, it is the partner who is in the critical position to validate and shape the woman's image of herself as a sexual being in the new context of coitus. Hence peers will not necessarily be a source of support when she takes the risk of sexual initiation.

Communication between the sexual partners is a major influence on the self-image as a sexual person—that is, on sexual identity. What is communicated depends on the vocabulary and social constructions available to the partners. Here, the sexual cultures in which they were raised have their effect, as do the sexual histories of the individuals.

The existence of a variety of sexual standards suggests a variety of social constructions of female and male sexuality which are compatible with each script—double standard, abstinence, permissive.

The Traditional Initiation: Information Dependence   In both versions of the traditional scripts—double standard and abstinence—courtship leads to marriage and monogamy, and to fertility (the focus of Stage 5). The social construction of female sexuality that best fits this script is of the essentially innocent woman awakened to genital sexuality (i.e., intercourse) by Mr. Right. De Beauvoir (1953: 352) has given us the most poignant portrait of the young girl approaching sexual initiation. This construction assumes no previous sexual experience: no homosexual or autoerotic history which has sexualized the genital area. The focus of traditional constructions of female sexuality is the vagina, which remains a sealed organ until sexual initiation. The traditional scenario of sexual initiation is dramatic. The role assigned to the female is passive, perhaps masochistic. It is the male who must forcefully rupture the hymen. The bloody sheets of the wedding night are proof of the bridegroom's potency and the bride's virtue. Some renditions of this scenario depict the virgin's pain being drowned in a tide of pleasure. She thus is permanently converted to penis-in-vagina sex, with orgasm portrayed as automatic. Of course, the lover is always experienced and skilled in giving pleasure, never hasty, clumsy, or clammy. And the virgin, naturally, develops a permanent passion for the man who deflowers her.

Clellan's *Fanny Hill* may provide an exaggerated rendition of this scenario, but it shares a sexual script which many people follow. Let us look at the social constructions of female and male sexuality that fit this script. The woman is essentially ignorant, the man experienced. If a woman is without substantial sexual experience, sexual initiation is a specific kind of learning experience. The male is cast as the teacher. One hackneyed image likens the male to a skilled musician, who can draw from the (inert) female instrument the most beautiful music.

We can accept the first part of this analysis without accepting the second. The woman who is essentially inexperienced will confront, in her first coitus, many sensations, interactions and thoughts that will be new. The extent to which the partner is qualified to label and interpret these is open to question. If the male is "experienced," it may mean only that he has had intercourse before. The limitations of his experience may be many. He may have had intercourse with one person, perhaps enough times to know that partner (but not his present one). More likely, he may have had a series of sexual encounters with partners he knew very slightly. Often these encounters have not been repeated (Simon, Berger, and Gagnon, 1972; Schofield, 1965; Kinsey et al., 1953). The physical locale of his sexual history may further limit his potential as a teacher. Sexual contacts frequently take place in cars, dorm rooms and other places where time is short and security is precarious. Almost always the "experienced" male has more experience in masturbatory release (alone or with other males) than with female partners (Kinsey et al., 1953). It seems possible that it is his experience with masturbation that he carries over into the context of heterosexual intercourse. For these reasons, he may have relatively little awareness of his own sexuality, and even less of his female partner's. The expectation, in the double standard script, that he is knowledgeable enough to be the teacher in a sexual contact may be too great for him to live up to.

Patterns of communication within and between the sexes may be protecting this myth of male competence. Among themselves, males seem to communicate about their sexual encounters in a vocabulary that lacks terms for quality. Of course, women are barred from these conversations and hence cannot contradict claims to success of their male partners. If women fail to communicate among themselves about sex, the inept partner or distasteful experience remains a secret. Nevertheless, the sex role script assigns the functions of initiation and pursuit to the male. Regardless of how inadequate he may be to assume leadership, he is likely to exercise control over the sexual situation by assigning meanings and directing the interaction. His capacity to label experience is determined by his own experience; he is likely to know more about ejaculation (and how to bring it about) than about female orgasm. Many aspects of the female's experience will escape him entirely, especially if she lacks the vocabulary and confidence to talk about them.

In sexual initiation the woman is confronting many experiences that are new. A new image of her body is reflected from her partner's reaction. Her own sexual reactions are new to her, and her partner's reaction can generate positive or negative feelings in her. Some women have reported feeling embarrassed by the sounds or motions of orgasm, and require reassurance from their partner. The "messiness" of lubrication and ejaculation or the mechanics of contraception can cause anxiety. If the partner is indifferent or shows distaste, the woman's learning will be far different from what it is when a partner shows delight and affirmation. Fear of rejection is always an underlying concern: fear that one's partner notices physical flaws, "test anxiety" about one's sexual competence, fear that the partner does not care about the person, only the body. Each of these aspects of sexual encounters has the capacity to be incorporated into sexual identity. If they are unlabeled and little discussed, they may not become firmly established. If they are labeled via alien experience (e.g., in a male vocabulary) they may be distorted.

It is reasonable to assume that, to the extent that the woman is inexperienced, lacks much sexual information or a context for discussing sex, and subscribes to traditional sex role ideology, she will be subject to information-dependence in her first sexual relationship. (And, in traditional scripts, her first relationship is her only relationship—ever.) Her definition of the whole world of sexuality is dominated by her partner.

In addition to information-dependence, others have traditionally posited an erotic dependence of the female on the male (de Beauvoir, 1953; Bernard, 1968). This seems to imply that women have no sex life, or can have no sexual satisfaction, without men. A critical dissection of this idea seems to reveal a distinctive construction of female sexuality. It assumes that the focus of sexuality is the vagina, hence the emphasis on sexual initiation (i.e., penetration). It denies the existence of self-stimulation and homo-erotic relationships. And it implies that the woman can only be sexually satisfied when she loves (a man, of course). This construction has been decisively challenged by recent research on female sexuality and by competing social constructions originating with the feminist movement and with the sexual revolution.

Scripts for Active Sexuality in Transition

The permissive standard provides a sexual script which differs in some ways from both the abstinent standard and the double standard. As a single standard, it does provide a social construction of female sexuality which is more on a par with constructions of male sexuality. Women are thought of as sexual beings, not merely as targets or reactors to male sexuality. Women's sexual desires are recognized. Though early texts on female sexuality sometimes asserted that most women are ''frigid''—i.e., inorgasmic (see Scully and Bart, 1973, for a review of standard gynecology texts). Masters and Johnson's (1966) justly famous work has made people think more objectively about female orgasm. As research accumulates, it becomes clear that most women are orgasmic under some circumstances and inorgasmic under others. Female orgasm is no longer to be thought of only in the context of certain male actions.

With the sexual revolution of the sixties, it became expected, at least in some subpopulations, that women were as interested in sex as men, and as willing to engage in coitus. In this context the idea has grown up of *women's right to orgasm*. Under the ''liberated'' sexual scripts, there is no ulterior payoff (marriage) for sex, so presumably the sex itself must be satisfying. Thus in the last ten years there has been much written about female orgasm. Often the male takes the female's orgasm as a tribute to his skill as a lover. Similarly, her ''failure'' to have orgasm is taken as a reflection on him. The male's ''obligation'' to provide his partner with an orgasm is often translated into an obligation on her part to produce one. This has resulted in an often-parodied pressure on the woman to fake orgasm, or to lie about it.

Though the permissive standard really only gives women the right to engage in sexual activity, the image of the sexually active woman has come to include a search for sexual satisfaction. This in turn has come to be interpreted narrowly as a search for orgasm. This new construction seems to parallel the common construction of male sexuality according to which ejaculation is the (sole) goal of sexual contact. Both constructions may leave out a good part of sexual experience. Little is known about the other aspects of male sexuality, in part because of a phallocentric orientation among sex researchers (Laws, 1973). But we do know something of female sexuality, and we cannot ignore women's repeated reports of sexual satisfaction that is not limited to, and may be distinct from, orgasm (Wallin and Clark, 1964). Moreover, a close look at these reports will show that there are dimensions of female sexual experience which heterosexual and homosexual contacts have in common. Existing social constructions have not yet incorporated these experiences, but we will examine them later in this section.

The permissiveness-with-affection standard has a number of elements in common with more traditional standards, as well as elements that are different. It does hold that love—in some form—is a prerequisite for sex, and it does assume a male partner. Moreover, as a social construction it does not challenge courtship as the context for the development of sexual intimacy, nor marriage as the ultimate goal. It implies monogamy. What it really is, then, is a script for *premarital* sexual behavior. It legitimizes the sexual script which many women have been covertly following since the 1920s (Kinsey et al., 1953, Table 83:339). Research findings corroborate this interpretation of the permissive standard. Women tend to be monogamous in their premarital sexual experience and to remain with their first partner. They stay with him not because of his skill as a lover, but because of their feeling for him (Simon, Berger, and Gagnon, 1972). They reserve coitus for a "serious" relationship. In the permissiveness-with-affection standard, love still plays an important part, and love and marriage are still linked.

Reiss (1960) has identified a fourth sexual standard which may be gaining in prevalence. *Permissiveness without affection* means that sex is acceptable when both partners want it and need not be "justified" by feelings of love between the partners. While affection is by no means ruled out, it does not, under this standard, dictate the nature of sexual contacts. There is no stated connection between sex and marriage, and sexual relations need not be monogamous.

Even when marriage is thought to be far in the future, the idea of it is still powerful in young women's lives. Upwards of 95 percent of young American women still expect to marry someday. As long as women's sexual behavior remains tied to their chances for marriage, abstinence, the double standard, and permissiveness with affection will continue to have their adherents. Nevertheless, some research evidence suggests a move toward the standard of permissiveness without affection. Davis (1970) finds that although college women apply the standard of affection to coitus, they report engaging in comparatively more intimate forms of sexual contact such as heavy petting with a variety of partners. Thus technical virginity is still tied to the kind of feeling associated with marriage— love and sexual exclusiveness—but other forms of sexual behavior appear less restricted.

Given the trends in sexual behavior, it seems likely that some patterns of sexual history are common but as yet unscripted. If females are engaging in sexual activity at ever younger ages, encountering a long series of partners, and anticipating an eventual marriage of essentially traditional dimensions, there are contradictions which none of the existing standards can resolve. Perhaps there are new sexual scripts which researchers have not yet interpreted. Very likely there are transitions between individual histories and adult sexual life-styles which remain unscripted. This would certainly be true for the young woman with extensive sexual experience who expects to enter into a monogamous, permanent, heterosexual marriage. It is equally true for the woman who is moving toward a lesbian or bisexual life-style, or from a traditional sexual standard to an open or nonmonogamous marriage style. And while the available social constructions are inadequate for many women's sexual life-styles in specific ways, they nonetheless seem to have some limitations in common. They all focus on heterosexual relationships and view females in terms of how they fit into men's sexual scenarios or sexual functioning.

Feminists challenge the available constructions, emphasizing relationships and the equality of partners in sex. In their view, sexual relations are reciprocal and mutual. Moulton (1972) has pointed out that the accepted word for sexual contact, *intercourse*, implies a symmetrical experience. In view of the way sexual encounters between women and men are orchestrated, this term is misleading in the extreme. It implies that sexual pleasure is produced in both women and men by the same means, by penetration and friction of the penis in the vagina. Stimulation which is sexually arousing to the female is termed *foreplay*, while ejaculation is the main event.

Making her point in a parable in which food stands for sex, Moulton likens our society to one in which women do all the cooking but men do all the eating. In her hypothetical society, the women are undernourished. There are many possible explanations (or social constructions) for this fact: for example, women do not like food, or their mouths and digestive systems (organs) are unsuited to the ingestion of food, etc. These are rationalizations for a social organization of eating which benefits men and not women. However, some women hatch a subversive scheme in the kitchen. It is called "foretaste." Although they still may not eat, once the man has started, they sneak a little taste in the kitchen during food preparation.

Social Constructions That Reflect Male Perspectives

Foreplay Moulton makes her point through the use of humor. In order to appreciate the way that female sexuality is seen through male lenses, we can look at three phenomena: foreplay, female orgasm, and penile penetration. In common usage, the term foreplay refers to the preliminaries preceding the main event (penetration and ejaculation) in a sexual interaction. Undertaken not for its own sake, for men, foreplay is a mere instrumentality. Thus, during the last decade, sex manuals have urged males to engage in foreplay in order to make their partners more receptive. If we think for a moment about what foreplay involves, we discover that for women it is often the main event. In reporting their own sexual experience, women say they like the holding and hugging, physical closeness and murmuring, kissing, touching, and caressing. It is only from a male point of view that such sexual contact is *fore*play. Women and men do appear to differ, not only in the meanings foreplay activities have for them, but also in time perspective. Some men appear to feel that foreplay is a necessary chore of little value to be got through as quickly as possible. For them, foreplay is instrumental, not an end in itself; it has value only if it facilitates sexual access or enables them to "bring" their partner to orgasm.

However, women's accounts of their own sexual feelings during foreplay reflect both an intensification of awareness relating to the partner and also awareness of a variety of sensations. The sexuality of women has been called diffuse, as contrasted with the concretely phallic focus of male sexuality. Women report sexual arousal from the touching of many body parts and enjoyment of sexual arousal, as well as enjoyment of sexual release (orgasm). Sustained periods of sexual arousal, and repeated sexual contacts, as well as the rarer multiple orgasms are also described as sources of enjoyment.

New research reveals that, particularly where the effect of sexual scripts is minimized, women's sexuality is more varied and more subtle than we have been taught to expect. One notable dimension is the sense of play—not *fore*play—and a luxurious and sensual pace. Rather than a hurry-up, goal-oriented activity, with overtones of achievement anxiety, sexual encounter has a quality of flow, a continuous high, punctuated by incidents like orgasm. Women do not necessarily conceptualize a sexual episode as "before and after" orgasm. From the female point of view, the term *foreplay* is a misnomer. Women like foreplay before, during, and after. As a social construction, foreplay clearly embodies male priorities and practices in the sexual encounter.

Orgasm   Hite (1976; especially chapters 2 and 3) reports the responses of the full 3,000 respondents to her nationwide questionnaire survey on orgasm. Questions and responses spanned many topics besides orgasm—techniques and preferences in masturbation, intercourse, clitoral stimulation, relations with women and with men, sexuality of older women, and attitudes toward the so-called sexual revolution—and Hite relies mainly on the respondents' own words in reporting the results. In the wealth and immediacy of the data she reports, it is difficult to distinguish emerging new scripts from scriptfree sexuality. Certainly there is evidence of women's concern with existing scripts, and especially with the reactions of the male partners designated as appropriate by those scripts. It appears, however, that women's experience is at odds with the sexual script in which penile penetration plays the starring role. Although some women report that intercourse is central to their sexual satisfaction, for many it is peripheral.

In speculating on the future of the institution of intercourse, Hite suggests that the form and pacing of intercourse could be varied so as to meet women's sexual preferences. New scripts for intercourse would displace the penetration-ejaculation sequence as the central focus.

Both the world of fiction, as exemplified by *Fanny Hill,* and the world of psychoanalysis, as defined by Freud, are phallocentric. It makes sense, perhaps, for men to attribute heroic powers and importance to the penis. It would make sense to glorify the clitoris, for many of the same reasons. The stimulation of these homologous organs is necessary to bring each of the sexes to orgasm. Yet, as indicated by Moulton (1972) and substantiated by Hite, it is obvious that the social constructions regarding such stimulation are not symmetrical. Research reveals that behaviors reflect this asymmetry. Respondents in Hite's study (1976: 213) report that most of their male partners are unskilled, some disinterested, and some downright resistant to stimulating the clitoris effectively. Yet it is reported by a number of women that male partners expect them to stimulate the penis, and will direct them in doing so. The males appear to have less hesitancy in asking for or even commanding the kind of stimulation they like, while many women feel uncomfortable or unjustified in doing the same. These feelings reflect an underlying premise that intercourse is for the benefit of the male partner.

Other responses of women in Hite's survey reflect the same premise. Hite asked women how they felt about not having orgasm as a result of intercourse (1976: 70–73). Some said they did not mind, for the payoff of the encounter has to do with intimacy and the partner's pleasure. Others expressed frustration and anger if a partner discontinued contact after he had climaxed, but before his female partner did. Both reactions appear to take for granted that the male has the prerogative of pacing and terminating intercourse.

Diverging from Male-Dominated Scripts: Female Sexual Preferences

These personal reports reflect the power of the sexual script on the sexual experience of individuals. As data accumulate, it becomes apparent that the preferences of women diverge from the script. The script is monolithic, and the preferences of women cover a broad spectrum. For some, penetration adds nothing to sexual arousal or enjoyment, and for still others it is a distasteful, painful, or antierotic experience.

Penetration involves distinctive sensations. For some women penetration is a specific kind of sexual thrill. Many women describe orgasms as very different, depending on many factors, including coital position. Some women report orgasms which differ in kind after childbearing. There may be wide individual differences in women's sensitivity to bodily events associated with sex, for example, the degree of awareness women have of uterine contractions accompanying orgasm. In addition to the physical sensations, penetration also has psychological meanings which enhance the experience for some women. Many women enjoy the feeling of physical strength and vigor which the body weight of a male partner and the rhythm of penile thrusting communicate. Others dislike the very same elements of the experience.

Women perceive a power dimension in the institution of intercourse. Although their sexual preferences may give penetration a low priority, they feel they risk social sanction from their partners by refusing:

> I think many of my sexual experiences arose out of my desire for sensual touching. I probably didn't want the sex, but after my partner would become very aroused, I felt obligated to have sex, because it always seemed that anyone who wanted to touch without having sex, especially sensual touching, would be a "cock-teaser"—some kind of anathema—some kind of castrator. (Hite, 1974: 49)

For women who prefer noncoital forms of sexual contact, the dilemma can be severe. If they do not insist on their own form of sexual activity, they will not experience orgasm: ". . . age (about) 13. I had my first orgasm petting. It was a very nice surprise. Once that person convinced me to 'go all the way,' the orgasm was only a memory" (Hite, 1974: 67). By conforming to male scripting, others lose sight of what is special in their own sexual preferences:

> But I loved "making out," which I would do for hours and hours. I became very excited by it, and derived great pleasure from it. At about the age of sixteen, I decided that I no longer wanted to be a virgin, and so I slept with the virgin boy I had been dating. In fact, I derived less pleasure from intercourse than I did from "making out" (petting, hugging, kissing); I remember that one of the reasons I liked intercourse was because when we were screwing I didn't have to deal with boys trying to touch my vagina (I didn't mind the penis in my vagina because it couldn't smell), and meanwhile I could have the pleasure of closeness, hugging and kissing. (Hite, 1974: 32)

When women's preferences are compared with the sexual script for penetration, it is clear that the former are often at variance with the latter. The experience of penile penetration is clearly nonessential for many women. The friction caused by penetration is much more essential to men than to women. Although this necessary stimulation can be caused by other means, heterosexual intercourse is, for men, the most socially approved. According to Blau's (1964) principle of least interest, then, the woman has more power in this situation than the man. In the light of this analysis, it is easy to see how necessary traditional social constructions of intercourse are to men. Doctrines which claim that sexual satisfaction for women depends on penetration help to bind women into an institution that benefits men more than it does women. From a female-centered viewpoint, penetration is reduced to the status of one of many options for sexual contact. It may rank high or low among a given woman's preferences, and to the extent that she is able to transcend the sexual scripts, her sexual behavior will resemble her preferences more than it does the script.

Since the publication of Masters and Johnson's research (1966), feminists have argued that penetration is irrelevant to female orgasm. What produces orgasm is "effective stimulation," which virtually always involves physical stimulation of the clitoris. Indeed, current research offers the conclusions that masturbation is the most efficient means of achieving female orgasm; in other words, it is a highly reliable method. Kinsey offers the statistic that most women can masturbate to orgasm in four minutes or less (1953, Table 83: 339).

For many women, effective stimulation ceases with penetration, at least in the male superior position. Thus, unless the partners accommodate themselves, they will not both enjoy orgasm through the same sexual contact, and certainly not simultaneously. When the ease and simplicity of orgasm through masturbation are contrasted with the difficulties, conflict, and ideological controversies surrounding orgasm through intercourse, it is easy to see why some women have decided to do without penetration, if not without men. The fact that women have this option is, of course, threatening to men both on a personal level and on a political level. When men can no longer control women's sexuality, the future of a number of social institutions is thrown into doubt.

Indeed, in a comparatively short time, sex research has produced a number of findings which have dramatically changed social constructions of female sexuality. With the discovery that orgasm is within the normal expectations of almost every woman *and* that clitoral rather than vaginal stimulation is the way to produce it, the whole picture changes. A revolution of rising expectations is under way for women. However, the social relations of sex lag behind. With the new concept of women's right to orgasm, power relations between the sexes are likely to change.

Women's Right to Orgasm: Battle Cry of Clitoral Imperialism?

In a sense, orgasm has become the battleground of clashing sexual scripts for women. As the sexual options of autoeroticism and lesbianism come to be perceived as offering women greater levels of sexual satisfaction than traditional heterosexual relations, some men may be left behind. Some writers have suggested that an "increase" in male impotence reflects a backlash against uppity bed partners.* Impotence is certainly a possible reaction to the uncertainty which many men must experience as they fail to establish the dominance they expect over their women partners.

The idea of women's right to orgasm has many consequences. Insofar as women turn to men as partners for their newfound sexuality, they must learn to communicate their desires to their partners, and insist on their own sexual pleasure. Hite's (1974) book reveals the difficulties many women have with these new responsibilities. Many men reportedly refuse or "forget" to do what their partner requests. Interestingly, many women report they feel obligated to comply with partners' requests even though the cooperation is not reciprocated. Some indicate that they feel guilty or selfish in seeking their own sexual satisfaction.

Feminist analyses (Koedt, n.d., and Atkinson, 1968) have facilitated the rise of alternate constructions of female sexuality which incorporate both the new insistence on orgasm and the preference for mutuality in sex which women have desired. The argument has been developed that in loving other women exclusively, women experience better human relationships and personal growth as well as better sex. Some lesbian feminists have urged a principled rejection of sexual relationships (i.e., with men) that include nonmutuality and inequality.

Other new constructions of female sexuality seem to be based on a popularization of the new feminist critique, grafted onto the old branch of the sexual revolution. It is argued that the clitoris is a superior organ, since it has no reproductive function but only serves pleasure. Hence women should seek to optimize sexual experience focused on the clitoris and its orgasmic capabilities. A potential danger of this "clitoral imperialism" is that it may lead to an essentially phallic construction of female sexuality that parallels the phallocentric constructions of male sexuality (see Laws, 1973). It encourages the objectification of the partner, who is seen mainly as a means to one's own sexual gratification and may be evaluated on this basis. The sexual liberation of women thus draws women into the sex-as-achievement syndrome, with test anxiety, competition, training in technical skills. We women now have the potential of developing a wham-bam-thank-you-sir kind of sexuality which is limited to the four-minute orgasm and parallels the male masturbatory style to which so many women have objected. But from our male partners we should have learned that a narrowly phallic emphasis leads to a body-centered, as contrasted with a

---

*Such claims must be viewed with great caution. Impotence is one of those phenomena on which we have no reliable baseline data against which to assess "change." To the extent that more men are consulting physicians about this problem, it may be as a result of the liberalization of sexual attitudes which makes it possible for people with a variety of sexual concerns to seek help.

person-centered, approach to sexuality and to sexual relations. This, in turn, leads our awareness away from the richer and more complex female sexuality which we have just begun to (re)discover. As the phallocentric male constructions leave out much of men's sexual potential, constructions of female sexuality which are modeled on the male will exhibit the same inadequacies.

Future Scripts for Female Sexuality

It appears that as a woman begins her sexual career, a range of alternative sexual scripts confronts her. In the future even more than at present, Stage 4 will involve a welter of sexual experiences which must be integrated into sexual identity. The social constructions which are more crystallized and legitimated will continue to have power over women's sexual self definitions, but as alternative constructions are articulated these too will appear to the individual as options. A major limitation on the forms that sexual identity can take will continue to be the set of available sexual life-styles (see Chapter 5). *Individuals must find some responsive community with which to share the formulation of sexual identity or suffer continual doubts and fluctuations in self definition.*

By no means are all the scripts articulated, nor are the sexual communities waiting. Nevertheless, sexual identity does not merely reflect social realities, but personal experience as well. If we think about the trends in the sexual experiences of women in Stage 4, we can speculate about some of the dimensions of future sexual identities.

Most women will have a series of partners.   Even those who follow the standard sexual script may find themselves divorced or widowed and may practice serial monogamy. Even in 1953, Kinsey found 26 percent of married women reporting at least one extramarital affair by the age of forty (Kinsey, 1953: 416). Premarital experience is now estimated to be more common than ever before, and nonmonogamous marriage forms, though a minority, also occur. Single women are virtually sure to have a series of sexual partners. This will be true for heterosexual, lesbian, and bisexual women.

Experience with a number of sexual partners will not have uniform effects across all individuals. One effect we might look for is more awareness of the self as a sexual being—that is, sexual identity. Identity, we recall, is the sense of self based on recognizing what is common and what endures across occasions. In the context of sexual experience, women learn about themselves by thinking about their sexual history, testing, selecting, and self-affirming.

Female sexuality will not be limited to experience with partners. More and more, women are receiving permission, instruction, and support in learning about their own bodies and the patterns of their own sexual response. Training in masturbation is currently a valuable experience for many women. Some experience their first orgasm through such learning programs, and many have increased their skill in producing their own sexual pleasure (Dodson, 1972).

Women will need to take more responsibility for their own sexuality than ever before. As sexual self-identity is strengthened by a range of experience and practice, we may expect changes in the character of female sexual behavior. Women will probably become more agentic and less reactive or passive in sexual situations. Their responsibilities will include contraception and precautions against the proliferating group of sexually transmitted diseases, knowledge about their own sexual preferences, and serious efforts to communicate about them. Ask for What You Want is a motto of the new female sexuality.

Women will also have to take responsibility for protecting themselves against bad sexual and human experiences: exploitation, danger, and alienation. It is particularly difficult for women to say no in an era of sexual liberation. The right of the individual woman to be selective and to respond to her own and not another's priorities has not yet been established.

Woman will be seen as continuously or permanently sexual, not merely in episodes, when she has a partner (and the "right kind" of partner at that). As women experience more partners, and as they take responsibility for their own sexuality, a new social construction of female sexuality may emerge. In a related development, *the sexuality of the individual woman will come to be seen as an attribute of her own person, not of her relationship with someone, and certainly not as anyone's property.*

Stage 4, the period in human development devoted to developing adult sexuality, comprises a great range and complexity of sexual experiences. The traditional sexual script—heterosexual/monogamous/married, permanently—seems remote from some of them. It specifies mate selection and marriage for the young woman in Stage 4. This sets the scene for the traditional developmental experience of Stage 5, fertility within the context of legal, heterosexual marriage. Clearly, the traditional trappings are not essential for the events of Stage 5 to take place: conceiving and bearing children are biological events. The social context does strongly condition the way the individual will experience these events, however, and may have an effect on the way sexual identity develops as a consequence of fertility.

Stage 5: Fertility

Almost all women are potentially fertile. When we speak of fertility as a distinct phase in the development of sexual identity, however, we are referring not to this potentiality but to the event of becoming pregnant and its consequences.

Fertility, like sexual intercourse, is a contingent rather than an essential aspect of female sexuality. Not all women engage in the activities which are the focus of Stages 4 and 5. More and more, we are beginning to think of fertility as an option rather than as a universal condition of women's lives. In part this is a result of improved contraceptive technology. It is only in the last fifteen years that the availability of reliable contraception and its widespread adoption have made pregnancy avoidable and hence an option. Many adult women can recall when their sex lives were governed by the fear of pregnancy. Though the Pill has drawbacks which are generally conceded, it has high reliability in contraception and is the most popular method ever known.

Improved technology is only part of the picture, however. When we consider popular terms for contraception, we can see that they invoke different constructions of female sexuality. *Family planning* implies a context of marriage and fertility, with contraception only an aid to the spacing and timing of pregnancies. This is a pronatalist construction of fertility control. On the other hand, neither *birth control* nor *contraception* implicates any social system larger than the woman herself. The assertion that women own their bodies and have absolute rights to control them comes from the feminist movement. The existence of this social construction can change the social meanings of fertility. It separates sexual intercourse from fertility, making these two distinct decisions. It denies that marriage is the sole context for sex. It implies that sexuality is an aspect of the woman, not a property of the relationship. It also implies that the responsibility for her sexuality—not only contraception, but decisions about sexual practices and sexual partners—is under the individual's control, and cannot readily be abdicated. Perhaps the most important element in the feminist construction of female sexuality, certainly for this developmental stage, is that *the only arbiter of her own fertility is the woman herself.* This means she has the right to practice contraception and abortion. It also means she has the right to determine the social relations she wants as a context for her fertility: a single household, a marital household, a lesbian household, a joint household.

Competing Scripts: The Traditional and the Insurgent

The changes of the last ten to fifteen years mean that there are now competing social constructions of fertility. We may think of these as the traditional script and the insurgent script. Although the former is the dominant construction, a number of trends seem to reflect the influence of the insurgent script. For the last ten years, the birthrate has been falling in the United States. This reflects a decrease in the number of children families desire and in fact have. And generally, it signifies a reduction in family size, not a transition from a life-style with children to a childfree life-style. Nevertheless, while only a few years ago the proportion of voluntarily childless couples was estimated at 1 percent or less (U.S. Bureau of the Census, 1975), attitude surveys suggest that this proportion may rise in the future. More college students report the intention not to marry, or not to have children, or both. Increasingly, fertility is seen as an option, not an obligation. Social scientists have identified a pattern of values which they call pronatalism, and demonstrated the ways in which many social arrangements foster pronatalism and discredit or deny other social constructions (Peck and Senderowitz, 1974). Organizations like the National Organization for Non-Parents (NON) spell out their arguments against childbearing.

If Berger and Luckmann (1966) are right, alternative constructions are in fact in competition, not in coexistence. Thus we find that arguments for childfree life-styles not only stress the advantages of childfree life-styles but also attack the myths of pronatalism. Conversely, in the recurring attempts to make abortion illegal we witness the backlash of the dominant social construction against the feminist alternative.

Much of the resistance to new constructions of female sexuality takes the form of counterattacks against what is perceived as an attack on the family. The social script does impose alterations of female sexual identity as the individual moves from stage to stage. With marriage, the woman is expected to abandon sexual display and sexual experimentation and remain faithful to her husband. The sexual element is virtually expunged from her relations with the social world.* With fertility, even the character of her sexual relations with her husband is likely to change. However, a new dimension is added to her female sexuality with pregnancy and the

---

*The controversy about the "weakening of the American family" can be seen as a conflict about control and about naming. In the dominant script it is apparent that female sexuality is subsumed under the unit of the family. The interests of women—or even their individual attributes—are subordinated to this social unit, which in its turn is thought to be valuable to society. Feminists deny that a woman ceases to be a person, and a sexual person, when she marries. The conflict of naming involves defining the wife as a member of the family unit versus defining her as a married female person.

addition of the maternal role. According to traditional constructions of female sexuality, a woman is less a woman who has not borne a child, just as the single woman is less womanly than the wife.

In the traditional script, pregnancy is recognized and applauded, within a context of social normalcy; the woman is married; the husband is present; the nuclear unit is solvent; and, increasingly, pregnancies are expected to be planned and few. In the traditional script, marriage is assumed as an intervening event. In some American subcultures, however, the positive evaluation of bearing children is not contingent on marriage.

Because our emphasis is on sexual identities, we will not go into detail about other aspects of wifehood and motherhood. The importance of the two statuses is, however, paramount, as our previous discussions have indicated. Marriage confers adult status on the woman. As a wife, she is a demonstrated success in the competition to which Stages 3 and 4 are devoted (unless, perchance, she should lose her husband; then she becomes a failure). As a mother, she takes on additional responsibilities, which are shared less and less by her partner as the family (and the workload) grow. Very few new mothers are prepared for the energy drain involved in caring for a newborn, and many mothers feel that the demands of time and vigilance do not abate until the child enters school. Moreover, in the child-centered American family, cultural values support reorganizing the life of the pair around the child and do not favor arrangements which segregate the child's schedule from that of the parents or which assign primary care of the child to someone other than the mother. Consequently the household is reorganized with the birth of children. Many aspects of the spouses' relationship alter, including the sexual.

Family Life: A Gradual Loss of Sexual Identity   Changes in patterns of sexual relating within marriage are surprisingly little researched, perhaps because the traditional script endorses a primary focus on family for the wife and on occupation for the husband. In what little research we have on marital sexuality, it is difficult to discover much about female sexuality. The unit of analysis seems to be the couple. Opportunities for sexual relations seem to be restricted to certain times, and the requirements of privacy restrict the locale of sexual contacts. In the traditional script, the wife is limited to her husband as a sexual partner. And whatever the script, the opportunities of housebound wives to meet other partners is very limited.

Sex between the spouses often becomes routine and even scarce (Wallin and Clark, 1964); it occurs at the husband's initiative and follows his rhythm and may often be disrupted or postponed by the demands of children. Although research suggests that female sexual drive and orgasmic capacity peak during the thirties, many factors in married life militate against the continued sexual development of women.

Because the focus of the sexual script shifts to family life at this stage, the assumption is sometimes made that the sexual relationship between the partners is frozen and remains the same from this point. Folklore has it that both women and men lose interest in sex in middle life and sexual desire and sexual behavior gradually diminish. Many events can intervene to change this script, of course. The loss of a partner, through divorce or death, places the survivor once again in a mating market which resembles that of Stage 4. Some couples remain together but experiment with nonmonogamous sexual life-styles. Extramarital relationships are not uncommon, and some spouses consider them a good antidote to the routinization of marital sex. Other individuals discover bisexual and homosexual desires, and after a heterosexual career, develop these aspects of their sexual identity in the middle years.

Some of the changes in sexual identity during Stage 5 are prefigured by the experiences of earlier stages. For some women, a combination of religious prohibition and inadequate sex education has made many aspects of sex forbidding or forbidden. Much unlearning can occur in the protected relationship of marriage. Many conflicts center on the need for contraception. A particularly dramatic case from Hite's research (1974) illustrates the way in which the spector of unwanted fertility can be the dominant aspect of a marital relationship:

> Contraception or lack of it affected my sexual life as food or lack of it affects a human's chances to survive. I used the rhythm method for 5 years complete with temperature taking, chart keeping and calendar eyeing, turning the bedroom into a laboratory. After my third unplanned baby born in as many years, I desperately wrote a letter to the good Bishop inquiring if there had been any change in Vatican policy. I never got a chance to use the blessed thermometer as I was already pregnant with the fourth. My husband was wild with disgust by now and insisted he'd divorce me if I didn't get an abortion. (Hite, 1974: 292)

Another history had a happier ending:

> The freedom I felt right after I went on the Pill was like some kind of explosion—incredible—and I think the first few times with my husband then were probably the wildest for sheer release of long pent-up feelings, even though we were still on terribly shaky ground as far as the whole marriage was concerned. I suddenly looked younger, felt younger, dressed younger, acted younger—there was simply no comparison. (Hite, 1974: 296)

In quite another area of marital sexual life, the effects of prior socialization can be seen. It appears that women, once they have children, feel impelled to deny or neutralize their children's sexuality, if not actually to punish it. Even those who can remember their own sexual experimentation and know that their sex lives did not begin on the wedding night seem to buy into the Big Lie in one way or another. They attempt to shield their children from the sexuality of adults, not only that of the proverbial stranger who offers candy, but of the parents as well. This imposes a further requirement of circumspection on married lovers.

Schaefer (1973) has analyzed the way the Big Lie affects the sexual learning of the young. A much studied phenomenon, the incest taboo, has a bearing here which has not been analyzed for its connection with sexual identity of women in this developmental stage. The incest taboo not only prohibits sexual relations between members of the nuclear family but, I believe, requires the desexualization of these relations as well. This has a particular impact on the sexual experiences women have which are specific to fertility, as we shall see. Though there are many interpretations of the necessity of the incest taboo, one aspect of this prohibition would appear to be the prevention of role conflict within the small social system of the family. If, as stated, the focus of the family unit shifts once there are children, then the preeminent role of the woman becomes that of mother. Given the sexual script which we have analyzed, she must then deny the child's sexuality and her own, *particularly vis-à-vis the child*. This avoidance shows up in the author's research in progress, in which young women overwhelmingly report nonsocial sources of information about sexual topics. The mother is the source for a few bits of information (mostly having to do with female bodily functions and not with interpersonal sex), and the father and other family members are virtually never mentioned (McDaniel, 1977).

Unscripted Dimensions of Fertility There are a number of dimensions of female sexual experience connected with fertility which remain unscripted. These include bodily sensations and changes in body image connected with pregnancy, birth, nursing, and sexual intercourse during and after pregnancy. Newton (1955) has suggested that these are omitted from the social constructions of female sexuality because as a culture we acknowledge only those aspects of female sexuality in which men have a direct interest. This observation is quite consistent with our analysis of social constructions relating to women in the stages of sexual identity development we have examined so far. The way in which the incest taboo fits into the sexual script seems to provide another reason for the neglect of a large part of women's experience with fertility. Insofar as sexual feelings are aroused by mothering, the incest taboo and the Big Lie combine to deny or cover up their existence.

Only in the work of female writers (and that rather recently) do we find explicit treatment of the sexual feelings evoked by nursing, by pregnancy, and by giving birth. It has long been thought that nursing speeds the recovery of muscular strength in the pelvis and uterus following childbirth, but only recently have we begun to pay attention to the potential for pleasure that the uterine contractions which accompany nursing can give.

Nursing is, of course, a pleasure that can exist in a household which does not include a male partner. Although no research is yet available on the experiences of lesbian mothers, a number of court cases have asserted the right of lesbian mothers to the care and custody of their children. This is an area of some controversy, and not all decisions have favored the mother. Though most persons would agree that conception requires, if not an ongoing relationship with a male partner, at least a cursory introduction to a viable sperm, the normal script goes further. *It assumes that a woman may not be a mother without being a wife.* Yet it is apparent that many aspects of female sexuality depend in no way on men, and this is as true of the experiences involved in fertility as it is in other developmental stages.

Another neglected aspect of female sexual pleasure has to do with sensations arising from the vagina, uterus, and other internal organs. While Masters and Johnson (1966) have demonstrated the importance of clitoral stimulation for orgasm, many women continue to report that they experience different sensations with vaginal penetration. The displacement of organs and varying sensations of fullness and pressure during pregnancy seem to alter sexual experiences. As mentioned above, some women find that they are much more orgasmic after the first pregnancy than before.

The availability of "natural" or "cooperative" methods of childbirth seems to have opened up some serendipitous sexual experiences, as well as providing an alternative to immobilization, fear, and pain, which are associated with the traditional practice of obstetrics in this country. Some women experience birth by natural childbirth as the most extended and intense orgasm of their lives. For others, the deep blending of sensual and tender feelings makes giving birth a sublime and deeply affirming experience.

As with other aspects of female sexuality, the context of childbirth has a profound effect on what kind of experience it is, and how it affects the development of sexual identity. The development of natural or cooperative childbirth was a reform movement, aimed at correcting unnecessarily alienating and even dangerous obstetrical practices. It opened up the possibility for parents to share an experience in which women and men had always been divided. The benefits of having a loving and supportive partner present during labor are not, of course, limited to situations where the partner is the father of the child, the legal husband, or a member of the male gender. Here again, however, individuals in more experimental lifestyles have encountered resistance from the authorities who preside over childbirth preparation classes and delivery rooms. The normal script makes its presence felt even (or especially) at the moment of birth.

Stage 6: Postfertility

The idea of a sexual script that is divided into age-graded stages implies that a woman is expected to be a different kind of sexual being at different stages. Although women exercise their individual options at each stage, they are in some sense judged according to the social standard. Although fertility is a contingent rather than an essential aspect of female sexuality in the emerging sexual script, the traditional script has it that the woman who does not bear children is less than a woman. This label is projected onto the woman who is past childbearing as well as the voluntarily childless.

In our culture, attractiveness is based on the standard of the nubile girl. And thus as, by definition, the individual woman's attractiveness wanes, so do her power and worth. This happens gradually, not overnight. But there is an event which serves as the focus for the transition from functioning woman to has-been: menopause. Being a menopausal woman is a distinct status. The image of the menopausal woman contains in exaggerated terms many of the disvalued stereotypes about women (irritability, irrationality, emotionality). It seems that without the countervailing influence of feminine, nubile sexual attractiveness, misogynistic attitudes of men emerge unalloyed and fasten on the older woman. Indeed, the image of the menopausal woman has many elements in common with the image of the witch.

More than any other, the menopausal woman is the victim of a peculiar feature of the social definition of female sexual identity: the tendency to evaluate the adequacy of female sexual identity in terms of (1) attractiveness to males and (2) fertility. Woman's own sexual drive is left out of this assessment, as are gains for the woman.

Social constructions of female sexuality in our culture reflect primarily its instrumental value *for others:* Attractiveness is valued because it facilitates sexual enjoyment and sexual fantasies of men; fertility is valued because it serves the society's need to perpetuate itself through new generations and because it confirms male virility. Although the woman in her mid-forties may be radiant, lively, healthy, and sexier than she has ever been in her life, by social definition she is a has-been. In order to assert her own sexual identity, she has to buck the social script. Moreover, the script allows men to take the initiative in sexual encounters, but not women. If men do not seek her out, the sexually interested older woman must buck the script in indicating her interest and pursuing it. And since the mating script defines eligible males as those who are older and more prestigious than their partner, the woman who chooses a younger male is defying convention in still another way.

The residue of Puritan culture is manifest in the scripting of the sexual life cycle. There is a lingering sense that all sex is bad, and special dispensations are required to permit some sex for some purposes (lawful reproduction within marriage, for example). This kind of thinking, subterranean and unconscious as it often is, is more apparent in the script provided for women than that provided for men. The period when women are permitted to flaunt their sexual attributes is limited to the relatively brief time they have the status of nubile female. A woman is allowed to be sexy only at that stage in her life when a man desires her.

The older woman, more than any other, is placed in double jeopardy by the sexual script. Even if she has faithfully followed the cultural script to middle age, she has not earned any credit as a sexual person. She can be a respectable married lady and a mother (or a widow), or even a grandmother, but she is not permitted to be a sexual person. Her years of sexual experience do not, at this stage, define her sexual status. In the normal script, she is considered postsexual, both because she is beyond childbearing and because no man desires her. This is bleak enough, but if she flouts the sexual script she may be exposed to ridicule or abuse. An examination of three images of the sexually active older woman gives some flavor of the options presented by the accepted sexual script.

Grandma is a regular feature of the Buck Brown cartoons in *Playboy,* and the way she is depicted indicates the limits of sexual liberation as represented in men's magazines. She is portrayed as a ridiculous and revolting figure, capable of frightening normal young men as she violates all the conventions of the sexy (passive) woman. She avidly pursues beautiful young males, and she is not above tricking or bribing them. In a parody of seductiveness, her costume, the standard brief and diaphanous nighty, reveals not the idealized and sexualized body of a nubile girl, but her long pendulous breasts and scrawny legs. What is the message?

Another contemporary morality tale, only slightly less a caricature than the Buck Brown cartoons, is found in the movie *The Graduate*. The sinister Mrs. Robinson, a middle-aged, sexually unsatisfied woman, is portrayed with some female glamour but with many traditionally unacceptable characteristics. She is punished for her unfeminine aggressiveness in initiating the seduction of Benjamin and for being too old to be his partner (and perhaps for using him as a sexual object, as well) by an unhappy outcome. Benjamin, of course, did not violate the script as did Mrs. Robinson; he was raped. Thus he is redeemed, finds a younger woman, and gets a happy ending.

The pairing depicted in this film is such an atypical one that we might ask—following the standard script: What does he see in her? Perhaps the answer is to be found in the sexual script. Of course, it is written from a male perspective: it specifies the advantages for the male, ignoring both the woman's interests and the possibility of mutual gain. A male tradition has it that older women are good sexual partners, for they do not risk pregnancy, they seldom talk about their sexual activities, and their gratitude for attention is unbounded. Also, their partners are not expected to wine them, dine them, and engage in courtship rituals. Indeed, to appear in public as a pair would expose both to ridicule.

While sexuality of older people is in general denied or tabooed, this is more true with respect to women than to men. The double standard persists: the older man may still pursue younger women, and although his *sexual* attractiveness may not be dazzling, it is understood that other attributes—power, money, experience—can make him a viable trader in the sexual marketplace. The older woman, however, is expected to be permanently out of circulation. Yet Stage 6 in our model spans a period of twenty years or more, and the social situations in which women find themselves can change drastically over that time. The normal script for Stage 5 provides that the woman loses interest in sex; with menopause, it is sometimes assumed, she loses the physical capacity for orgasm or perhaps intercourse, instead of merely the capacity to conceive. Social myths have impeded research on the sexuality of aging persons (Rubin, 1973). There may be some diminution of erectile capacity among men over forty, and this might suggest some adjustment in sexual patterns. *In women, there is no evidence that menopause has any physical effect on sexual desire,* although psychological sequelae range from mild to substantial, and from euphoria to grief, depending on the individual's feelings about childbearing.

Social status, too, has its effects on sexuality after menopause. Often society conveniently assumes that the widow or divorcee has no sexual desires, since she has lost her partner. Sex differentials in mortality rates may create a real shortage of partners for women in their sixties, corresponding to the shortage specified in the sexual script. Some of Hite's older respondents ruefully cited the problem of finding partners. In the words of one unhappy woman:

> I am now forty-four and have had some sensational love trips, but my increased age has made a difference in sex for me, because of the culmination of my choosiness and the world's present insistence on sex as a youth symbol. I had thought that if a person (woman) were terrific in her own right and togetherness, her sexual attractiveness would remain self-evident for her lifetime. With what I know I'm capable of, and with what's available to me on the 'sexual marketplace,' it looks like it's gonna be a long cold winter for us single over-forty ladies. *Damn Damn Damn!* (Hite, 1976: 352)

Some respondents, however, had found a new lease on their sex life with a younger partner, often ten years younger or more. Others had discovered, late in life, sexual relationships with women. Older women, too, were becoming skilled at masturbation, some for the first time.

Sexual Identity of Older Women

In every stage of sexual development, we have found discrepancies between social constructions of female sexuality and individuals' experiences. These disparities are more extreme at the earliest and latest stages, where the female person is essentially defined as sexless. Social sanctions underscore the prescriptive nature of these statements of fact. Yet we have found young children manage to evade these, and we are beginning to find that older women do too. The existence of a sexual script means that there are approved and disapproved ways of being sexual. The sexual identities of individuals reflect their experiences with approval and disapproval but are not determined by them.

We can anticipate much more research on the sexuality of older women in the future. We should expect to find that sexual experience is limited by some of the factors discussed here—the availability of partners, physical limitations and general health, living arrangements, and social climate. Counterbalancing these limitations, we can expect to find evidence of a cumulative sexual identity and confidence in that identity, a valuing of their sexual history, awareness of their own preferences and responses, and the capacity to participate actively in structuring sexual activity in satisfying ways. Older women may be more able than most to construct their own sexuality in postpatriarchal ways.

Sexual identity is not made by one's sexual history, but by making sense of that history. Social constructions which legitimize experiences have a role to play, and in the future we can anticipate that, for postmenopausal as for younger women, new social constructions will become available and bring some experiences out of the shadows.

References

Atkinson, T.-G. (1968). Vaginal Orgasm as a Mass Hysterical Survival Response. New York: The Feminists.

Bem, S.L., and S.A. Lewis (1975). Sex Role Adaptability: One Consequence of Psychological Androgyny. Journal of Personality and Social Psychology 31(4): 634–643.

Berger, P., and T. Luckmann (1966). The Social Construction of Reality. Garden City, N.Y.: Doubleday.

Bernard, J. (1968). The Sex Game. Englewood Cliffs, N.J.: Prentice-Hall.

Blau, P. (1964). Exchange and Power in Social Life. New York: Wiley.

Block, J. (1973). Conceptions of Sex Role: Some Cross-cultural and Longitudinal Perspectives. American Psychologist 28(6):512–527.

Blumstein, P., and P. Schwartz (1974). Lesbianism and Bisexuality. *In* Sexual

Deviance and Sexual Deviants. E. Goode and R. Troiden, eds. New York: William Morrow.

Brown, R.M. (1973). Rubyfruit Jungle. Plainfield, Vt.: Daughters.

Chicago, J. (1975). Through the Flower: My Struggle as a Woman Artist. Garden City, N.Y.: Doubleday.

Davis, K. (1970). Sex on Campus: Is There a Revolution? Medical Aspects of Human Sexuality, Winter 1970.

de Beauvoir, S. (1953). The Second Sex. New York: Knopf.

Dodson, B. (1972). Liberating Masturbation. Union, N.J.: Survey Research Corporation.

Fagot, B.I., and G.R. Patterson (1969). An In-Vivo Analysis of Reinforcing Contingencies for Sex-Role Behaviors in the Pre-school Child. Developmental Psychology 1(5):563–568.

Gagnon, J.H., W. Simon, and A.J. Berger (1970). Some Aspects of Sexual Adjustment in Early and Later Adolescence. *In* The Psychopathology of Adolescence. J. Zubin and A. Freedman, eds. New York: Grune and Stratton.

Hite, S. (1974). Sexual Honesty by Women for Women. New York: Warner Paperback Library.

———(1976). The Hite Report. New York: Macmillan.

Kinsey, A.C., W.B. Pomeroy, and C.E. Martin (1948). Sexual Behavior in the Human Male. Philadelphia: Saunders.

Kinsey, A.C., et al. (1953). Sexual Behavior in the Human Female. Philadelphia: Saunders.

Koedt, A. (n.d.). The Myth of the Vaginal Orgasm. Boston: New England Free Press.

Kohlberg, L. (1966). A Cognitive-Developmental Analysis of Children's Sex Role Concepts and Attitudes. *In* The Development of Sex Differences. B. Maccoby, ed. Stanford, Calif.: Stanford University Press.

Kohn, M., and E. Carroll (1960). Social Class and the Allocation of Parental Responsibility. Sociometry 23:378–392.

Laws, J.L. (1973). Exotica ≠ Erotica: A Plea for Continuities in the Study of Human Behavior and Sexual Behavior. Paper presented at the meetings of the American Psychological Association.

Libby, R., and R. Whitehurst, eds. Marriage and Its Alternatives: Exploring Intimate Relationships. Glenview, Ill.: Scott, Foresman.

Masters, W.H., and V.E. Johnson (1966). Human Sexual Response. Boston: Little, Brown.

McDaniel, J. (1977). The Role of Significant Others in the Acquisition of Sex Information among College Women. Ph.D. dissertation, Cornell University.

Money, J. (1968). Sex Errors of the Body. Baltimore: The Johns Hopkins Press.

Morris, J. (1974). Conundrum. New York: Signet Press.

Moulton, J. (1972). Philosophical Confusions in Descriptions of Sexual Behavior. Unpublished.

Newton, N. (1955). Maternal Emotions: A Study of Women's Feelings toward Menstruation, Pregnancy, Childbirth, Breast Feeding, Infant Care, and Other Aspects of Their Femininity. New York: Paul B. Hoche.

Peck, E., and J. Senderowitz, eds. (1974). Pronatalism: The Myth of Mom and Apple Pie. New York: Crowell.

Pleck, J. (1973). New Concepts of Sex Role Identity. Paper presented at the Society for the Scientific Study of Sex, New York.

Reiss, I. (1960). Premarital Sexual Standards in America. New York: The Free Press.

Ross, S.A. (1971). A Test of Generality of the Effects of Deviant Pre-school Models. Developmental Psychology 4:262–267.

Rubin, I. (1973). The "Sexless Older Years": A Socially Harmful Stereotype. *In* Sexual Development and Behavior. A.M. Juhasz, ed. Homewood, Ill.: The Dorsey Press.

Schaefer, L. (1973). Women and Sex: Sexual Experiences and Reactions of a Group of Thirty Women as Told to a Female Psychotherapist. New York: Pantheon.

Schofield, M. (1965). The Sexual Behavior of Young People. London: Longman, Green.

Schwartz, P. (1973). Social Games and Social Roles: Effects of a College Dating System. Ph.D. dissertation, Yale University.

Scully, D., and B. Bart (1973). A Funny Thing Happened on the Way to the Orifice: Women in Gynecology Textbooks. American Journal of Sociology 78(3):1045–1050.

Simon, W., A.S. Berger, and J.H. Gagnon (1972). Beyond Anxiety and Fantasy: The Coital Experiences of College Youth. Journal of Youth and Adolescence 1(3):203–222.

Stoller, R. (1968). Sex and Gender: On the Development of Masculinity and Femininity. New York: Science House.

U.S. Bureau of the Census (1975). Fertility Expectations of American Women. June 1974. Table 3. Current Population Reports, Series P-20, No. 277. Washington, D.C.: U.S. Government Printing Office.

Wallin, P., and A.L. Clark (1964). Religiosity, Sexual Gratification, and Marital Satisfaction in the Middle Years of Marriage. Social Forces 42(3):303–309.

Chapter Three

Woman's Body–Woman's Mind: Biological, Psychological, and Social Interactions

Rejecting Biology as Destiny

"The female anatomy, *mentality,* and reproductive biochemistry are initiated, maintained, and controlled by hormones" (Collins and Newton, 1974: 1, emphasis added). So reads the first sentence of a recent book on the biochemistry of women, a volume which claims on its copyright page that "this book represents information obtained from authentic and highly regarded sources. . . . Every reasonable effort has been made to give reliable data and information." Women's *mentality* is initiated, maintained, and controlled by hormones? Nonsense. Reliable scientific data are not available to support a generalization of this sort. Statements like the one by Collins and Newton are distortions of the most basic principles of scientific discourse; they would be unworthy of attention, much less concern, if it were not for one important fact. They serve an ideology about the "nature of woman" which justifies and perpetuates a set of beliefs, attitudes, and actions which many women and some men experience as oppressive. *Biology is destiny* is a phrase which has been used as a rough characterization of this ideology, and the suggestion that the "raging hormonal influences" of the menstrual cycle render women "unfit for top jobs" (New York Times, 26 July 1970) is a direct expression of just one of its political functions.

A review of the literature suggests that the viewpoint quoted above, while unusually explicit, is not untypical. Scientists who have studied the psychology of human female reproductive processes have looked almost exclusively to biological factors as the sole causes of the phenomena being investigated. This limited perspective may be related to the fact that biological causes, seemingly immutable, fit most readily into an ideology which justifies and maintains the status quo in the relations between women and men. Arguments directed against scientists' self-interested

motives do not, of course, bear directly upon the substance of their research. But such arguments do suggest where one might look in this
research both for lacunae and for overstatement. Unfortunately for the
development of knowledge, both are easily found in research on women
and their bodies.

In our review here of the psychological research on menstruation, birth,
and menopause, we suggest that it does not give an adequate picture of
women's experience largely because investigators have been limited by
their beliefs that a woman's biology is closely related to her destiny as a
social being. Further evidence will be discussed which suggests that the
same beliefs which guide and limit the scientific research also influence
what women actually do and experience in connection with the major
events in their reproductive lives. Thus in its most general form the argument put forth in this chapter will be that the scientific picture of women's
experience and the subjective realities to which women attest have each
been constructed by social processes: science as a social activity and
individual experience as a product of a person's interactions with her
social environment. The thrust of this argument, it will become clear, is
different from the usual assumptions that women's reproductive biology
fairly directly causes certain psychological events, and that these psychological events are in turn fairly accurately depicted in the scientific
studies. These usual assumptions seem not only unwarranted but untrue,
since they ignore the demonstrable effects of social variables both in shaping the psychological experience of reproductive events and in the activities involved in doing science.

It is a truism that the study of psychological consequences of changes in
bodily states is unavoidably contaminated by cognitive and social factors;
the psychological state of an individual is always a product of the interaction of social and biological processes. It is less often noted, however, that
there may be no scientific reason why investigators should find it useful to
make inferences about direct causal connections between physical states
and behavior or experiences. What we are ultimately aiming for, surely, is
a description of biological, psychological, and social *interactions*. We want
to know whether and why certain psychological events occur in particular
individuals in particular social circumstances in particular physical states.
To regard biological processes as "causes" of psychological events and
social and psychological variables as "contaminants" or sources of variance to be controlled seems to reflect undue and unwise reliance upon a
simplistic version of a natural science cause-and-effect model.

Since the social and psychological factors influencing a woman's experience and behavior have been so often ignored or "controlled for" in
scientific studies of menstruation, birth, and menopause, the following
review will place relatively more emphasis on them than is usual. This will
provide a necessary context within which existing data on interactions

between female biological processes and female behavior may be interpreted.

The Menstrual Syndrome: Truth or Fiction?

Anthropologists, psycholinguists, and sociologists have observed in a variety of contexts that the language used by a social group in talking about things or events can tell us much about the way that group conceptually structures physical and social reality (Whorf, 1956; Brown, 1958; and Thorne and Henley, 1975). Societies seem to make relatively fine distinctions in their vocabularies among events or phenomena that are of functional importance to them, while they do not make distinctions among things that, for them, do not need to be differentiated. The language thus both provides and represents a social construction of reality which affects the ways in which individual speakers of that language encode their experience. The Eskimo language, for example, has several words for what speakers of English simply call "snow," and it is reasonable to suppose that this linguistic differentiation reflects a distinction among several culturally significant types of snow.

Research on attitudes suggests that speakers of a single language may exhibit a somewhat related tendency on the psychological level. That is, individuals seem to make differentiations among things that are important to them (and to which they will respond differentially) and to lump together under a single label things they consider less significant. People with strong liberal or conservative political views, for instance, might make very fine distinctions among politicians with views somewhat similar to their own but dismiss all those whose views differ by some critical degree as "hidebound conservatives" or "radical liberals."

The vocabulary for female reproductive processes, then, would seem to indicate the meaning and importance that society attaches to them. A specific event may have many or no labels, and such labels may have positive or negative connotations, but in any case they reveal something about the ways in which both the society and the individual members of it are likely to think, talk, and act with respect to the event. Ernster used the material in the Folklore Archives of the University of California at Berkeley as a basis for her analysis of English-language slang expressions, "euphemisms," for menstruation. She found that not only are there a very large number of such expressions but also a large number with negative connotations: "the curse," "under the weather," "lady troubles." In general, such expressions imply that the menstrual flow is unpleasant, painful, embarrassing, and/or disabling (Ernster, 1975; see also Joffe,

1948; Boone, 1954). Lupton (1973) and Weideger (1976) have attempted to put these data in a broader context by noting similarities between the negative views of menstruation embodied in the slang vocabularies of English speakers today and the cultural practices surrounding menstruation (for example, the menstrual taboos) in other societies both in the past and in the present.

Analysis of vocabulary items, however, is only one way of scientifically exploring the significance of menstruation for members of a society. Another way is to use some of the standard techniques of psychological research to identify attitudes and behavior related to the menstrual cycle. For reasons to be discussed below, these research techniques have so far provided only limited information, but the data they provide suggest ways research might go in the future.

At least since the early 1960s, psychological research based on questionnaire surveys has shown that women associate certain physical symptoms and negative mood changes with the premenstrual and menstrual phases of the reproductive cycle (Coppen and Kessel, 1963; Moos, 1968). Much of this research has focused on the existence of a "premenstrual tension syndrome." This syndrome is variously defined by different investigators, but in general it is described as an experience of tension, irritability, and depression during the premenstrual phase in the cycle, accompanied by tendencies to cry and behave erratically, perhaps especially in antisocial ways. Men's responses on a "menstrual distress" questionnaire suggest that they, too, believe in the existence of a premenstrual tension syndrome. According to the data obtained, men think that women experience a wide range of negative mood and behavioral changes in the premenstrual and menstrual phases of the cycle (Parlee, 1974). College-aged single males, furthermore, seem to think these changes are more extreme than do married men in their late twenties and early thirties (Parlee, unpublished data).

Different groups of women, too, give varying responses when asked about premenstrual and menstrual symptoms and mood changes. Paige (1973) has found, for example, that religious background is related to the nature of questionnaire responses. Women from Catholic homes report more numerous and more severe menstrual symptoms than do women from Protestant and Jewish homes. Paulson (1961) found differences in reports of premenstrual tension symptoms among groups of women who differ in their attitudes toward the traditional female role of wife and mother. Women who reported the most severe symptoms were those who did not verbally endorse the traditional role. Paulson did not describe his data in terms of the women's attitudes toward traditional roles, however. Instead, he characterized women who reported having menstrual and premenstrual symptoms as "more inadequate and less able to fulfill maturely the psychosocial and psychosexual roles which society and their own femininity expect of them'' (1961: 737). Research in Sweden and India has shown that women in these countries respond somewhat differently on questionnaires regarding menstrual distress than do women in the United States (Culberg, 1972; Parlee, unpublished data). Other investigations, not using a standardized questionnaire, suggest that women in other countries report a wide variety of key, or most important, symptoms during the premenstrual and menstrual phases (Janiger, Riffenburgh, and Kersh, 1972). Whether an individual woman believes that the negative changes associated with menstruation are more or less severe, then, seems to be related to certain sociological variables such as religious and cultural background as well as whatever psychological factors are involved in verbal endorsement of the traditional female role. There is little reason to believe that U.S. women of different religious backgrounds or women living in other countries are different enough *biologically* to account for the observed variation in responses on menstrual distress questionnaires.

If the responses on these questionnaires are not based solely on the experience of the biological changes of the menstrual cycle, however, then social and psychological factors must also play some as yet unidentified role. And of course *men*'s responses on a questionnaire about what women experience during and prior to menstruation cannot be determined by their own experiences of biological changes. Yet these nonbiological determinants of responses to questions about menstrual distress have been ignored by scientists. While men's responses have not even been examined, women's responses have been assumed simply to represent accurate reports of personal experience. They have been taken, without further scientific confirmation, as evidence that at least some women experience a psychological syndrome of tension, irritability, and depression in the premenstrual and menstrual phases of the monthly hormonal cycle. An alternative interpretation, that responses on "menstrual distress" questionnaires might be regarded as evidence of socially shared *beliefs* about menstruation—beliefs which may be true or false, leads one to consider the data from a different point of view (Parlee, 1974).

Almost by definition, members of a society hold shared beliefs about a wide range of things, including beliefs about matters of physical fact and social fact. Beliefs about social facts are different from beliefs about physical facts in at least one important respect. The beliefs that something is true about the social world can lead to or be the basis for actions that tend to ensure the "truth" of that fact. Social reality is in this sense constructed by social actions, by shared beliefs and acts based upon them.

Research by Koeske and Koeske (1975) suggests that beliefs about the psychological concomitants of menstrual cycle may indeed form the basis for social actions. They found that an observer's interpretation of the causes of a woman's behavior differed depending on whether or not the observer believed the woman was in the premenstrual phase of her cycle.

When the woman was believed to be in the premenstrual phase, her actions were attributed to biological changes of the menstrual cycle, while they were attributed to environmental causes if she was not believed to be in this phase of the cycle. Thus responses by persons in the woman's social environment might reinforce or perpetuate those of her behaviors that conform to the shared beliefs about the psychological concomitants of the menstrual cycle. For example, if it is believed that hormonal changes cause females to be more irritable during the premenstrual phase of the cycle, those in a woman's environment might respond more tolerantly to her expressions of anger during this phase than at other times, thus reinforcing a pattern of irritable behavior immediately prior to menstruation. In this way, behavior toward women based on socially shared beliefs about menstruation may well produce behavior patterns which tend to confirm the beliefs.

Socially shared beliefs about the menstrual cycle might affect women's experience in other ways, too. Schachter and Singer's classic experiment (1962) demonstrated that when people are in an altered bodily state for which they have no appropriate explanation, what they experience is influenced by their social environment. Subjects experiencing the aftereffects of an adrenalin injection who were in the presence of a euphoric companion reported themselves to be happier than did those whose companion was depressed. The physiological stimulus (the effects of the drug) was the same across all conditions, but the subject's experience was defined by "information" from the social environment. The meaning (cognitive label) the subjects assigned to their altered bodily state, in other words, was affected by their expectations about what moods it was "appropriate" to feel in the particular situation. These expectations constitute the psychologically relevant feature of what might in other contexts be termed social or cultural influence.

The implications for the interpretation of women's moods at different phases of the cycle seem clear. If the language and the social environment provide a set of expectations in the form of shared beliefs regarding mood changes in the premenstrual and menstrual phases of the cycle, then the bodily changes during these phases might well be labeled in accord with the expectations. The cross-cultural data suggesting that in different countries different symptoms are associated with the premenstrual and menstrual phases are consistent with the hypothesis that the effects of changing physical states on moods is mediated by cultural attitudes. An individual woman's experience of these cyclical changes in her body would be determined in part by the way the society in which she lives perceives them.

It is perhaps relevant to note in this connection that some societies, the Kung bush, for example, seem to provide no labels for psychological experiences related to the premenstrual and menstrual phases of the cycle (Marjorie Shostack, November 1974: personal communication). Interestingly, the Kung bush do seem to have a concept like premenstrual tension, but it is applied to the psychological experiences associated with pregnancy rather than with the menstrual cycle. But the concept of premenstrual tension does not seem to be of sufficient importance among the Kung bush and in other such societies even to require a word to identify it in a general way.

In our society, as noted above, there are no shared beliefs about or labels for the feelings of well-being which many women seem to experience at the ovulatory phase of the cycle. Women are not alerted by the language to expect such feelings or to verbally encode them when they do occur. Yet scattered scientific data, as well as spontaneous reports of personal experiences, suggest that women may experience a sense of well-being around ovulation at least as consistently as they are subject to dysphoric moods in the premenstrual phase (Benedek and Rubenstein, 1939a,b).

What might be the social significance of the existence of the concept of premenstrual tension and the absence of any similar concept of ovulatory well-being, if such a phenomenon exists? It is tempting to speculate that a society that emphasizes the negative psychological consequences of the ''raging hormonal influences'' of the menstrual cycle rather than the positive ones thus ascribes an innate disability to women and in so doing conveniently justifies certain kinds of social and economic discrimination based upon sex.

Here, one would think, is where scientific research could be especially useful: What are the objective facts concerning psychological changes associated with the menstrual cycle? Are there positive changes as well as negative ones? Are there specific emotional and behavioral changes which are hormonally determined, or are such changes merely associated with bodily changes through cultural labeling? Such questions can be answered only very tentatively on the basis of data currently available. One reason for this unsatisfactory state of empirical knowledge is that scientists seem to have approached their investigations of menstruation from the viewpoint embodied in the socially-shared beliefs discussed above. That is, scientific investigations of psychological aspects of the human menstrual cycle have focused almost exclusively upon negative moods and symptoms in the premenstrual and menstrual phases of the cycle, and data have been interpreted almost exclusively in terms implying biological causes unmodified by psychological and social processes.

Assessing the Gaps in Research

Existing research on psychological aspects of the menstrual cycle can be grouped into three general categories according to the methods used in the study. One category, discussed above, consists of studies using questionnaires which ask about psychological experiences at different times in the cycle. These "menstrual distress" questionnaires contain mostly items asking about negative moods and symptoms in the premenstrual and menstrual phases of the cycle. A woman's answers on such a questionnaire are regarded as evidence of the *degree* to which she has "menstrual distress" or "premenstrual tension." Religious or cross-cultural differences in attitude and experience are not explored, nor are the implications of the fact that men give very similar responses when asked what women experience.

Questionnaire data are always difficult to interpret, but it'is noteworthy that little effort has been made to provide external validation (confirmation of self-reports by other kinds of measurement) of the data obtained from "menstrual distress" questionnaires. Studies which would seem to involve direct measures of some of the psychological characteristics that are the concern of these questionnaires, such as concentration and emotionality, have failed to demonstrate differences in nonverbal behavior at different phases of the cycle. Thus, while women might say on a questionnaire that they have difficulty concentrating during the premenstrual and menstrual phases of the cycle, repeated attempts by scientists have failed to demonstrate a decreased ability to concentrate on intellectual or sensory-motor tasks during these phases (Parlee, 1973; Sommer, 1973). Apart from questionnaire data, in other words, there is no direct evidence that women in the premenstrual and menstrual phases of the cycle are more irritable, depressed, inefficient, or antisocial than at other phases.

Most writers cite psychological studies of another type, correlational studies, as evidence that women do in fact behave erratically and in a socially undesirable way during the premenstrual and menstrual phases of the cycle. According to these studies, women who have committed violent crimes, entered a mental hospital with an acute illness, or had an accident at work are more likely to have done so during the four days preceding or the four days following the onset of menstruation than in the remainder of the cycle (Dalton, 1959, 1960, 1961). Such studies are undoubtedly the best evidence of a significant association between specific phases of the menstrual cycle and behavioral acts.

But how is this association between hormones and behavior to be interpreted? The usual response, one which is consistent with (and appears to confirm) the socially shared beliefs about menstruation, is that the hormonal changes of the menstrual cycle *cause* the behaviors. The hormonal changes, in this view, produce a psychological state of premenstrual tension which predisposes the woman to commit the negatively valued action under study. And this certainly seems a reasonable interpretation. There is, however, another interpretation, with data to support it, which seems equally reasonable. This alternative interpretation, however, does not confirm the socially shared beliefs about the negative consequences of the hormonal influences, and it may be for this reason that it has not been considered in discussing the implications of correlational studies of the menstrual cycle.

Every psychologist knows that a correlation, in this case between cycle phase and behavior, does not establish causation and that either member of the correlated pair may cause the other, or both may be the result of some third causal event or circumstance. In the case of correlational studies of the menstrual cycle, however, it is rarely considered that psychological states may affect hormones as well as the reverse. Yet all of the behaviors examined in correlational studies of premenstrual tension seem to involve stress in some loose sense of the term. Perhaps the stress of committing a crime and being arrested delays or precipitates menstrual onset. If so, one would expect a relatively larger proportion of women under such stresses to be menstruating or to be "premenstrual"—i.e., their menstrual period is expected but its occurrence is delayed.

There is good evidence to suggest that this alternative interpretation of correlations between phases in the menstrual cycle and behavior needs to be carefully considered. In an investigation conducted in exactly the same way as the correlational studies discussed above, an association was found between the act of taking an important examination and the phase of the cycle a woman was in when she took the exam (Dalton, 1968). As in the studies of crimes and accidents, women taking the examination were more likely to be in the four days preceding or the four days following the onset of menstruation than in other phases of the cycle. Yet this was an examination which was scheduled for a large group of women; their menstrual cycles could not have had an effect on the time of its occurrence. The usual interpretation of hormone-behavior correlation seems most implausible in this case. A hormonally caused state of premenstrual tension did not predispose the women to commit the act of taking the examination. Since hormones could not affect the timing of the behavior in this study, some other interpretation of the correlation must be found.

Data from the same study, in fact, suggest that the examination affected the timing of the menstrual cycles of the women who took it, possibly because of the stress of the test's impending occurrence. A record was kept of the number of women menstruating prior to and during the days the examination was given, and it was found that in a significant number of women expected menstrual onset was delayed, while in others it was earlier than anticipated. The study seems, therefore, to demonstrate the effects of the examination on the timing of menstruation rather than the effects of hormones on behavior. It should be emphasized, however, that the results of this investigation are not reported in such a way that the association between premenstrual and menstrual phases of the cycle and the act of taking the examination is clear. One must reanalyze the actual data presented in the paper in order to see the similarity between the results of this investigation and the results of other correlational studies of the menstrual cycle (Parlee, 1975).

In addition to questionnaires and correlational studies of the menstrual cycle, there is a third category of investigations in which women's behavior is studied throughout the cycle in order to demonstrate changes over time. Longitudinal investigations have the clear advantage of being able to draw conclusions about psychological changes which do not, as the questionnaires do, have to rely on subjects' memories.

Results from studies using questionnaires to assess mood states on a day-to-day basis have been largely inconclusive. Either no significant changes are found over the cycle, or the data are presented in such a way that the presence or absence of fluctuations cannot be determined—for example, the total number of negative symptoms during the entire cycle may be reported (McCance, Luff, and Widdowson, 1937; Altman, Knowles, and Bull, 1941; Rees, 1953; Abramson and Torghele, 1961; Moos et al., 1969). A longitudinal study done by Gottschalk and Gleser (1969), however, does seem to indicate differences between the mid-cycle and premenstrual/menstrual phases. Using the content analysis method, five-minute samples of speech during the various phases of the cycle were scored for mood or affective state. And two separate studies based on the same method have reported that hostility and anxiety scores are higher in the premenstrual and menstrual phases than at mid-cycle (Ivey and Bardwick, 1968; Paige, 1971).

Like studies in the first two categories, however, longitudinal investigations have focused primarily upon negative moods and, consistent with the socially shared beliefs, have described any resulting changes as *increases* in negative affect during the premenstrual and menstrual phases. If positive moods had also been studied, the descriptions of any cycle-related changes might be more complex: a relative increase in positive moods at mid-cycle, perhaps, and a relative increase in negative moods in the premenstrual and menstrual phases. This latter description is not so easily characterized as a demonstration of the premenstrual tension syndrome. At present, however, we cannot know whether it is correct because scientists have almost exclusively studied negative moods and described any resulting changes as increases in negative affect during the premenstrual and menstrual phases. Yet an equally accurate description of such data may be that there are decreases in negative affect at mid-cycle. Changes can be judged only against the background of a baseline. In the case of the menstrual cycle, we should know the normal mood levels at each phase of the cycle in order to be able to assess fluctuations. Lacking such background, the baseline implicitly adopted in describing these psychological changes over time is one which suggests that the changes are consistent with the socially shared beliefs about premenstrual tension.

In addition to the issues of conceptualization raised by the implicit baseline and the study of negative affects only, there are two more strictly methodological points which also have implications for the way psychological phenomena associated with the menstrual cycle are conceptualized. One is the use of group data. Recent longitudinal studies of the menstrual cycle almost invariably report data from a group of subjects rather than the records of individual women. Endocrinologists have shown that there are large individual differences in the physiological changes involved in the menstrual cycle and probably also differences from cycle to cycle for a single woman (Whalen, 1975). If psychological changes are related to hormonal changes, or even if they are not, one might expect similar inter- and intrasubject variability in the psychological measures. While we do not know what the answers will be, it is clear that the interactive effects of biological, social, and psychological factors will be obscured so long as individual or group differences at any one of these levels of analysis are ignored.

A second methodological problem in these longitudinal studies of the menstrual cycle is the lack of control groups. Unless hormonal measures are taken along with psychological measures, one can only *assume* that any long-term changes in moods in women are causally related to the menstrual cycle. To make this point by overstating it: It is logically and empirically possible that moods in women fluctuate in association with some environmental or social events, the phases of the moon, or holiday celebrations, for instance. It is conceivable that these events might also affect the timing of the menstrual cycle. Moods and hormone levels in men might also fluctuate in association with environmental or social events. Unless one uses men as a control group in longitudinal studies, one may be erroneous in assuming that any mood fluctuations in women are causally related to the menstrual cycle. In light of empirical evidence suggesting the presence of cycles of approximately thirty days in a variety of biological processes in men and women, it would seem unwise to attribute any psychological fluctuations found in women to biological changes of the menstrual cycle unless the study has included a control group of men (Richter, 1968).

What is needed is longitudinal research which examines a range of positive and negative moods and behaviors. If possible, the investigative interest in the menstrual cycle should be disguised to minimize the effects of subjects' beliefs about mood changes and menstruation on their reports of moods. In order to see if an *individual* exhibits rhythmic changes in moods and behavior, measures must be taken over a fairly long period of time. Time series analysis of individual records of data of this sort requires measurement over an interval two and a half to three times the period of the longest rhythm sought. Control groups of nonmenstruating individuals must be included if any fluctuations in behavior are to be interpreted as related to the menstrual cycle.

In sum, we do not have a complete scientific picture of the nature and extent of psychological changes associated with the menstrual cycle because the kinds of questions scientists have asked have been limited by their apparent prior belief in the significance of a premenstrual tension syndrome. Research efforts have focused almost exclusively upon the question of whether negative affects increase in the premenstrual and menstrual phases of the cycle and have failed to explore fully a broader range of moods, positive as well as negative, at other phases of the cycle.

The socially shared belief in the existence of a premenstrual tension syndrome may also have limited the kinds of interpretations women make and the kinds of bodily changes they consciously experience throughout the cycle. A set of socially shared beliefs which emphasizes the notion that the premenstrual and menstrual phases of the cycle are accompanied by negative affects and antisocial behaviors may well increase the probability that women will label their altered bodily states and behave in ways in accordance with these beliefs. Or perhaps bodily changes play no role at all. Women may simply learn (consciously or unconsciously) to take advantage of cultural attitudes and understandings to exhibit more hostility and aggression at the phases of the cycle when such behaviors are tolerated. Indeed, both our available scientific knowledge and women's subjective experience and behavior may be influenced by social constructions like our socially shared beliefs about the "raging hormonal influences" of the menstrual cycle. The persistence of these beliefs and their power to shape both scientific activity and personal experience may derive in large part from their functional significance to the society as a whole.

Pregnancy, Birth, and the Postpartum Period

Beliefs and attitudes in our society surrounding pregnancy, birth, and the postpartum period are much less easily identifiable, either in scientific literature or in popular culture, than are those related to the psychology of menstruation. Until recently, in fact, psychologists have done very little research on such topics (Parlee, in press); beliefs and attitudes about these aspects of reproduction must be inferred from the socially patterned behavior (including scientific activity) surrounding it.

What scientific research and medical literature there is on the psychology of pregnancy, birth, and the postpartum period has focused largely on either hormonal determinants of states such as nausea in early pregnancy or the blues in the early postpartum period, or on psychoanalytic descriptions of dynamic changes occurring in individual women when they become mothers. The social context within which the biological and psychodynamic processes occur has been almost totally ignored. Since a woman's experience of pregnancy and birth, like that of the menstrual cycle, is probably best characterized as an interaction among biological, psychological, and social factors, it may be that the scientific silence about the social context of birth represents a distortion of scientific activity in service of an ideology.

This silence, in fact, may serve a useful function for the society as a whole by failing to expose or emphasize the social and cultural patterns of behavior related to reproduction which have negative psychological consequences for women. Evidence of these negative consequences, though they are usually not identified as such, can be found scattered throughout the scientific literature. The consistency and persistence with which such evidence is ignored or given other interpretations suggests that the forces shaping scientific activity—and women's experiences—must be very strong indeed.

Consider the following example: In a longitudinal investigation of monozygotic female twins, Kaij and Malmquist (1971) found that as middle-aged women, twins who were mothers had significantly more psychiatric and somatic symptoms than did their sibling twins who had not had children. From these data the authors conclude: "Our hypothesis that pregnancy undermines the psychiatric and somatic health of women even in the long term seems to be supported by our investigation." Do they really mean to imply that it was, literally, the *pregnancy* that affected the women's health, or do they simply mean to say that motherhood as a social role seems to have negative consequences for physical and mental health?

The discussion that follows is intended to draw together some scattered scientific evidence regarding the psychological effects of the social context within which the biological process of birth occurs. Again, it is not our purpose to prejudge the relative importance of physiological factors vis-à-vis others as determinants of women's experiences, but rather to provide a perspective for assessing the possible interactions among biological, psychological, and social factors.

Pregnancy

From a sociological point of view, the role of the pregnant woman in our society seems to be more ambiguously defined than most other social roles. Rosengren's investigations of "pregnancy as a sick role" (1962*a,b*), in fact, were based upon the explicit assumption that the social expectations regarding the behavior of pregnant women are sufficiently vague that some women might choose to enact the more clearly defined sick role as a way of resolving ambiguity about their status. (The sick role as defined here was based on Parsons's [1951] analysis of it as a role which exempts the person from normal role responsibilities and a sense of personal responsibility for the illness and requires the person to want to get well and to seek technically competent help to do so.) Rosengren's data tentatively suggest that some women, but not all, do view pregnancy as a sick role—a role in which they are exempted from normal responsibilities because of a body "condition" which may entail pain and suffering, and a role whose management requires them to assume a position subordinate to that of a medically trained expert.

The women who view pregnancy this way, Rosengren found, were those who were socially mobile: Both upward and downward mobility seemed to be associated with what he called sick role expectations regarding pregnancy. Rosengren suggests that the psychologically significant aspect of mobility in this case is that it means a separation from an established network of family and friends. Since the role of the pregnant woman is socially ambiguous, it is suggested, a supportive network of family and friends might serve to provide a coherent set of expectations regarding behavior during pregnancy. This would reduce the need for the woman to adapt her behavior and experience to an unambiguously defined (but less appropriate) role—the sick role—which is recognized as legitimate by the society at large. In further research along these lines, McKinlay (1972) has pointed to the importance of subcultural differences in the extent to which a pregnant woman is pressured by others to adopt the sick role. One of the implications of both Rosengren's and McKinlay's work, of course, is that the biological changes of pregnancy do not in and of themselves unambiguously determine the way a pregnant woman feels and behaves.

An interesting series of experimental studies has attempted to explore systematically the kinds of responses evoked in others by the sight of a pregnant woman (Taylor and Langer, 1977; Langer et al., 1976). Since the pregnant woman is undoubtedly influenced by these responses, they may be regarded not only as indicators of socially shared attitudes surrounding pregnancy but also as factors which affect or determine the way she interprets the bodily changes she experiences. Taylor and Langer found that people seem to respond to a pregnant woman as if she suffered a social stigma (in the sense of the term as used by Goffman, 1963). That is, a pregnant woman is treated differently from nonpregnant women because (in this case) of an easily identifiable physical feature which, according to the shared beliefs of the participants, interferes with normal social interaction. Social behavior in the presence of a pregnant woman was found to differ from behavior in the presence of a nonpregnant woman. Persons tend to stand farther away from a pregnant woman in an elevator and to stare more at her stomach. When a woman is thus "stigmatized" by being visibly pregnant, in other words, the usual norms regarding physical distances between individuals and looking behavior are disrupted. Further research led to the conclusion that the response to a pregnant woman could best be characterized as a "novelty" response; the difference in physical appearance that accompanies pregnancy stigmatizes—it marks an individual as different or nonnormal—because it is a social stimulus which occurs fairly uncommonly. When subjects were allowed to satiate their curiosity regarding the novel stimulus provided by a pregnant woman by looking at length at her without her knowledge, subsequent social interactions with the pregnant woman proceeded as smoothly as with a nonpregnant woman.

The suggestion that pregnancy is responded to by others as a novel stimulus serves to underscore the ambiguity of social expectations regarding the role of the pregnant woman. In light of evidence that pregnant women are viewed by others as nonnormal and given the ambiguity about what roles they could or should play, it is perhaps not surprising that the sick role is adopted by at least some pregnant women as a way of resolving their uncertainties.

It seems clear that one important social institution, the medical profession, does encourage, perhaps even pressure, pregnant women to adopt at least one feature of the sick role: the assumption of their subordination to the medically trained expert. This is illustrated by the following quotation from the twelfth edition of the widely used medical text *Williams' Obstetrics* (Kanner, 1961: 354): "For nearly 12 months the obstetrician takes over the guidance of an adult woman, answers her questions, clarifies her puzzlements, advises her about the handling of her baby when it comes, and generally charts her conduct during the 24 hours of the day."

Apart from what would seem to be fairly strong social pressures exerted by physicians for the pregnant woman to regard herself as having a medical condition, there is another line of evidence which may suggest that socially shared beliefs and attitudes surrounding pregnancy attribute physical symptoms and "illness" to it. Studies of men whose wives are pregnant indicate that these men report greater numbers of physical symptoms than do men whose wives are not pregnant (Trethowan, 1968). Such data suggest that when pregnancy is salient for an individual, reports of physical symptoms increase even when the individual himself does not experience the physical changes of pregnancy. While these data in existing form cannot be interpreted as evidence of shared beliefs that pregnancy entails physical illness, they do imply some cultural association of pregnancy and illness and suggest that women's self-reports of pregnancy-related symptoms must be interpreted with care.

As in the case of the menstrual cycle, scientific research does not provide an adequate picture of psychological changes during pregnancy. Scientific studies of the nature and causes of psychological changes during pregnancy, whether these take the form of increases in physical symptoms or in feelings of well-being, are few and inconclusive. In spite of fairly widespread beliefs that nausea and vomiting occur during the first trimester of pregnancy, for example, it is not known what proportion of women actually experience these symptoms then. Nor is there agreement among investigators as to what biological, psychological, or social factors are associated with such experiences (Trethowan and Dickens, 1972).

Lennane and Lennane (1973) have suggested that in much of the medical literature it is assumed that nausea and vomiting have psychogenic origins, while existing data in fact point to the importance of hormonal changes as causal factors. Sherman's excellent review (1971) of this topic, on the other hand, points up the considerable lack of agreement as to the causes, hormonal or psychogenic, of nausea and vomiting. Sherman suggests the usefulness of distinguishing between persistent and/or severe vomiting and milder, more transient nausea with or without vomiting. It seems likely that such a distinction among phenomena at the psychological level will indeed prove useful in assessing the relative importance of different kinds of causal factors for explaining different kinds of experiences.

While available scientific evidence seems to provide little basis for generalizations or conclusions about the causes of nausea and vomiting in early pregnancy, one feature of this literature does seem worthy of note. A number of investigations have explored—with inconclusive results—the relationship between nausea and vomiting and ambivalence toward the pregnancy or acceptance or rejection of it. Other investigators not studying nausea and vomiting have also been concerned with, or have at least commented upon, the stage of the pregnancy at which women come to accept their pregnancies. While it is true that much of this research was carried out before women's right to abortion was legally recognized, one looks in vain in the resultant data for some exploration of the possibility that some, perhaps many, women were pregnant and did not want to be.

It seems undeniable that subtle conscious and unconscious processes create a state of ambivalence in many women regarding pregnancy. Caplan's research (1957) suggests, in fact, that such ambivalence is normal and is perhaps best resolved by facilitating whatever emotionally supportive networks of family and friends are available to the pregnant woman or creating new ones where necessary. It seems equally undeniable, however, that if a woman persistently maintains, for whatever reasons, that she does not want to be pregnant, the appropriate research question is not how or when she comes to accept the pregnancy, but why investigators and clinicians assume acceptance is necessary. The scientific silence on the psychological implications and consequences of an unwanted pregnancy seems to point to an implicit pronatalist bias on the part of investigators. One might agree or disagree with this bias, but surely implicit assumptions guiding research on a controversial issue should at least be made explicit and the implications of alternative interpretations of existing data should be considered.

At present one can only speculate on ways in which a strongly enforced pronatalist bias in the culture might affect the way an indivdual woman experiences her pregnancy. Particularly for women who do not want a pregnancy, there may be consequences both for them and for the children born of their unwanted pregnancies. There is some behavioral evidence, however, that in a sample of Czechoslovakian women who twice requested and were denied an abortion, the children born ás a result of these unwanted pregnancies were slightly less well-adjusted socially and intellectually at age ten than were children from a sample of control mothers who had not requested an abortion (Dytrych et al., 1975). While it is often an empty gesture to call for further research in an area where little or no data exist, the present availability of safe and legal abortions makes it more feasible to explore not the acceptance of a pregnancy, but rather the psychological consequences and concomitants of pregnancies that are wanted in differing degrees.

Birth

Social practices surrounding the biological processes of birth in the United States have manifested little concern for the psychological and even the physical well-being of the woman giving birth. The experience of giving birth in the United States, in contrast to that in industrialized western European countries, is determined to a very great extent by the fact that it routinely occurs in a hospital setting under the supervision of a surgically trained physician. Until fairly recently, parturient women were isolated, drugged, and subjected to medically unwarranted procedures (routine episiotomy, enema, shaving, delivery in a prone position, standard medications) without regard for their individual needs and desires. While some of the strongest indictments of traditional obstetrical practices have come from women who have experienced them (see Tennov and Hirsch, 1973), others within and outside of the medical profession have also been critical (see Howells, 1972; Atlee, 1963; Lomas, 1964; Shaw, 1972).

Criticism of traditional obstetrical procedures has focused largely on their adverse effects on the infant (Tennov, 1973), but attention has also been directed to their potentially negative effects on the psychological relationship between mother and child. With regard to this latter question, one study found that mothers who had more extended contact with their infants immediately after birth showed different behaviors toward them a month later than did mothers who had experienced the prompt and relatively prolonged separation from the infant that is usual in most hospitals in the United States (Klaus et al., 1972). The mothers whose contact had been more extensive tended to align their faces with their infant's while engaging in direct eye contact with them more than did the control group of women who had experienced the usual routine separation.

These findings were interpreted in terms of the possible existence of a critical period immediately after birth for maternal attachment to the infant. The importance of such a biologically based mechanism for the survival of the species seems clear. It is not clear, however, whether the only significant element in the attachment process is the biological condition of the woman who has just given birth (although this could be inferred from the notion of a critical period) or whether the stimulus properties (visual, acoustic, olfactory) of the newborn infant also play some role. Again, a control group is lacking in the research design. Does a male who is allowed extended contact with a newborn infant show behaviors toward the infant a month later different from those of a male who has not had such contact? Without data on this point, we cannot know whether what was demonstrated in this study was the existence of maternal attachment or of parental attachment.

Observations of fathers' behavior toward newborn infants suggest some similarity between their responses to newborn infants (patterns of touching, eye contact) and those of mothers (Greenberg and Morris, 1974). Although such behavior in fathers has been described as "paternal engrossment," it could perhaps equally well be interpreted as manifesting an attachment phenomenon. The fact that it has not, that the research emphasis has been almost exclusively focused on the attachment of *mother* and child, probably reflects a tendency among scientists to accept the traditional conception of the maternal role as "given" rather than as at least in part a social construction (Wortis, 1971).

There may be two primary reasons that research on psychological aspects of birth is relatively sparse. One is that birth is not an event that fits readily into psychologists' preferred research methodologies. Some of the problems are "practical" in the sense that they have to do with access to subject populations, issues of informed consent, and the like. Other problems, however, are more intrinsic to the discipline of psychology itself. Manipulation and control of variables is neither possible nor appropriate in studying birth, and intrusive measurements of any kind are unsuitable. Until research perspectives and methods are developed which allow for greater use of purely observational techniques, it seems unlikely that scientific psychologists will have much to contribute to our understanding of birth.

A second possible reason that there is so little psychological research on birth may have to do with the role of science vis-à-vis the social status quo. As mentioned above, a woman giving birth is certainly not granted the kind of care and respect which we might expect in light of the high cultural value ostensibly placed on the social role of mother. The social practices surrounding birth and the attitudes which support them certainly play a role in the way an individual woman experiences childbirth. To explore in detail the kinds of psychological and physical maltreatment women have experienced as a result of these practices and acts would probably reveal a mass of evidence that directly contradicts the cultural myth that women and motherhood are highly valued. Thus the scientific silence on the topic of the psychology of birth may be partly the result of the scientific inadequacies of psychology as a discipline, but it may be functional as well in obscuring the contradictions between cultural values related to motherhood and actual practices surrounding the process of becoming a parent.

The Postpartum Period

Medical and psychiatric literature on "postpartum depression" is large relative to that on pregnancy and birth, but it is less informative than it might be because investigators have frequently failed to be clear about what it is that they are studying. (Some of this research has been reviewed by Kaij and Nilsson, 1972; Jansson, 1963; Thomas and Gordon, 1959; Tetlow, 1955). For present purposes, we will not consider the results of studies on psychoses with onsets in the postpartum period or studies on the transient weepiness and depression that some women experience in the first few days after birth. The discussion here will be limited to studies bearing on some women's experiences of clinical depression, ranging in degree from mild to severe, beginning any time after the first postpartum week and extending as long as a year after birth.

Some of the literature from the women's health movement (Boston Women's Health Book Collective, 1976; Rozdilsky and Banet, 1972) is a more useful guide to the nature, prevalence, and treatment of postpartum depression than is the research and clinical literature. In part this may be due to the fact that the medical literature focuses on problems that are operationally defined as medical because they require the attention of a physician. If women become depressed after childbearing but do not seek the advice of a doctor, their experiences may not be noted by those medical investigators interested in postpartum depression. The nature and prevalence of depression occurring under these circumstances, therefore, would be difficult to assess simply from reading the medical literature.

It is clear from this literature, however, that even when such depression is noted, obvious causal factors may be overlooked. In particular, medical investigators studying the postpartum period have almost totally ignored the psychological implications of the social fact that in giving birth to a child a woman becomes a parent. That is, she becomes an occupant of a social role (mother) that derives its meaning largely from cultural sources. Scientists have focused instead on biological changes associated with birth or on the psychodynamic makeup of the individual woman as factors which might lead to postpartum depression. It may well be that failure to look into the social causes of depression in the postpartum period serves the same function as the scientific inattention to the psychological aspects of pregnancy. By failing to explore negative consequences, in this case of becoming a parent, scientists fail to raise questions and produce data which might pose an implicit challenge to the social status quo. By failing to make such information available to women, scientists perpetuate a one-sided picture of motherhood.

Even more than the literature on the psychology of the menstrual cycle and birth, the literature on psychological aspects of the postpartum period seems to be infused with unexamined assumptions about women and women's roles and with an inability or unwillingness to explore data which might challenge existing cultural values. Since the assumptions held by investigators seem to be similar to the assumptions or explicit values of the society as a whole, it seems reasonable to suppose that they affect not only the kind of scientific information we find in the literature on the postpartum period but also the way individual women experience the transition to parenthood. Scientific findings on the postpartum period may be social constructions based on a set of implicit assumptions about women. These are similar to the assumptions that underlie research on the menstrual cycle. Because these *assumptions* (though not necessarily the research findings) are shared by all members of the culture, women's experiences as reported through research may reflect the social constructions. Thus both the experience of women and the products of researchers have a common source which is distinct from the biological events themselves. The way in which women give expression to their experiences, and consequently the way they report them to researchers, is conditioned by the social constructions of female sexuality.

Because, until recently, women had little support for talking about their experiences and feelings when these did not seem to fit the customary cultural assumptions or values, it is relatively rare to find direct expressions of the variety of ways in which women have felt and behaved as they become mothers. When one does find such direct expressions, as in *Our Bodies, Ourselves: What Now?* (Boston Women's Health Book Collective, 1976) and other literature from the women's health movement, they serve to underscore the ways in which scientific research has distorted and omitted facts relevant to an understanding of the psychology of postpartum depression and, more generally, to an understanding of the transition to parenthood. Given what women say about their experiences, it seems clear that research on the postpartum period has been distorted by investigators' failure to consider the role of social factors in their descriptions and explanations of the psychological phenomena. In particular, they have failed to take seriously evidence of negative psychological consequences of the social role of mother.

Disregard for the negative aspects of this role is manifested in scientific research in both subtle and obvious ways. In considering biological factors as possible contributors to postpartum depression, for example, most investigators have placed greater emphasis on readjustments in estrogen and progesterone levels after birth than on the kinds of biological changes that result when an individual is deprived of substantial periods of uninterrupted sleep. Yet even in the scientific literature there is evidence that loss of sleep is subjectively experienced as one of the major stresses of the postpartum period (Larsen, 1966). Since a change in sleeping patterns is probably a highly predictable consequence of becoming a mother, failure to explore and take into account the psychological effects of such a change is a serious omission.

More obvious examples abound. Sixty-four percent of the women in one study of postpartum depression, for instance, reported major or moderate increases in feelings of "entrapment" after the birth of their first child. Yet the investigator offered no comments on the possible causes or significance of this finding (Melges, 1968). Another author, a psychoanalyst, has noted a phenomenon similar to feelings of entrapment, and suggests that expressions of a fear of being enclosed are conscious representations of an unconscious fear arising out of identification with the baby (Heiman, 1965). One need not be unsympathetic to a psychoanalytic perspective to suggest that possible sources of entrapment feelings may lie not only in the unconscious of the woman but also in the traditional conception of a mother's role which holds that she is the one best caretaker for a very young infant. When the activities of an adult are closely structured by the needs of an infant in a society that has few facilities for meeting such needs outside the home, the psychological consequences for that adult may well be feelings of entrapment, regardless of whatever satisfaction other aspects of the relationship with the infant provide.

Other, scattered data suggest even more strongly that social factors that may cause or affect postpartum depression have not been explored with adequate care. These data are impressive not only because they are consistently reported in a variety of studies (though not commented upon), but also because they seem on the surface to be precisely what investigators interested in postpartum depression are looking for. That is, they seem to be useful in predicting which women are likely to become depressed in the postpartum period and which are not—a goal of much of the research on postpartum depression in which either biological or psychodynamic factors are studied.

Women with a strong commitment to work outside the home seem to become depressed when they leave work and become "full-time mothers" after the birth of their first child. Although the association between work commitment and postpartum depression appears in the reports of a number of studies, it is frequently described in a way that obscures the relationship (Dyer, 1963; Douglas, 1968; Biskind, 1958; and Ostwald and Regan, 1957). Certainly this association is never emphasized. For example, in the psychoanalytic literature, women who become depressed in the postpartum period may be described as "rejecting femininity," or as having "masculine identifications," or as engaged in the "struggle to be or not to be a woman." Yet it may be that the fact that a woman has worked outside the home is taken as prima facie evidence of her rejection of femininity. Sometimes the assumption of an equation between masculine characteristics and a career outside marriage is explicitly stated (as in Ostwald and Regan, 1957); elsewhere it can be inferred from the language used in these articles. One author, for example describes a woman suffering from postpartum depression as "an ambitious career girl . . . who had always tried to rival men at their *own* game" (Lomas, 1959; italics added).

Sociologists who have studied the transition to parenthood in nonclinical populations have also noted an association between previous strong work commitments outside the home and postpartum depression, but they, like the medically trained investigators, have not commented on the predictive value of such an association (LeMasters, 1957). If research on such depression is at least partly aimed at prediction and prevention, this failure to pursue evidence that certain kinds of role changes may predict postpartum distress seems hard to understand on scientific grounds. It may be significant that what scientists have not explored in their studies of postpartum depression is a set of social variables. In focusing on biological or psychodynamic causes of postpartum depression, they have neglected to examine the social role of motherhood, a role inextricably embedded in a network of other roles and institutions which have proved stable over time. Research evidence that motherhood may be detrimental to health, both physical and mental, might be seen as an implicit challenge to that time-honored network. Perhaps research in the future will be less constrained by concerns for the maintenance of existing roles and institutions and will be directed towards a more complete understanding of the psychology of the postpartum period as a process of biological, psychological, and social interaction. As is the case in research on birth, research on postpartum depression at present seems to bear so little relation to what women say about their experience as to be irrelevant, both to scientific understanding of the psychological processes and to the kinds of changes in health care and social institutions that women are beginning to demand.

Menopause

There is very little systematic research on the psychological aspects of menopause. In a review and methodological critique of this literature, McKinlay and McKinlay (1973) concluded that most of the "evidence" with regard to psychological aspects of menopause rests on the clinical experience of physicians and is not supported by adequately controlled scientific research. The only hormonally caused symptom concerning which there seems to be both clinical and scientific agreement is the "hot flash," which many, if not most, women experience in varying degrees at some time during the climacteric. The precise nature of a more general "menopausal syndrome" of depression, irritability, and various psychosomatic symptoms has only rarely been explored in a reliable way (Neugarten et al., 1963). The only systematic studies of the psychological effects of menopause have used questionnaires, thereby raising some of the same interpretive issues posed by research on the menstrual cycle: Are control groups (of nonmenopausal women and of men) used? Are positive as well as negative moods and behaviors examined? Do women's beliefs about menopause affect their responses on questionnaires?

Perhaps more importantly, however, research and speculation on the psychology of menopause has, like research on the postpartum period, consistently disregarded the possible importance of social variables in interpreting women's reports of their experiences at menopause. Apart from hot flashes, most of the so-called menopausal symptoms seem at least as likely to be the results of role changes experienced by middle-aged women as they are to be biological changes or psychodynamic responses to the loss of femininity supposedly represented by the cessation of menses. Although it is rarely mentioned in the medical and psychiatric literature, middle-aged women frequently experience a number of significant changes in social roles at the same time their menstrual cycles gradually cease: children leave home, parents die, mates experience "mid-life crises." To attribute, either implicitly or explicitly, the psychological concomitants of these major life changes to biological or individual psychological causes seems premature at best. Scientists who fail to explore the potential significance of social factors in the psychology of middle-aged women may continue to describe their experiences as menopausal, but it should be clear that there is no sound scientific basis for the implication that biological factors are of paramount importance. Again, biological, psychological, and social processes undoubtedly interact, and an exclusive emphasis on any one of them misrepresents the complexity of the whole.

References

Abramson, M., and J.R. Torghele (1961). Weight, Temperature Changes, and Psychosomatic Symptomatology in Relation to the Menstrual Cycle. American Journal of Obstetrics and Gynecology 81:223–232.

Altman, M., E. Knowles, and H.D. Bull (1941). A Psychosomatic Study of the Sex Cycle in Women. Psychosomatic Medicine 3:199–224.

Atlee, H.B. (1963). The Fall of the Queen of Heaven. Obstetrics and Gynecology 21:514–519.

Benedek, T., and B.B. Rubenstein (1939a). The Correlations between Ovarian Activity and Psychodynamic Processes: I. The Ovulatory Phase. Psychosomatic Medicine 1:245–270.

———(1939b). The Correlations between Ovarian Activity and Psychodynamic Processes: II. The Menstrual Phase. Psychosomatic Medicine 1:461–485.

Biskind, L.H. (1958). Emotional Aspects of Prenatal Care. Postgraduate Medicine 24:633.

Boone, L.P. (1954). Vernacular of Menstruation. American Speech 29:297–298.

Boston Women's Health Book Collective (1976). Our Bodies, Ourselves: What Now? Second ed. New York: Simon and Schuster.

Brown, R. (1958). Words and Things. Toronto: Collier-Macmillan.

Caplan, G. (1957). Psychological Aspects of Maternity Care. American Journal of Public Health 47:25–31.

Collins, W.P., and J.R. Newton (1974). The Ovarian Cycle. Biochemistry of Women: Clinical Concepts. A.S. Curry and J.V. Hewitt, eds. Cleveland: CRC Press.

Coppen, A., and N. Kessel (1963). Menstruation and Personality. British Journal of Psychiatry 109:711–721.

Culberg, J. (1972). Mood Changes and Menstrual Symptoms with Different Gestagen/Estrogen Combinations. Acta Psychiatrica Scandinavia, Supplement 235.

Dalton, K. (1959). Menstruation and Acute Psychiatric Illness. British Medical Journal 1:148–149.

———(1960). Menstruation and Accidents. British Medical Journal 2:1425–1426.

———(1961). Menstruation and Crimes. British Medical Journal 2:1752–1753.

———(1968). Menstruation and Examinations. Lancet 2:1386–1388.

Douglas, G. (1968). Some Disorders of the Puerperium. Journal of Psychosomatic Research 12:101–106.

Dyer, E.D. (1963). Parenthood as Crisis: A Re-Study. Marriage and Family Living 25:196–201.

Dytrych, Z., et al. (1975). Children Born to Women Denied Abortion. Family Planning Perspectives 7(4):165–171.

Ernster, V.L. (1975). American Menstrual Expressions. Sex Roles 1:3–13.

Goffman, E. (1963). Stigma: Notes on the Management of Spoiled Identity. Englewood Cliffs, N.J.: Prentice-Hall.

Gottschalk, L.A., and G.C. Gleser (1969). The Measurement of Psychological States through Content Analysis of Verbal Behavior. Berkeley: University of California Press.

Greenberg, M., and N. Morris (1974). Engrossment: The Newborn's Impact upon the Father. American Journal of Orthopsychiatry 44:520–531.

Heiman, M. (1965). Psychiatric Complications: A Psychoanalytic View of Pregnancy. *In* Medical, Surgical, and Gynecologic Complications of Pregnancy. Second ed. J.J. Rovinsky and A.F. Guttmacher, eds. Baltimore: Williams and Wilkins.

Howells, J.G., ed. (1972). Modern Perspectives in Psycho-Obstetrics. New York: Brunner-Mazel.

Ivey, M.E., and J.M. Bardwick (1968). Patterns of Affective Fluctuation in the Menstrual Cycle. Psychosomatic Medicine 30:336–345.

Janiger, O., R. Riffenburgh, and R. Kersh (1972). Cross cultural Study of Premenstrual Symptoms. Psychosomatics 13:226–235.

Jansson, B. (1963). Psychic Insufficiencies Associated with Childbearing. Acta Psychiatrica Scandinavia, Supplement 172.

Joffe, N.F. (1948). Vernacular of Menstruation. Word 4:181–186.

Kaij, L., and A. Malmquist (1971). Motherhood and Childlessness in Monozygotic Twins: I. Early Relationship. British Journal of Psychiatry 118:11–21.

Kaij, L., and A. Nilsson (1972). Emotional and Psychotic Illness Following Childbirth. *In* Modern Perspectives in Psycho-Obstetrics. J.G. Howells, ed. New York: Brunner-Mazel.

Kanner, L. (1961). Psychiatric Aspects of Pregnancy and Childbirth. *In* Williams' Obstetrics. Twelfth ed. N.J. Eastman and L.M. Helman, eds. New York: Appleton-Century-Crofts.

Klaus, M.H., et al. (1972). Maternal Attachment: Importance of the First Postpartum Days. New England Journal of Medicine 286:460–463.

Koeske, R., and G. Koeske (1975). An Attributional Approach to Moods and the Menstrual Cycle. Journal of Personality and Social Psychology 31:473–478.

Langer, E.J., et al. (1976). Stigma, Staring, and Discomfort: A Novel-Stimulus Hypothesis. Journal of Experimental Social Psychology 12:451–463.

Larsen, V.L. (1966). Stresses of the Childbearing Years. American Journal of Public Health 56:32–36.

LeMasters, E.E. (1957). Parenthood as Crisis. Marriage and Family Living 19:352–355.

Lennane, M.B., and R.J. Lennane (1973). Alleged Psychogenic Disorders in Women: A Possible Manifestation of Sexual Prejudice. New England Journal of Medicine 288:288–292.

Lomas, P. (1959). The Husband-Wife Relationship in Cases of Puerperal Breakdown. British Journal of Medical Psychology 32:117–132.

———(1964). Childbirth Ritual. New Society, December, p. 31.

Lupton, M.J., in cooperation with J. Delaney and E. Toth (1973). The First Pollution: Psychoanalysis and the Menarche. Mimeographed.

McCance, R.A., M.C. Luff, and E.E. Widdowson (1937). Physical and Emotional Periodicity in Women. Journal of Hygiene 37:571–605.

McKinlay, J.B. (1972). The Sick Role: Illness and Pregnancy. Social Science and Medicine 6:561–572.

McKinlay, S.M., and J.B. McKinlay (1973). Selected Studies of the Menopause: An Annotated Bibliography. Journal of Biosocial Science 5:533–555.

Melges, F. (1968). Postpartum Psychiatric Syndromes. Psychosomatic Medicine 30:95–108.

Moos, R.H. (1968). The Development of a Menstrual Distress Questionnaire. Psychosomatic Medicine 30:853–867.

Moos, R.H. (1968). The Development of a Menstrual Distress Questionnaire. Psychosomatic Medicine 30:853–867.

Moos, R.H., et al. (1969). Fluctuations in Symptoms and Moods during the Menstrual Cycle. Journal of Psychosomatic Research 13:37–44.

Neugarten, B.L., et al. (1963). Women's Attitudes toward the Menopause. Vita Humana 6:140–151.

Ostwald, P., and P. Regan (1957). Psychiatric Disorders Associated with Childbirth. Journal of Nervous and Mental Diseases 125:153–165.

Paige, K.E. (1971). Effects of Oral Contraceptives on Affective Fluctuations Associated with the Menstrual Cycle. Psychosomatic Medicine 33:515–537.

———(1973). Women Learn to Sing the Menstrual Blues. Psychology Today 7:41–46.

Parlee, M.B. (1973). The Premenstrual Syndrome. Psychological Bulletin 80:454–465.

———(1974). Stereotypic Beliefs about Menstruation: A Methodological Note on the Moos Menstrual Distress Questionnaire and Some New Data. Psychosomatic Medicine 36:229–240.

———(1975). Menstruation and Voluntary Participation in a Psychological Experiment. Presented at the Symposium of the 83d Annual Meeting of the American Psychological Association, Chicago.

———(In press). Psychological Aspects of Menstruation, Childbirth, and Menopause. *In* Psychology of Women: Future Directions of Research. J.A. Sherman and F.L. Denmark, eds. New York: Psychological Dimension.

Parsons, T. (1951). The Social System. Glencoe, Ill.: The Free Press.

Paulson, M.J. (1961). Psychological Concomitants of Premenstrual Tension. American Journal of Obstetrics and Gynecology 81:733–738.

Rees, L. (1953). Psychosomatic Aspects of the Premenstrual Tension Syndrome. Journal of Mental Science 99:62–73.

Richter, C.P. (1968). Periodic Phenomena in Man and Animals: Their Relation to Neuroendocrine Mechanisms (A Monthly or Near Monthly Cycle). *In* Endocrinology and Human Behavior. R.P. Michael, ed. London: Oxford University Press.

Rosengren, W.R. (1962*a*). Social Instability and Attitudes toward Pregnancy as a Social Role. Social Problems 9:371–378.

———(1962*b*). Social Status, Attitudes toward Pregnancy, and Child-Rearing Attitudes. Social Forces 41:127–134.

Rozdilsky, M.L., and B. Banet (1972). What Now? A Handbook for Parents (Especially Women) Postpartum. Seattle: What Now.

Schachter, S., and J.E. Singer (1962). Cognitive, Social and Physiological Determinants of Emotional State. Psychological Review 69:379–399.

Shaw, N.S. (1972). ``So You're Going to Have a Baby . . .'': Institutional Processing of Maternity Patients. Ph.D. dissertation, Brandeis University.

Sherman, J.A. (1971). On the Psychology of Women: A Survey of Empirical Studies. Springfield, Ill.: Charles C Thomas.

Sommer, B. (1973). The Effect of Menstruation on Cognitive and Perceptual-Motor Behavior: A Review. Psychosomatic Medicine 35:515–534.

Taylor, S.E., and E.J. Langer (1977). Pregnancy: A Social Stigma? Sex Roles 3:27–35.

Tennov, D. (1973). The Relationship between Obstetrical Procedures and Perinatal Anoxia. Journal of Clinical Child Psychology 2:20–22.

Tennov, D., and L. Hirsch, eds. (1973). Proceedings of the First International Childbirth Conference, 1973. Stamford, Conn.: New Moon Communications.

Tetlow, C. (1955). Psychoses of Childbearing. Journal of Mental Science 101:629–639.

Thomas, C.L., and J.E. Gordon (1959). Psychosis after Childbirth: Ecological Aspects of a Single-Impact Stress. American Journal of Medical Science 238:363–388.

Thorne, B., and N. Henley, eds. (1975). Language and Sex: Difference and Dominance. Rowley, Mass.: Newbury House.

Trethowan, W.H. (1968). The Couvade Syndrome: Some Further Observations. Journal of Psychosomatic Research 12:107–115.

Trethowan, W.H., and C. Dickens (1972). Cravings, Aversions and Pica of Pregnancy. *In* Modern Perspectives in Psycho-Obstetrics. J.G. Howells, ed. New York: Brunner-Mazel.

Weideger, P. (1976). Menstruation and Menopause: The Physiology and Psychology, the Myth and the Reality. New York: Knopf.

Whalen, R.E. (1975). Cyclic Changes in Hormones and Behavior. Archives of Sexual Behavior 4:313–314.

Whorf, B.L. (1956). Language, Thought, and Reality. Cambridge, Mass.: Technology Press.

Wortis, R.P. (1971). The Acceptance of the Concept of the Maternal Role by Behavioral Scientists and Its Effects on Women. American Journal of Orthopsychiatry 41:733–746.

Chapter Four

Sexual Transactions

In Chapter 2, the focus of analysis was on the individual. A developmental script was traced, from birth to old age. Sexual identity was viewed as a process of correspondence and noncorrespondence of the individual's experience with an age-graded sexual script. That script, for women, is defined as heterosexual/monogamous/married—permanently. We also noted that in the later stages of development of sexual identity there was a proliferation of options for women, permitting the development of sexual identities at variance with the standard script. Still that script, the marriage script, is always the backdrop, whether for the development of sexual identities or for the sexual transactions that will be analyzed here. In this chapter we will try to show how individuals' behavior is scripted—how it follows the limits of transactions as defined here. In this chapter, too, the role of peers becomes clear, as audience to sexual transactions. In Chapter 4 it will become even clearer that in order for there to be a sexual life-style, there must be a community which shares behavior and social constructions which validate that behavior. The idea of sexual life-style is developed in Chapter 5.

A transaction is the negotiation of an exchange between two or more people. The individuals involved in a transaction want to exchange what they have for the best possible return, presumably something of equal or greater worth. A transaction can be completed through barter for different things of equivalent worth or through the use of some currency of recognized worth. A transaction can be a simple exchange, or it can involve several rounds of bids and counteroffers.

Sexual exchange requires a marketplace where people who want to make such transactions can meet. College mixers obviously provide such a meeting place, as do singles bars and gay bars. *In a market situation, it is generally known what commodities are available and what their prices are.* There may be specialization of markets. In many cities gay bars frequented by men may be known as "leather bars" and may specialize in ''rough trade.'' Similarly, in cities with several educational institutions, there may be specialization among colleges as to the ''kind of girl'' males seek as dates. This is particularly true of women's colleges.

A market regulates both price and commodity, *placing limits on the kind of transactions that can take place.* Theoretically, the market can permit competition that is virtually unrestricted, or it can permit monopoly. Traditional marriage resembles a monopoly, with no competition permitted. Yet as we will see in examining swinging, some competition is permitted under certain special rules.

Sexual transactions in marriage are ordinarily limited to the two lawfully wedded partners. Their joint history includes the sexual transactions peculiar to courtship. Under traditional sexual standards, sexual access to women was scarce, and many of the features of traditional dating and courtship exchanges are based on a scarcity mentality. Some individuals may view the current liberalization of sexual standards as akin to price wars, in which sellers attempt to undercut each other's prices and thus drive the profit down for all. Popular folklore has it that the average man has more sexual opportunities now than in previous times. Sexual access that can be gotten ''cheap'' drives down the ''value'' of sexual access to more reluctant partners. Hence the perception of a price war both in the realm of courtship and in the realm of marriage. A price war may be a situation in which the seller is forced to engage in unprofitable transactions just to stay in business. In marriage or in the courtship market, a woman may engage in sex at times, in ways, or with partners unsatisfactory to her, under the threat of the man taking his business elsewhere. Traditionally, where sexual access was restricted, virginity was highly prized. Marriage (and consequently courtship) was a seller's market, with the prize being awarded to the highest bidder. Under liberalized sexual standards, courtship, if not marriage, is usually perceived as a buyer's market. If the seller does not meet his terms, the buyer can try other sellers.

Courtship and Dating Scripts

Sociologists have been studying courtship for generations. The original researchers viewed courtship simply as a mechanism for mate selection. In earliest times, courtship consisted of mechanisms which would place the young on the track of the traditional sexual script: heterosexual/monogamous/married—permanently. It was assumed that courtship was a prelude to, and expeditiously followed by, marriage. The original sexual standard for courtship, the single standard of abstinence, fit the social conditions of earlier times. The young were chaperoned, and courtship was serious business. The stage of nubility (the period between puberty and marriage) was expected to be comparatively short.

In some societies, the stage of nubility is much shorter than in ours. In some, marriages are contracted before puberty. And in others, sexual contact between the sexes is not restricted to marriage, so that while marriage is taken seriously, sexual activity is not. The sexual bond is a part of marriage, but matters of property and lineage are of much greater concern.

Our society has a distinctive pattern: the lag between puberty and marriage is long, and premarital sex is disapproved. Yet the young are not chaperoned; the responsibility for maintaining premarital chastity is left with them. The features of our institution of courtship are adapted to these constraints. In our society, the institution called dating has evolved as an offshoot of serious courtship, or permanent mate selection. Dating begins ever earlier, and age at first marriage has recently risen, with the result that the period of nubility is quite long. Dating has become a pastime in itself, with its own routines and norms, and is a recognized way for single persons to meet and relate. Dating has no serious purpose, and is usually characterized as involving superficial interactions. Courtship, on the other hand, is thought to involve more "real" relationships, with an ultimate goal of permanent mating.

Though an analytical distinction between the characteristics of dating and courtship may be made, this distinction is not always apparent in real life. Dating is often seen as a prelude to courtship, which is itself a prelude to marriage. Later in this chapter, when we look at dating as an option for single adults, its distinctive characteristics may become clearer. But during the stage of nubility, the two processes—dating and courtship—and their two scripts are often confounded.

Both scripts have two important dimensions: the institutional and the interpersonal. The institutional aspects of courtship relate closely to those of marriage, and the closer partners get to marriage, the more their relationship takes on the institutional aspects of marriage. Arrangements regarding finances, division of labor, sex, and many other items in a joint life become habitual, or institutionalized. The *form* of such habitual arrangements is most often patterned after marriage. As courtship progresses, there is an increasing commitment, not only to the individual who is the partner, but to the role obligations of marriage as an institution. Courtship is thus closed-ended, while dating is more open-ended. Another way of saying this is that courtship has a direction; it is "going somewhere" (toward marriage), while dating is "going nowhere." These constructions, of course, remind us that marriage is the expected destination for the adult woman in our society. Libby (1976) has pointed out the limiting effect of the "primrose path of dating" as contrasted with the more open-ended "getting together" script. He questions the destination of the "going somewhere" script and sees more advantage in the kind of relationship which might be viewed as "going nowhere."

Dating and courtship can be distinguished in terms of their institutional status. They can also be distinguished in terms of the kind of personal relationship which obtains. Insofar as the courting relationship is serious, it is oriented toward a lasting commitment and planning for a joint future. It is emotionally intimate and usually sexually exclusive. The dating relationship lacks this future orientation. It is expected to persist only so long as the exchange of benefits in present time is mutually satisfactory. However, the status of a given relationship is frequently ambiguous. Changes in sexual standards mean that certain behaviors—e.g., coitus—which once demarcated "serious," monogamous relationships from casual, multiple ones, no longer do so. Cues are ambiguous; competing social constructions apply. Parents do not talk to their adolescents about sexuality (Libby and Nass, 1971). The young are thrown back on themselves, their partners and their peers for a definition of the situation. In some sense, the definition of the relationship is always a private matter, based on negotiation and communication between the partners. At the individual level, there is always ambiguity. Nevertheless, scripts exist which provide interpretations for events that occur in the couple's history. Some of these are sexual scripts.

Sexual Transactions in Dating

Dating has often been analyzed as a form of barter, an exchange of goods and services for esteem and sex. Individuals are motivated to make an exchange in which they get something of greater value than they give. Fears of exploitation exist on both sides, and they may be justified. The gold digger induces a suitor to take her to expensive places and spend money on her. This can enhance his image and self-esteem, where money is equated with potency or importance. Escorting a beautiful or desirable woman can also add to his prestige. Equally familiar is the scenario in which the male attempts to persuade a female to give him sexual access or sexual favors in exchange for a social life or expressions of esteem.

Each partner aims to enhance his or her own social status and image. Status in one's own sex peer group, however, depends in part on avoiding exploitation by the other sex. Thus some social analysts see the dating pair as adversaries in a zero-sum game in which one partner loses when the other wins. Both individuals in the pair are vulnerable not only to their partners, but to the peer group of their partners as well, since this peer group has a strong influence on how their partners perceive their desirability.

The key to success in this kind of market situation lies in creating a *perception of scarcity*. What is scarce is presumed to be valuable, and this equation of scarcity with value runs all through the dating and courtship situation. The female strategy of playing hard to get is one means of creating the impression of scarcity. A comparable male strategy is to "play it cool," to appear not to notice or be attracted by females vying for attention.

Although the peer group backs up the individual to some extent, there is a limit to same-sex solidarity. In the dating market, persons compete against others of their own sex to appear as the most desirable and hence be chosen by the most desirable partner. Research has discovered many strategies by which individuals seek to enhance the perception of their own desirability:

> Nothing succeeds like success. Therefore, the clever coed contrives to give the impression of being much sought after even if she is not. It has been reported by many observers that a girl who is called to the telephone in the dormitories will often allow herself to be called several times, in order to give all the other girls ample opportunity to hear her paged. Coeds who wish campus prestige must never be available for last-minute dates; they must avoid being seen too often with the same boy, in order that others may not be frightened away or discouraged; they must be seen when they go out, and must, therefore, go to the popular (and expensive) meeting places; they must have many partners at the dances. If they violate the conventions at all, they must do so with great secrecy and discretion; they do not drink in groups or frequent the beer-parlors. Above all, the coed who wishes to retain Class A standing must consistently date Class A men. (Waller, 1937: 731)

The audience of peers is an essential part of impression management. In the women's dorm or sorority setting, peers have the opportunity to observe the individual woman's success with men and to rate her. In addition, their approval of a given date heightens his desirability in her eyes, and their disapproval makes her reluctant to be seen with him. Female peers are not just a passive audience, however; they often play an important part in dating. They frequently have some prior knowledge of a given partner and can offer an opinion on whether his intentions are exploitative or sincere. They also serve as middlemen or panders. They sometimes supply partners for women in their group (older brothers or visiting relatives), and they may carry messages between potential partners who are in the delicate early stages of a dating relationship. It is common among adolescents for the peer group to give encouragement to individuals, assuring them that their potential partners really do like them and coaching them in how to become more desirable in the eyes of their partners.

As we would predict from our review of sexual standards in Chapter 2, female and male peer groups do not operate in the same way. The male peer group encourages its members in conquest and applauds their "scores." Almost any sexual contact enhances a male's reputation, including exploitative or casual contacts. Under most conditions, however, sexual contact detracts from a woman's reputation, and the response of her peer group reflects this. The woman is not likely to receive social support for bragging about the sexual exploitation of her partners: there is no *approving* slang term comparable to *stud* that designates a woman famed for sexual conquest.

This difference in female and male reference groups has a history. There is evidence that even before individuals become involved in dating, males have a peer group which shares sexual experience and knowledge, while females do not. Most boys learn about masturbation from other boys, while girls learn by trial and error (Kinsey et al., 1953). When boys have their first heterosexual experience, they tell their male friends; girls keep it to themselves. In fact, as many as 27 percent may not have told anyone, even six months after the experience. Studies of college students' expectations of approval or disapproval for potential sexual acts seem to reveal the same pattern. Males anticipate much more approval and females much more disapproval. A number of studies have shown that women do, indeed, have more conservative sexual standards than men (Schofield, 1965).

Manipulation and Exploitation

The strategies individuals employ in attracting a desirable partner rely, in large part, on *manipulating their perceived scarcity,* since scarce commodities are valued. Some of these, as we have seen, depend on creating a certain impression in the audience of female and male peers.

Using threats to *make the partner feel insecure* is another way of enhancing bargaining power. The "teddy bear tricks" urged by *Cosmopolitan* magazine in the seventies exemplify such threats. At least one of these, the post card ploy, is an old trick, used with effect by Zelda Sayre on her fiancé, F. Scott Fitzgerald, in the twenties. *Cosmopolitan's* version is to leave post cards from exotic places where a waiting date cannot help seeing and reading their far-from-casual messages from unknown rivals. Zelda's version was to send to Scott, "accidentally," a letter intended for another suitor.

The basic strategy of dating, for both sexes, is holding back, manipulating scarcity, and, coincidentally, the insecurity of one's partner. Dating is governed by the *principle of least interest:* the partner who cares less is in a stronger bargaining position, since the other partner fears the loss of the relationship more. The more interested partner will accommodate more and will yield in conflict situations. Thus, in situations governed by the principle of least interest, the potential for exploitation is high. By definition, power is unequal in such situations. One partner can be compelled to do things which benefit the other partner exclusively. The potential for alienation is also high, when the only motivation for one of the partners in the relationship to participate in certain transactions is fear or bribery. One consequence of alienation is a deadening of feeling about the area where coercion and powerlessness is experienced, and the abdication of any attempt to make a choice or influence outcomes (Phelps, 1975). This alienation may characterize persons who have a great deal of unsatisfying sexual contact early or under conditions of nonintimacy.

Rejecting the Dating Script

A number of critiques of dating have pointed out the negative effects of relationships based on manipulation and exploitation. Many young people have rejected the game-playing aspects of dating, expressing frustration at the superficiality of relationships that result from manufacturing and manipulating artificial impressions of desirability and scarcity. The rejection of these traditional dating techniques often implicitly holds up marriage as the ideal of the intimate and honest relationship and, as we shall see, many of the emergent forms which replace dating are no more than shortcuts to marriage.

Thus the practice of going steady can be seen as a protomonogamous alternative to ''playing the field'' in conventional dating. In a sense, it is a nostalgia trip: a hearkening back to a (possibly mythical) time when mating was for life and feelings did not change. Going steady, as well as a number of other alternatives to dating, is a way of changing the definition of the situation from dating to courtship.

Competing Standards of Behavior

In dating a variety of sexual standards are potentially applicable. Only the single standard of abstinence puts severe restrictions on sexual behavior. Schwartz (1973) characterizes the contemporary dating pattern as one in which there is pressure for an early physical relationship. The occurrence of sexual interaction is not sufficient, however, to define the relationship. Often sexual intercourse has the meaning of commitment, with the implication of exclusivity. This standard of *permissiveness with affection* is most common in courtship.

In the absence of such a serious relationship, however, sexual interaction may be construed according to the *double standard,* which legitimates the male but not the female role, or the *recreational standard,* according to which both female and male sexual activity occurs without expectation of any future commitment or repercussions. The two partners, of course, can construe their shared sexual contact differently. The woman may operate under a recreational sex philosophy, while the man is operating under a double standard philosophy. Interestingly, in her study of contemporary sexual mores at Yale, Schwartz (1973) found considerable evidence of the kind of thinking we associate with the double standard. Even though recreational sexual contact was expected in dating, nonetheless women (but not men) tended to be downgraded by such contact. Schwartz calls this the dilemma of "the pit and the pedestal." Apparently, neither the so-called sexual revolution nor the enlightened atmosphere of an elite university contains the antidote to the double standard script. As we have seen, the limits of sexual permissiveness have shifted over the last few years, but as long as the social consequences of sexual relations differ for women and men, a double standard persists.

Many typical transactions in dating reflect the persistence of the double standard. Reiss (1960) has analyzed some of the transactions which result from this habit of mind. Thinking of women as good (chaste and marriageable) and bad (sexually available and ineligible for marriage) sometimes produces a curious kind of locomotion in males. When seeking sexual partners, they travel to a locale outside the market from which they expect to select a bride. This may be the local red light district or just another school or community. This practice may well have originated in times when men would raid other communities for women but would protect "their own" women, their wives and sisters, in the home community. The raiding male expects to protect his "own" women when he has a wife and daughters.

Given the way contemporary dating is organized, however, this pattern no longer serves the function of protecting the property value of "good" women. Fathers and brothers exercise little control over young women's behavior, and "good" and "bad" women are members of the same community. A "good" woman is no longer a woman who comes from a respectable family or neighborhood, but one who refuses sexual contact. In an era of liberalized sexual standards, the male operating under the double standard is vulnerable on this point: somebody else may have "scored" where he failed to do so.

The value placed on virginity, where marriage is the desired outcome for women and where the double standard obtains, pits the dating pair against each other in a zero-sum situation: what one partner wins, the other loses. Given incompatible goals, some compromise might be expected. Reiss (1960) discusses the institution of petting as such a compromise. Petting standards specify the level of sexual intimacy permissible to a given degree of acquaintanceship. They govern kissing and caressing, degrees of nudity and physical closeness, and petting—even to orgasm, but stopping short of penetration by the male. Degrees of sexual intimacy are thus calibrated—and there is research evidence that the stages are known and agreed on—but technically virginity is maintained. This emphasis on technical virginity evidences the continuing strength of the ideal of premarital abstinence. The social significance of technical virginity is also evidence of the phallocentric origin of traditional scripts for women. Penetration is what counts. Sex and all other experience are negated.

Standards for lesser intimacies in petting tend to be less restrictive than for activities approaching penetration, permitting hand holding or kissing with less familiarity and commitment and more partners. More intimate behavior, however, tends to be restricted to one partner, with whom there is substantial commitment. The dominant standard here seems to be permissiveness with affection: as long as there is affection, fairly intense sexual activity is permissible. Living under this standard is, as we have noted, training for monogamy.

We have characterized dating as an exchange of sex and esteem. Under all the traditional sexual scripts, sexual access to the female is scarce. Thus sexual transactions lend themselves to the scarcity = value equation and imply a script for female personality as well as female sexual behavior. Under one such script, the nubile woman is encouraged to think of herself as something special, destined for some future triumph which is *passive rather than active:* being chosen by "Mr. Right." She dispenses sexual favors sparingly and with solemnity. Virginity, of course, is the ultimate gift and is exchanged only for something equally scarce and valuable: marriage, or the promise of marriage. This script, a courtship script, involves a progression of sexual intimacies, personal commitment, and public commitment for both partners. The following quote, from Baumgold's analysis of the "Jewish American Princess," illustrates a clash between this script and a dating script:

> If you meet a Jewish girl, and shake her hand, that's dinner. You owe her a dinner. If you should take her home after dinner and rub and kiss in the doorway, right. That's already a small ring, a ruby, or something. If, God forbid, anything filthy should happen amongst you, it's marriage and the same grave. They do expect a lot for a little fooling around. (Baumgold, 1971)

The female in this interaction is available only for courtship. Her expectations are not out of line for that script. Her partner's expectations, however, are tied to a recreational sex script ("just fooling around").

The conflict represented in this quote illustrates a dilemma which runs through the book. How do individuals match their experience to sexual scripts? How does the individual make a transition from one script to another? Few transitions are scripted. But even the scripting that does exist, as that between dating and courtship, does not provide answers to many questions. How do people determine which script governs their relationship, or what kind of a relationship they have? Beyond this, what are the alternatives for persons who wish to reject or transcend available scripts?

The Traditional Courtship Script

The traditional form of courtship in America relies on dating in the initial stages of the search for a permanent partner. Dating provides a slight exposure to a wide variety of potential partners and fits the strategy of casting a wide net so as to have the maximum field to choose from. However, dating is only a preliminary to narrowing down the field. The partners who appear to have less potential are weeded out, and a provisional selection is made. The transition to a courting relationship is marked by progressive increases of personal and public commitment. These correspond to the interpersonal and institutional aspects mentioned above.

The stages of courtship—from going steady to "pre-engagement," engagement, and marriage—are socially recognized. Courting couples work out their relationship in private, yet sooner or later they make a public declaration and seek a formalization of it. At different stages in this process of couple formation, various forces work for or against it (Ryder, Kafka, and Olson, 1971). The folklore holds that "success" in courtship is due to the woman's efforts, particularly her skill in the maneuvers analyzed above. Yet the burden of finalizing and formalizing the commitment between the partners is on the male. In the institutional aspects of courtship, then, the roles assigned to the partners are asymmetrical. The awarding and accumulation of tokens which is part of the public sequence is, perhaps for these reasons, asymmetrical as well.

Thus, for example, it is still customary for the male to award the female some token of commitment signifying, perhaps, ownership. In the early stages of the relationship it is often some piece of jewelry which is quite obviously the property of the male (an outsize class ring or the insignia of his fraternity) and can be taken back if the relationship disintegrates. At later stages, it may be an outright gift of some value, which the male cannot recover. Only when the commitment is formalized in marriage, however, does the male wear any outward and visible sign of his pledge—a wedding ring—and then not in all cases. Interestingly, this asymmetrical pattern of awarding tokens is often carried over into marriage. There it serves the function of "conspicuous consumption" (Veblen, 1899); the husband advertises his success by decorating his wife with the luxuries of furs, jewelry, cars, or vacation cruises. While the relationship is different, the transaction here has overtones of the gold digging discussed earlier.

The institutional aspect of courtship has received more study than the interpersonal aspect. Young people, however, have become increasingly disenchanted with social institutions and wary of the ritual and formal conditions for marriage and courtship. They emphasize instead their personal relationship, and in so doing they cause social scientists to focus on a series of difficult problems: individuals' feeling states, the labeling of feelings, communication and scripting of feelings, and the negotiation of relationships based on both feelings and labels. This new emphasis often finds individuals involved in feelings and relationships which are unscripted or which diverge from the familiar scripts in important ways.

There are thus two problems here. Individuals must attend to and identify their own feelings and needs in an intimate relationship, and they must then construct such a relationship with a partner who is willing and able. It should come as no surprise that the *ideas that individuals take as guides for constructing new personal and relationship scripts are borrowed from existing scripts.*

Romantic Love: Basis for a Traditional Script

One such traditional concept is romantic love. Most people understand love to be an elemental, essentially irrational force which is so great as to prevail against prejudice, custom, and caution. Love is also thought to be good: a force for transcendence and a source of joy. The script that is based on this traditional view of love reflects these two elements: *power* and *moral good*. Love is a kind of white magic, and the lover a divine fool.

The woman in love is understood to behave irrationally, to suffer certain delusions (e.g., love is blind), as well as disruptions of normal life (e.g., loss of appetite and sleep). In short, the woman in love is not responsible. In her state of temporary derangement, she is free of her normal role obligations and also free of the anxiety-producing calculus involved in dating games. She cannot fight the power of love and hence must go along with it. Love, then, becomes the guide to action. It supersedes all other rules and motivations for behavior.

Romantic love affords the delights of passive abandonment. Recall de Beauvoir's (1953) definition of magic as *passive* force. Identifying and giving oneself up to love permits the individual woman to have what she wants, without exercising force (or even volition). In love, she is not responsible. This may be particularly appealing to women, given the restraint and responsibility the standard script imposes on them. Romantic love has a specific role in courtship and marriage scripts. Because it is evaluated so highly, it is accepted as legitimate grounds for making (and breaking) serious commitments. *Our courtship script says that falling in love is the magic by which the individual passes from the routines of dating to the rewarding and "real" relationship she has been seeking.*

In our culture, love is linked to marriage; hence many of the behaviors in which the person engages once she is labeled as in love are oriented toward this end. Because of this connection, *social expectations hinge on falling in love, and the essentially private emotion of love assumes public significance.* In our culture, love is the most socially acceptable reason for getting married. Conversely, it is expected that people who are in love will want to get married and will make a serious effort to do so. Indeed, we find it more respectable for married persons to divorce their spouses in order to marry others they love than for people in love who are free to marry to choose not to do so.

It would seem that the blessed irrationality of love would afflict women and men in the same way. However, because of its link to marriage, this may not be the case. The traditional sociological literature on courtship assumes that marriage is more essential to and more desired by women than men. Certainly marriage is more consequential for women than for men in that it involves many more status changes and material constraints. Hochschild (1975) has observed that women are more likely than men to engage in "feeling-work," that is, to consciously analyze and transform feelings. Women are also more likely to treat feelings as resources of value than are men. Thus, they would appear to be more cautious in investing their love and committing it to a relationship, and we may speculate that they work harder at maintaining the relationship, so as not to lose their investment. This "serious" approach contrasts with the greater "romanticism" several studies found to be characteristic of men. Men are quicker to label their feelings as love than women are (Kanin, Davidson, and Scheck, 1970), perhaps because the double standard and the standard of permissiveness with affection permit them to be in love without being committed to monogamy.

Blau (1964: 81) suggests that women can use the transactions of dating to cause their partner to fall in love: "By prolonging the challenge of the chase until a boy has become intrinsically attracted to her, a girl exploits the significance of conquest to promote a more fundamental attachment that makes this incentive for dating her superfluous." But Blau's analysis is incomplete. In focusing on the manipulation of a power relationship by the less powerful individual, he takes that power relationship for granted. He cannot see the woman in any other role, nor does he analyze how her partner may cause her to fall in love.

One current theory argues that the "thrill" of romantic love is based on the risk, insecurity, and distorted perceptions engendered by the dating situation. Anxiety produces a heightened physiological state which, under the right social conditions, is labeled love (Walster, 1971). Because being in love is a recognized social construction, the person who labels herself this way knows how to behave subsequently, as a *person in love.* In the traditional script, love leads to marriage. Marriage appears to offer the "possession" of the partner whom the lover longs for and thus an antidote for the insecurity and jealousy that dating engenders. Monogamy is expected to provide security, and permanence to provide the stability many people feel they need to develop an intimate relationship.

The Serious Relationship Script

Courtship and, ultimately, marriage provide the model for the "serious" relationship. The serious relationship involves love, commitment, and sex. Traditionally, dating involved no serious sexual relationship. Sexual intimacy, along with deeper feelings, was reserved for the serious relationship, which was a recognized stage in the progression to marriage. At present, however, many young people experience sex outside of such relationships, and the *significance of sexual intimacy as a cue for marriage has decreased.* Neither love nor sex is reserved for a relationship which will end in marriage. What is special about the contemporary serious relationship is its interpersonal quality.

Sociologists have had no more luck than songwriters in defining what the subjective and intersubjective essence of love is. However, when most young people refer to their relationship as serious, what they mean is that they have reached an understanding that love is involved. Two individuals desire to love each other and to be loved; these strong impulses do not necessarily flow harmoniously together. According to Schwartz (1973), couples who are "serious" expect their relationship to embody certain values, many of which are the opposite of those the dating relationship involves. They expect a great deal of communication and honesty and a sharing of power and of feelings: a spirit of cooperation and a cooperative way of doing things. Implicitly or explicitly, they expect an egalitarian relationship, in which maleness and femaleness are complementary rather than antagonistic, and in which each is equally valued. The desire is for the authentic self, and not some superficial or partial manifestation, to be loved and affirmed. Courtship, much more than dating, implies a partnership, perhaps for life. The partner is someone to talk to, someone to share decisions with, someone to build a life with.

This set of expectations may seem idealized, and no doubt it is. Nevertheless, the lure of such a relationship is strong. The attendant risks are also great. The desire to be loved involves the possibility of rejection. Loving involves the possible costs of accommodation and compromise. Giving love without receiving it in return can hurt a woman's reputation in a way that does not occur with men. But the vulnerability that comes from caring for another person affects both sexes.

Developing intimacy requires taking risks. Yet as we have seen, dating teaches the person to be self-protective, not self-disclosing; in dating the individual learns to evaluate others hastily and on superficial grounds. Young people experience this as a personal dilemma, and sociologists analyze it as a sociological dilemma: if the serious and lasting relationship is where people want to end up, and dating is where they start out, how do they get there?

There are at least three possible solutions. The first is a traditional sequence of steps from casual dating to serious courtship, culminating in marriage. The second is falling in love, which counteracts the gamelike aspects of dating by transforming and prescribing the individual's perceptions. The third is circumventing dating by inventing other social forms.

Alternative Transactions: Rejecting the Dating Script

Insofar as dating is viewed as a game, though a very serious one, there are winners and losers. The total adolescent culture, including both female and male peer groups, forms the audience for this contest and judges the outcome. It is very difficult for individuals to define their own goals, for in the dating game, as indicated above, prestige and popularity are the explicit bases of evaluation, while a fundamental tension between the desire for sexual activity and ultimate marriage ability complicate the female role. When people have tried to re-invent courtship, new forms have evolved which are intended to minimize the stresses caused by competition and the necessity of impression-management.

Group Dating

Social activities are organized not by pairs but in sometimes amorphous groups of females and males in group dating. In this context, there is no stigma to participating without a date, and the elaborate minuet of boys asking and girls accepting or refusing is avoided. A more egalitarian management of money can be a part of the pattern. Individuals tend to pay their own way, and this arrangement circumvents some of the covert transactions implicit in the pattern in which males bear all the costs of entertainment.

Group dating is not new. In earlier decades it was a stage preceding pair dating. Now it is common among older persons—college students rather than junior high students. Now, as then, however, pairing takes place, and couples emerge from within the group nexus. The argument for this form of social mixing is that it permits persons to move toward courtship without assuming the high risks of dating.

Going Steady

This second pattern has many features in common with marriage. It tends to be exclusive and intimate, often including sexual relations; it is defined as a love relationship rather than a casual exchange. Steady relationships are sometimes short-lived, but rather than changing the pattern, participants often change partners. The pattern thus resembles the serial monogamy—a succession of monogamous relationships—practiced by adults.

Going steady and serial monogamy shortcut the dating phase and plunge a pair immediately into the expectations governing serious relationships, often prematurely. Such hasty pairing also circumvents the refined selection process which longer and less exclusive association between partners permits. Going steady and serial monogamy are responses, opposite in direction, to the same problem to which group social life is a reaction. Persons who adopt this pattern also seek to avoid the rating- and dating-game and superficial relationships.

Cohabitation

Unlike the "anticipatory monogamy" of our parents' generation, cohabitation is not trial marriage. It does not occur late in the development of a committed relationship and does not necessarily involve plans for marriage. In more mundane ways, however, it resembles marriage more than it does courtship.

The study of cohabitation as it is practiced by college students reveals several parallels with marriage. The place of domicile is controlled by the male; by far the commonest pattern is for the female to move in with him, rather than their seeking a common dwelling or his joining her. Moreover, the female cohabitant very often undertakes the domestic tasks which, in the traditional marriage, are assigned to the wife: cleaning, cooking, laundry. Then, too, she must pass muster with her partner's friends and find some way of getting along with them, since he continues to see them after cohabitation is initiated. She, however, may lose touch with her female friends (Macklin, 1972).

In looking over the innovative transactions some persons have chosen in preference to dating, it is apparent that most of them are merely shortcuts to courtship or even (proto) marriage. They may succeed in circumventing some of the distasteful features of dating—the "meat market," the risk of not being sought out as a partner, and time wasted in superficial interaction—only to deliver the individual into the dilemmas of courtship. Some of the dilemmas of courtship center on assuming the public status of couple and the constraints which role prescriptions then impose: the issue of stability or commitment and the issue of exclusivity. The alternative scripts described here are not innovative enough to offer solutions to these problems.

Sexual Transactions within Marriage

The courtship script involves a sequence of increasing commitment to a loved partner and ends with marriage. The script for marriage is already established: heterosexual/monogamous/permanent. The nature of the individual marriage, however, is influenced by factors other than the sexual script. The kinds of sexual transactions that occur in marriage reflect two simultaneous realities: marriage as an institution and marriage as a relationship.

In some respects, the relationship formed during courtship is carried over into marriage. A couple's interpersonal relationship may be paramount in defining their marriage. However, the institutional and cultural aspects of marriage set some limits on the development of that relationship. Married couples are legal entities defined in our state civil codes. They also have a place in the kinship structure, the more so when children are born into the marriage. *The social organization of marriage affects the couple relationship increasingly as the couple moves through the family life cycle.*

Sociologists have distinguished a *companionate* form of marital relationship and a *traditional* form. The companionate marriage is based on courtship ideals of sharing and psychological intimacy. The traditional marriage is founded upon complementarity rather than similarity. It involves a division of labor, most commonly with one partner as breadwinner and one as domestic laborer. The delineation of functions and division into separate functional worlds appear to affect psychological intimacy (Oakley, 1974). The traditional pattern of marriage has been associated with couples of working-class background, and the companionate with couples having a college background.

Research on marital satisfaction tends to show that couples are satisfied with their marriages as long as their expectations are met, whether these be for a traditional or a companionate marriage (Laws, 1971). We may ask, however, if the companionate model is becoming more and more the ideal for all young people and what effects this will have on marital satisfaction. Finally, we should note the *tendency for all marriages, including those founded upon a companionate basis, to revert to the traditional form with the advent of children* (Geiken, 1964).

Although many individuals do not know it, the law does not define the rights and obligations of wives and husbands as symmetrical and equal. This is as true of sexual rights and obligations as it is of other aspects of the marital relationship. The law provides that men have sexual rights in marriage; hence *there is no rape in marriage.* The wife who denies her husband his conjugal rights has no legal justification. However, the law does not specify any sexual rights of the wife in marriage (although non-consummation or infertility may be grounds for annulment). These facts in themselves suggest the development of certain types of sexual transactions in the context of marriage.

Additional sexual transactions stem from other aspects of marriage as an institutional arrangement. Only children born within marriage have the legal status of legitimacy, and married couples are expected to have children. Hence the inception and timing of marital fertility often prescribes the timing of sexual transactions. After children are born, the marriage script provides that the female partner, in her role as mother, is to subordinate her individual interests to the children. By implication, the father's priorities may also be modified by the demands of children. The quality as well as the quantity of parents' sex life can be affected by their parental obligations.

If the presence of children, their direct demands, or the mother's consequent state of fatigue limits opportunities for sexual outlet, the double standard may come to the rescue for the father. This script holds that men have "a" strong sexual drive which is, by implication, unmodifiable and must find an outlet. Prostitution has often been cited as a necessary accommodation to this "fact of life." Interestingly, Stein (1974), in her recent study of call girls, found that a number of their clients patronized them when their wives were indisposed. These clients felt that no disloyalty or threat to the marriage was involved in this behavior; indeed, it was the honorable thing to do, far preferable to initiating an affair with a nonprostitute. We cannot use Stein's study to estimate the prevalence of this behavior, but it does afford us a picture of one kind of transaction associated with marital sexuality.

To the extent that the institutional aspect of the marital relationship follows the traditional model, the division of labor may be reflected in the nature of the personal relationship, particularly its sexual aspects. If the man assumes the role of breadwinner, his "potency" may be assessed in terms of his financial success and the consumables he showers on his family. Many men experience impotence in periods of occupational setbacks, and some women are less attracted to men viewed as economic failures than to "successes." Veblen (1899) noted the function women play in conspicuous consumption: by wearing, driving, consuming or otherwise displaying the fruits of their partner's success, they advertise him. Tokens the man gives the woman to display as symbols of his success are often "rewarded" in their turn by sexual receptiveness.

The other side of such transactions has received less comment by social scientists. If a woman's assignment in the division of labor is to keep house adequately, present herself attractively, and have successful children, she may find herself spurned if she fails in any of these obligations. It is sometimes reported that a weight gain results in rejection. If a man finds his partner's housekeeping too slatternly, he may refuse to spend time at home. If he judges her a poor mother, he may withdraw or even divorce her. One man refused to "give" his wife another baby because he disapproved of her as a mother. Another refused to have intercourse with his overweight wife, insisting on oral sex.

Marriage illustrates the fundamental dilemmas of intimate relationships: the tension between mutuality and individuation and between security and excitement. Marrying is a way of routinizing the love relationship. It affords a degree of security, but at the expense of romance. If, as Walster (1971) suggests, the excitement of being in love is in part based on thrill and risk, excitement declines as risk recedes. Although the relationship aspects tend toward intimacy and mutuality, the institutional aspects of marriage may be conducive to role segregation and individuation.

The "problem of romance" in marriage reflects these dilemmas. The role of housewife is defined mainly in terms of services to others. Women limited to this role are particularly eager for affirmation of their nonservice attributes: the uniqueness that caused their partner to love them in the first place. Hence wives desire the kinds of attentions that were part of their courtship relationship with their partner: going out, compliments, declarations of love, expressions of passion, a sense of intimacy, affirmations of commitment, expressions of feeling. But marriage, as an institution, contains an element of unavoidable routinization which may bring a decrease in the intensity and unique quality of a couple's personal relationship.

As the culture's emphasis on the interpersonal aspects of marriage increases, marriage may become a victim of a "revolution of rising expectations." Bernard (1971) has noted that the high rate of failure of marriages in our country is a function of the high expectations Americans have for marriage. In former times, when the interpersonal and institutional aspects were not so distinct, it might have seemed incomprehensible that partners could be well satisfied with the institutional aspects of their marriage—their routines, their home, their children—but dissatisfied with their personal relationship. Yet research on divorce confirms that this is so.

Alternative Marital Transactions

A number of different sexual transactions seem to grow out of the dilemmas of marriage. One is conventional adultery, or sexual relations without the spouse's knowledge (as distinct from consensual adultery, extramarital sexual relations with the spouse's consent). The double standard has always condoned extramarital affairs for men, and current data suggest an increase in the incidence of extramarital activity on the part of women. A recent survey indicated that 38 percent of women married ten years or more had engaged in extramarital affairs (Levin, 1976). A rough comparison is afforded by Kinsey's (1953: 416) data. He found that 26 percent had had extramarital coitus by the age of forty. Adultery ordinarily involves deception, and this should give caution in interpreting the increase as a change in sexual standards.

Adultery, however, is not the only response to marital dissatisfaction. Today's marriages manifest a broad range of sexual life-styles, including consensual adultery or swinging, group marriage, and serial monogamy. Each of these involves relaxing one or more of the strictures of the traditional marriage script while retaining heterosexual marriage as the framework. In swinging and group marriage, monogamy is discarded. In serial monogamy, permanence is sacrificed, but only temporarily. The romantic model of marriage is retained, and the individual intends to be heterosexually/monogamously/permanently married to the *next* partner. In all of these variant constructions, marriage remains "serious."

Swinging

Swinging is discussed as a sexual life-style in more detail in Chapter 5. Here we will focus on the sexual transactions it involves. If traditional adultery involves deception of one partner, *swinging is consensual adultery.* For this reason Smith and Smith (1970) have coined the term *co-marital sex* to refer to sexual transactions which, though violating the monogamy tenet of the dominant script, occur in designated and highly structured ways.

The practice of swinging is the temporary exchange of spouses for purposes of sex. Recent research (Smith and Smith; 1970; Bartell, 1971) indicates the basic features of this exchange, in which, as in dating, sex is marketed: (1) Men initiate it. Generally they learn of magazines where couples advertise their availability and may begin correspondence with others before telling their wives. (2) Men barter their wives. Although the husband's attractiveness is a consideration, the real selling point is a photograph of the wife in a sexy outfit. Photos of men often show them in business suits, as success objects rather than as sex objects (Farrell, 1974). (3) The women go along with the arrangements set up by the men. The researchers already cited have reported that the wives are initially reluctant to give up their monogamous arrangement, but that once the practice is initiated, women tend to like swinging better than their husbands do. (4) Among the arrangements set up by the men is often a homosexual contact between the women. This appears to function as a re-creation of a common theme in commercial pornography, for the purpose of arousing the men. It is apparently not intended as spontaneous sexual interaction between the women for their own enjoyment. Men avoid sexual contacts with each other in swinging. (5) At swinging parties, the women do not initiate sexual contacts; they only respond to men's initiatives. They may refuse an invitation, but most do so with a polite evasion. They do not express sexual agency. (6) The emphasis is on performance, "being good," having a lot of techniques, having a good reputation in the group.

Swinging appears to represent the incorporation of recreational sex into the most "serious" relationship of all: marriage. Though many may find this kind of behavior shocking, it nonetheless exhibits many continuities with the standard script. Most studies agree that men remain heterosexual and married in the swinging situation. The meaning and outcome of sexual contacts between women in this situation have not been explored, perhaps because of a heterosexist bias among researchers. But traditional sex role scripts are followed: men initiate, women react, and the flesh market of dating and courtship is reactivated; once again, it is the attractiveness of women that is the medium of exchange.

Just as premarital sexual activity takes place within the implicit context of marriage, so the preexisting marriage is the framework for swinging. Contacts between the swinging partners are taboo except within the party setting. Often spouses will be present when one swinging partner is engaging in coitus with another. Social controls act to limit the intimacy which can develop: Comarital sex is a refreshing interlude. It is not romantic. No one gets carried away. Couples tend to avoid swinging repeatedly with the same couples, thus reducing the potential for the development of intimate extramarital relationships. Sometimes couples rehash their evening's experience as they ride home together in the car. This way husband and wife share the seeming intimacy of their respective sexual contacts and lessen their spouse's potential sense of threat. This behavior can be seen as a means of reaffirming their couple solidarity and the primacy of the marital relationship over all others.

The emergence of swinging would seem to fly in the face of the process inherent in traditional courtship: the progressive narrowing of sex and commitment so as to exclude all but one partner. The traditional assumption has been that exclusivity and permanence are necessary conditions for true intimacy. In a recent book, Masters and Johnson (1974) reassert the desirability of monogamy. Yet we know that more permissive sexual standards are increasingly prevalent. Sex and commitment are no longer coterminous. More and more people come to marriage sexually experienced. Some of these contract a traditional, monogamous marriage, while others opt for some alternative variety of marriage. Smith and Smith (1970) see the emergence of swinging as a response to a cultural clash between pre- and postmarital sexual standards. For some couples, the recreational and varied sexual experiences of comarital sex seem an acceptable way of avoiding the impoverishment of either or both partners' sex lives. Particularly when recreational sex is firmly separated from marital commitment and where both parties participate (or at least have the option), some of the usual grounds for jealousy appear to be neutralized.

We should note that some recruits to swinging do not find it a satisfactory arrangement. One researcher studied swinging dropouts (Bartell, 1971). How their defection is viewed depends, one assumes, on the observer's own sexual standard. From a swinger's perspective, the dropouts were simply unable to cope with the bartering arrangements or their own jealousy. From a more traditional perspective, the dropouts are those who cannot find satisfaction in truncated or casual relationships.

Similarly, opposing sexual standards impute different meanings to swinging. Swingers have turned the traditional argument concerning intimacy on its head by asserting that rather than weakening the pair bond, swinging strengthens it. Smith and Smith (1970) propose that consensual adultery is less disruptive of couple solidarity than is conventional adultery, which involves deceit and jealousy. From this perspective, the new swinging script for marriage is like an incest taboo that permits sex. In swinging, intimacy and not sex is the threat to the stability or permanence of the marriage. The uniqueness and irreplaceability of the primary partner (the spouse) are maintained, through keeping other partners at a distance and on rotation.

Group Marriage

Group marriage involves quite different premises from swinging, and consequently different sexual transactions. So little research has yet been done on group marriage that we cannot offer generalizations about this form of married life. Accounts of experiments to date do, however, give some idea of the complexities involved.

Different starting points may affect the form a group marriage takes, and its outcome. It appears that most group marriages originate with a couple who have an established marital relationship. The incorporation of couples or singles into the ongoing marriage may have distinctive effects. The group marriage analyzed by Clanton and Downing (1975) was initiated by the male, who retained direction over virtually all aspects of its multiple relationships until its demise. A sexual relationship between the husband and the female single was sustained. An anticipated sexual relationship between the single and the wife failed to flourish. Sexual relationships of each of the partners with others occasioned some problems of jealousy within the marriage.

In its isolation from other group experiments, this marriage lacked social supports. Its individual partners, too, had virtually no intimate relationships outside the marriage. When the marriage was under strain, the partners had only their own resources on which to rely. In this instance, although the partners received social support for their own individual life-styles of sexual openness and experimentation, there were no models or support for the growth and development of the arrangement as a marriage.

In an in-depth study of a small number of multilateral marriages (Constantine and Constantine, 1973), a wide range of duration and specific arrangements was found. While sexual transactions followed a variety of patterns, the modal arrangement was generally some sort of regular rotation of partners. Most sexual contacts occurred in heterosexual pairings; homosexual contacts were rare, and group sex only occasional. (The Constantines' study contains data on many aspects of child rearing and child outcomes, as well as financial and domestic arrangements.)

Though research on group marriage is still in its infancy, the available findings do suggest some possibilities for characterizing them. Both values and structure of group marriages imply *high transaction costs*. When transactions are not routinized, they require more energy, communication, and time to accomplish and are thus more costly. This is characteristic of all nonscripted sexual life-styles, as Chapter 5 reveals. Participants in group marriages are committed to openness in personal as well as sexual relationships. Such values, even in the conventional or closed marriage, require high interaction rates and a high level of intensity in interactions. *Where the life-style is unscripted, ways of solving the problems of living together require much discussion and negotiation.*

The extent to which partners possess interpersonal skills may be much more crucial in these situations than where structure is provided by fixed roles and supported by other social structures, for example, the kinship structure. Perhaps because variant life-styles are rare, people who choose them may have exceptionally high standards, particularly for the relationship aspects of their marriage. The group marriage is therefore under considerable stress, from both external and internal forces. Participants' commitment and their feelings of success must be continually renewed in order for the group marriage to be sustained. And values aside, the structural demands of multilateral intimacy are high. If a two-person marriage contains two relationships, a three-person marriage contains six, and a four-person marriage, twelve.

The traditional marriage may have more tolerance for nonoptimal functioning, both because of the assumption of permanence and because of role segregation. This may help partners in a traditional marriage to weather (though not necessarily overcome) bad periods and problems. As research accumulates, we may find that many group marriages (like many traditional marriages) are casualties of the revolution of rising expectations.

Communes   While in group marriages the emotional relationship is the basis for forming a common household, in communes the basis may be economic.

Communes, with their multilateral sexual relationships, are another form of variant sexual life-style. Here the commitment to marriage as a model and the individual commitment to others in the group is often less than in the group marriage, whose participants ideally make an emotional commitment to all partners comparable to their commitment to the first partner. Aspects of the life-style other than sexual relationships may also be unconventional in communes. Many communes have foundered on economic problems. This is particularly true of the subsistence farming communes established in the sixties by individuals who rejected the success script of American society but who lacked a farm background. A number of such communes have been emphatically criticized by feminists for perpetuating a traditional, sexually determined division of labor and for exploitative sexual patterns.

Prostitution

Of all the relationship forms discussed in this chapter, prostitution is probably the only one that is *ordinarily* thought of as a transaction. It is generally considered more contractual than other relationships, and certainly the terms of the exchange are made explicit. Prostitution is often thought of as a one-way transaction rather than a reciprocal relationship. But while many persons appear to see prostitution as an unequal or exploitative transaction, some see the client as the exploiter and others, the prostitute.

Traditionally ostracized and excluded from the marriage market, the prostitute or call girl has been viewed with horror, disdain and/or pity. Yet some now portray her in quite a different light—as the only honest woman.

In this view, all women, married, dating, or courting, sell their sexual favors for a price, but only the prostitute does so without pretense. Indeed, prostitutes have frankly stated that they have chosen their line of work for the benefits it provides: access to a life-style and an income bracket that many women might envy and few can attain by their own efforts (Millett, 1971).

Current opinion that prostitutes have lost their monopoly on sexual availability through competition from "amateurs" is based on the assumption that scarcity is the dominant factor in the sex market. If any kind of free sex is available, so the reasoning goes, clients will not pay prostitutes for sex. Yet this view overlooks the distinction between quantity and quality, assuming that all sexual contacts are basically the same. In fact, there appears to be a division of labor in the current sexual marketplace. Prostitutes are the specialists. They provide aids and exotica to enhance the sexual experience of their clients. They deal in sexual specialties, with a graduated scale of fees, and they are expected to be more expert, as well as more versatile, in sexual techniques than nonprostitutes. There is probably some basis for this expectation, since call girls and prostitutes typically receive explicit training in sexual techniques—the use of voice, demeanor, body, and accessories as instrumentalities to produce desired effects ranging from reassurance to sexual arousal—which very few other women in our society do.

The sexual transactions discussed in this chapter, as we have indicated, are often influenced by sexual scripts. The prostitute or call girl violates the script. She initiates sexual intercourse, and she explicitly discusses items and prices. She does not withhold the experience of her body as something to be bartered for a prestigious marriage but engages in sex without love, commitment, or romance. Subject to the social construction of female sexuality in their time, early theorists found it unthinkable that a woman would prostitute herself by choice and looked for individual psychopathology or extreme trauma to explain the life history of the prostitute. Now, however, we are beginning to see continuities between prostitution and other kinds of sexual transactions. The sexual experience of today's woman is not so distant from that of the prostitute as it was fifty years ago. Many women have had sex with partners to whom they pledged neither love nor commitment. Recreational sex is a prevalent alternative to the traditional sexual script. Sex without love is no longer synonymous with prostitution. Although most women probably do not ask for money in return for sexual access, as previously indicated, there is an economic exchange of material goods for sexual favors in dating that is fairly well understood.

The study by Stein (1974), based on hundreds of hours of observations of clients' interactions with call girls, provides a source of unusually detailed information about such transactions. The findings from this study make it clear that these sexual transactions involve far more than the exchange of money for sexual services. Some clients pay to inject a bit of romance into their lives. They want to treat the call girl as a mistress: they send gifts and remembrances, take her on dates and outings, and check in by phone just to chat even when they do not have a date. They want to be special, to be remembered in their turn; they want the relationship to be their ideal romance, and they idealize the call girl.

Others use the call girl as an adjunct to their business. Like a wife, she helps with their business entertaining. Sometimes a party with a call girl is a reward or a bribe to sweeten a business deal. In addition, some clients pay for release from the obligations of reciprocity in sex. They want to direct the sexual interaction and orchestrate it around their own sexual fantasies and sexual release. Particularly where the client's sexual fantasies are central to the interaction, the call girl is supposed to read his mind and play up to his desired fantasy, bypassing direct and explicit communication which could break the thread of fantasy. Clients do not want to have to woo or persuade their partner; they want a girl on call, ready when they are.

Stein likens the call girl's skills to her own skills as a trained social worker. The call girl, like the social worker, is not insincere—but the client is not her one and only, or her first. The relationship between call girl and client is not one of reciprocal benefit or symmetrical participation. The call girl's obligation is to *produce benefit for her client.*

Clearly, there are parallels between the role of call girl and that of wife. The responsibility for sexual satisfaction is rather one-sided. At the same time the call girl is to provide the client with the sexual satisfaction he desires, she is also expected to provide psychological reassurance that he is a fantastic lover and has rendered her ecstatic. Many wives fake orgasm for the same reason.

For all the expense in dollars (a client may pay $50 for a half hour), in several respects patronizing a call girl costs the client less than having the same kind of sexual transaction with his wife. Because the wife is often not so conveniently located, sexual interaction between spouses at non-traditional times of the day may require the rearrangement of complex schedules. The wife may be more demanding—and in terms of the marital contract, may have the right to be so—than the call girl. And sex often cannot easily be separated from the many other concerns spouses share.

Many of the clients in Stein's study saw their call girl during the working day, on a regular basis, over a period of years. This was presumably not known to their wives, although it may well have been known to their male peers. For some, call girls provided a sexual outlet without threatening their marriage, for while adultery usually involves a psychologically intimate relationship, prostitution does not. Again, the call girl is not in the marriage market, and a man cannot incur any obligation to her.

The question of "making an honest woman of her" does not arise. In addition, no comparison need arise between the call girl—nice, but naughty—and the wife—a good woman.

Somewhat uncritically, Stein passes along an idea that has long served as a rationalization for married men's recourse to prostitutes, to wit: if they were getting (enough, or the right kind of) sex at home, husbands would not be seeking sex in the cash marketplace. This sounds suspiciously like blaming the victim (for Stein concedes that the wives may be just as dissatisfied as the husbands). There appears to be more to it than that, however. In fact, Stein suggests on the basis of her study that all the sexual transactions between husband, wife, and call girl reflect certain constraints of the male sex role. On the one hand, some clients feel that their role as breadwinner has eclipsed all others at home: to have fun, they must have recourse to a call girl. On the other hand, Stein's account suggests that these men are resistant to investing anything but money (time, empathy, confrontation) at home. As a result, their wives may be just as dissatisfied as they are. Turning to the relationship with the call girl, we find once again that while the client seeks empathy, flattery, and the sexual services of a specialist, he does not reciprocate. His contribution is once again money. In both contexts the client's attitudes are essentially the same. He may assign different functions to his wife and his call girl and reward them both, but the focus remains himself, and the desired outcome, his well-being. Thus the transactions involving wife and call girl may be more similar than we have supposed.

Cruising: The Singles Scene

This chapter began with an analysis of the sexual transactions commonly observed in dating and courtship. When dating coincides with nubility, it is assumed that dating will give way in time to courtship and courtship, in turn, to marriage. A sequence of feeling states and sexual relations is also scripted. Individuals who do not follow the script or, having followed it, do not "live happily ever after," remain in or regain the single status.

To the extent that singles are out of synchrony with those peers who originally formed the "pool of eligibles" for dating, courtship, and marriage, they require social institutions that take the place of school, church, and neighborhood as a context for pairing. In a world where the unit is the couple, both the never married and the formerly married seek a milieu tailored to singles. Singles groups, singles apartment complexes, singles clubs, and especially singles bars have developed to provide the right context for cruising—making temporary contacts for the purpose of recreational sex. They are characterized not only by a specific kind of clientele, but by a specific kind of interaction. The sexual transactions which typify singles bars also characterize gay bars, a specialized kind of singles bar.

Schwartz (1973) suggests that the prototype of the singles bars is the college mixer. This is a special occasion, created to provide an opportunity for pairing. Ostensibly the mixer is an entertainment in and of itself, but the person who ends the evening alone probably does not feel satisfied. The sexual transactions of the cruising scene are organized around being on display and being available to be chosen, while at the same time canvassing the crowd in order to make a choice. Most analyses of heterosexual cruising cast the male in the active or agentic role. Once an attractive possibility is marked out, an approach is made. There is only a short time in which to make an impression, perhaps the duration of one dance or one drink.

After the approach is made, there is an attempt to persuade the selected partner to leave. If successful, this accomplishes two goals: it removes the chosen partner from competition, and it promotes a more private and overtly sexual contact. There is always a time constraint. Not only do singles bars and their prototypes, the college mixers, have a closing hour, but competition for desirable partners is keen. There is a distinct advantage to being able to move fast. In the straight mixer situation studied by Lever and Schwartz (1971), the males initiated contact and followed a script embodying a traditionally masculine construction of reality. The mixer was construed as a win or lose situation. Men approached it with a "game plan" and were more likely than females to play as a team.

The singles scene, whether a straight or gay bar or a college mixer, is a specific kind of sexual marketplace. It is fairly well understood that contacts are made for the purpose of finding a temporary partner for recreational sex. Value is placed on variety and novelty. Some individuals may rely on this specialized sexual marketplace as a regular or even exclusive source of contacts. Others use it only occasionally.

Especially for those who do not have other communities in which to seek partners, the cruising scene may be frustrating and lacerating. Fraught with performance anxiety and fear of rejection (Schwartz, 1973), it is a situation that is also specialized for a style of relating that many persons find alienating. It permits neither real self-disclosure nor real knowledge of the partner. The pattern of quick meetings, superficial exchange, hasty judgment, and precipitous sexual contact does not make a good beginning for a serious relationship. Yet most participants expect sooner or later to find a partner with whom they can build a relationship of genuine personal commitment. Indeed, the fantasy of finding true love and forming a lasting marriage colors such unlikely transactions as prostitution and pairing off in gay bars as well as where such expectations are traditional: in "serious" courtship.

In this chapter we have analyzed some of the sexual transactions embedded in the more familiar sexual scripts. In sexual transactions, two or more people negotiate the terms of a sexual exchange, each with the idea of gaining something of equal or greater value. Some exchanges are systematically regulated. Worth is understood; appropriate partners are designated; stages are choreographed; and rule violations may cause the transaction to be terminated. In short, some sexual transactions are extensively scripted.

Sexual transactions are, however, complex. In part this is because sexual transactions are seldom for the sake of sex alone. Many other commodities are bonded to sex and enter into sexual exchanges: prestige, security, reassurance, affirmation, commitment, and love, to say nothing of revenge, novelty, and risk.

Another complexity is that traditional scripts prohibit some actors—especially women—from acknowledging one aim of the transaction as sex. In the traditional scripts for women, sex is always for the sake of something or someone else, not for oneself. We do not know how such scripting affects the ways in which women engage in sexual transactions. If sexual self-interest is not a permitted motive for women, does this cause them to bargain less hard than their partner, or to settle for a bargain that is different from what they desire? Is communication distorted by the language of love or duty that women must use and men accept?

The great variety of sexual transactions examined in this chapter, with their underlying commonalities, evidence the importance of social scripting of human sexuality. Although for the most part transactions involve only two people interacting in comparative privacy, the meanings they impute to each other and their sexual contact reflect social constructions of sexuality and the resultant sexual scripts. Stein's (1974) work suggests that the partners in call girl prostitution define their contact in a way quite different from the way society may define it. Lever and Schwartz (1971) suggest that persons who pair off at mixers rely on same sex peer groups to make sense of their sexual connection. In other words, partners in sexual transactions need to have their experience interpreted in a context which already has meaning for them.

Sexual scripts provide ways of knowing how to behave and how to respond to others in specific situations—on a date, with a call girl, at a swingers' party. Sexual scripts also provide occasions for learning, for acquiring definitions of the self and the partner(s) which may carry over into later life. In novel situations, an old hand often takes the neophyte aside and explains the repertoire of accepted roles and behavior and the rules for sexual conduct. Individuals fall back on the sexual scripts they have learned when confronting new situations. But while sexual scripts may serve as a guide to action, smoothing the way and lessening awkwardness in the individual who confronts a new situation, they may also limit the possibilities for behavior in a new setting.

The sexual scripts now available are particularly limiting for women. We have seen in this chapter how sexual transactions in a variety of contexts reflect such scripts. In their sexual transactions, women act out a female script of receptivity and reactivity, not of sexual agency. They allow themselves to be judged and graded on standards ranging from their attractiveness to the tastiness of the meals they cook. They suffer the consequences of not being chosen, and of not being valued. The occasion for sexual expression is too often love or duty—and these too are instigated or defined by men. The "new look" in sexual transactions fits within the confines of the old scripts. In surveying the new forms of sexual transaction, we must conclude that without challenge and change in the dominant female scripts, female sexuality will not expand and develop.

The unscripted transactions, as we have seen, involve more effort and more self-exposure. Yet exchanges which are not to be exploitative or stereotyped must move away from the sexual scripts, and toward more personal connection.

References

Abbott, S., and B. Love (1972). Sappho Was a Right-On Woman. New York: Stein and Day.

Bartell, G.D. (1971). Group Sex. New York: New American Library.

Baumgold, J. (1971). The Persistence of the Jewish American Princess. New York, March 22:25–31.

Bernard, J. (1971). Women and the Public Interest. Chicago: Aldine-Atherton.

Blau, P. (1964). Exchange and Power in Social Life. New York: Wiley.

Clanton, G., and C. Downing (1975). Face to Face to Face: An Experiment in Intimacy. New York: Dutton.

Constantine, L., and J. Constantine (1973). Group Marriage. New York: Macmillan.

de Beauvoir, S. (1953). The Second Sex. New York: Knopf.

Farrell, W. (1974). The Liberated Man. New York: Random House.

Geiken, K.F. (1964). Expectations Concerning Husband-Wife Responsibilities in the Home. Journal of Marriage and the Family 26:349–352.

Hochschild, A. (1975). Attending to, Codifying and Managing Feelings: Sex Differences in Love. Paper presented at the meetings of the American Sociological Association.

Hoffman, M. (1968). The Gay World: Male Homosexuality and the Social Creation of Evil. New York: Basic Books.

Kanin, E., K. Davidson, and S. Scheck (1970). A Research Note on Male-Female Differentials in the Experience of Heterosexual Love. Journal of Sex Research 6:64–72.

Kephart, W. (1967). Some Correlates of Romantic Love. Journal of Marriage and the Family 29:470–474.

Kinsey, A.C., et al. (1953). Sexual Behavior in the Human Female. Philadelphia: Saunders.

Laws, J.L. (1971). A Feminist Review of the Marital Adjustment Literature: The Rape of the Locke. Journal of Marriage and the Family 33(3):483–516.

Lever, J., and P. Schwartz (1971). Women at Yale. Indianapolis: Bobbs-Merrill.

Levin, R.J. (1976). The Redbook Report on Premarital and Extramarital Sex: The End of the Double Standard? Redbook 145(6):38.

Libby, R. (1976). Social Scripts for Sexual Relationships. *In* Sexuality Today and Tomorrow: Contemporary Issues in Human Sexuality. S. Gordon and R. Libby, eds. N. Scituate, Mass.: Duxbury Press.

————(1977). Creative Singlehood as a Sexual Lifestyle: Beyond Marriage as a Rite of Passage. *In* Marriage and Its Alternatives: Exploring Intimate Relationships. R. Libby and R. Whitehurst, eds. Glenview, Ill.: Scott, Foresman.

Libby, R., and G.D. Nass (1971). Parental Views on Teenage Sexual Behavior. Journal of Sex Research 7:127–136.

Macklin, E.D. (1972). Preliminary Summary of Study on Heterosexual Cohabitation among Unmarried College Students. Unpublished, Cornell University.

Masters, W.H., and V.E. Johnson (1974). The Pleasure Bond: A New Look at Sexuality and Commitment. Boston: Little, Brown.

Millett, K. (1971). Prostitution: A Quartet for Female Voices. *In* Woman in Sexist Society. V. Gornick and B.K. Moran, eds. New York: Basic Books.

Oakley, A. (1974). The Sociology of Housework. New York: Pantheon Books.

Phelps, L. (1975). Female Sexual Alienation. *In* Women: A Feminist Perspective. Palo Alto, Calif.: Matfield.

Reiss, I. (1960). Premarital Sexual Standards in America. New York: Free Press.

Ryder, R.G., J.S. Kafka, and D.H. Olson (1971). Separating and Joining Influences in Courtship and Early Marriage. American Journal of Orthopsychiatry 41:450–464.

Schofield, M. (1965). The Sexual Behavior of Young People. London: Longman, Green.

Schwartz, P. (1973). Social Games and Social Roles: Effects of a College Dating System. Ph.D. dissertation, Yale University.

Simon, W. (1968). Youth Cultures and Aspects of the Socialization Process. Unpublished report.

Smith, J.R., and L.G. Smith (1970). Co-marital Sex and the Sexual Freedom Movement. Journal of Sex Research 62:131–142.

Stein, M. (1974). Lovers, Friends, Slaves. New York: Berkley Medallion Books.

Veblen, T. (1899). The Theory of the Leisure Class. Reprint. New York: Mentor, New American Library, 1953.

Waller, W. (1937). The Rating and Dating Complex. American Sociological Review 2:731.

Walster, E. (1971). Passionate Love. *In* Theories of Attraction. B. Murstein, ed. New York: Springer.

Chapter Five

Sexual Life-Styles

If we have come to think that the nursery
and the kitchen are the natural sphere of
a woman, we have done so exactly as English
children come to think that a cage is the
natural sphere of a parrot—because they
have never seen one anywhere else.

George Bernard Shaw
The Womanly Woman in
Masculine/Feminine

The pattern and context of an individual's sexuality can be called a sexual *life-style*. It becomes concretized by the acknowledgment and judgment of peers. It is more than the sum of an individual's acts. Each act occurs within a context that makes it understandable to both actor and observer. Each sexual life-style has its own customs that make it recognizable to those who practice it and, if people are not being secretive, to those who do not. Marriage, for example, is expected to be monogamous, and marriage partners are expected to intermingle their living arrangements, material goods, and social circles. Public cues such as wedding rings are not necessary, but common. Peer groups do not have to be other married couples, but they are likely to be. None of this, of course, necessarily follows from the choice of heterosexual monogamy, but it is the model we have come to expect.

Of course there are variant constructions—real options that are available but that receive no support from society and are unfamiliar in detail to the population at large. People know, for example, that homosexuals exist. But since homosexuality is not positively valued by our society, information about how to live a homosexual life is withheld.

Nonetheless, when we take the time to look at different kinds of sexual life-styles, we can note individual patterns, expectations, and rules. Indeed, the aim of this chapter is to show the norm and its alternatives, to describe the life-styles that evolve from certain choices and their effect on individual lives. We will took at what are probably the most important choice dimensions in these life-styles: the decision to be alone or with someone, to be married or not married, to be monogamous or non-monogamous, and the decision—or happenstance—of being heterosexual or homosexual. There are, of course, many variations on these choices, but the above are central. Our discussion will begin with monogamous marriage, since it is the most accepted and expected model, and proceed then to nonmonogamous marriage, singlehood—of both those who prefer cohabitation and those who choose to live alone—and finally homosexual and bisexual life-styles.

Before considering marriage, however, it is important to understand how the general construction of female sexuality, its proper form and outlet, affect the choice of a sexual life-style.

Female Sexuality and the Female Sexual Life-Style

In the expected and approved script for intimate relationships in the United States dating evolves into serious courtship and monogamous marriage. Based on the assumption that each individual has a need for sexual and affectional bonds and that these needs will ultimately be best served in the long-term relationship that is recognized by both state and family, this script provides a pattern and context for female sexuality: a sexual life-style. *There is no sexual life-style that is as fully scripted as monogamous marriage.* The behaviors learned during the courtship period, the direct tuition of family and friends, and the institutional directives of church and state are all very clear on this. Few networks or subcultures inform girls about alternatives to the monogamous lifetime pair bond.

In our society, if a woman does not marry, she is judged deficient. If she is unattractive or "not marketable" for some other reason, her inability to find a mate is usually understood and accepted; in such cases she generally finds sympathy and support in her extended kin grouping. But if she is attractive and yet chooses to remain single, or even if she is not attractive but makes no effort to develop or pursue courtship opportunities, society's judgments are harsher.

The woman who chooses an unscripted sexual life-style is commonly characterized in one of three ways: (1) She is *bad;* by having sex outside the approved context of marriage, she is flaunting the rules of society and is therefore personally responsible for endangering her market value.

(2) She is *asexual*—without sexual feelings and thus strange or sick and in need of psychological help, an object of some ridicule or pity. (3) She is *homosexual* and therefore sexually deviant.

It is hard to know which characterization is more stigmatized. While sexual freedom and experimentation may receive verbal support in our contemporary culture, recreational sex, or sex without affection, is still basically viewed as a male prerogative. As an alternative female sexual life-style, it is considered demeaning, although it may be tolerated among small liberal subcultures. Most people find the sexually active, unattached female who has no intention of limiting her sexual experiences to one person disturbing. As such, she may be labeled sick, in the belief that her sexual life-style is due to her inability to form commitments or that she is using her sexuality to act out unresolved psychological problems. Or she may be considered malevolent, destructive to established homes and families—a woman who dismantles what she cannot or does not have. On the other hand, such a "bad" woman may be viewed as somewhat more natural than women who are characterized as asexual or homosexual.

Whether its application to human sexuality is appropriate or not (see Simon and Gagnon, 1970), the concept of sexual drive receives particular emphasis in our culture; we assume sexual drive is either expressed or repressed but never unimportant in the evaluation of human acts. Therefore, a woman considered asexual (having no drive) may be even more stigmatized than a woman considered too sexual (having too much drive). Once she reaches the age at which the accepted female script demands the establishment of sexually oriented relationships, the sexually inactive woman is labeled a deviant and a failure. Her only recourse in counteracting this stigmatization lies in expending all her energy in "good works" or activity like child care that is generally considered appropriate for women. Although homosexuality is now seen by some experts as merely one of several sexual options, the general populace still regards homosexuality with hostility and fear (Tripp, 1975). While male pornography seems to exploit female homosexual *acts* (many films have an obligatory lesbian scene), female homosexual *identity*—which excludes men from the field of eligible partners—is considered highly undesirable and deviant.

Interestingly, if any of these deviations from the traditional script occur on only a temporary basis, they may not cause stigmatization. It is somewhat more socially acceptable to be sexually active *temporarily* (either premaritally or between marriages), homosexual *for a moment* (as in a swingers' party where normally heterosexual women often have momentary homosexual contacts), or abstinent *for a short period* or before sexual maturity. But if these types of behavior develop into life-styles, they become quite threatening to the dominant script of sex within marriage and thus incur condemnation.

A major aspect of unscripted life-styles is therefore that those people who are untraditional, either through conscious choice or circumstance, are without guidebooks. This lack of models for behavior, rationales for picking an option, and encouragement for pursuing those models must be acknowledged when we look at nonnormative sexual life-styles. For example, two individuals who choose to live together and not marry are without certain kinds of advice and support. Their kin can neither advise them as to what makes a relationship like theirs successful nor warn them when they are behaving in a way that is likely to undermine their personal contract. Well-meaning people may treat them according to a definition of their relationship different from their own. Some may wish to interact with them as if they are married when they themselves have extreme objections to that definition of the situation. They may not want to be invited everywhere as a couple, or they may want to see other people in a way that marriage partners do not. On the other hand, the reverse may be true, and the cohabiting pair may be dismayed when people act as if their relationship is more transitory in nature than marriage.

The consequences of such disparities between society's and a couple's own definition of the relationship are serious. The impact of the social reaction to this variant life-style may be oppressive enough to cause the couple to change their definition of the situation. To paraphrase W. I. Thomas, "What is defined as real is real in its consequences." With no other models and no support, the cohabitants may begin to feel that they are wrong. The outside world's definition becomes more powerful than their own, and they eventually either marry or break up.

Of course, some couples can resist social pressure and remain together. But this is never done without cost. Once people depart from approved social relationships, they become aware of their aloneness in the endeavor. Whether it is negative sanctions or mere lack of guidance and norms they are struggling to overcome, those who depart from the traditional scripts are pioneers. So we must keep in mind, as we look at some of these sexual life-styles that are less common and often seem to be unsuccessful, that they are attempts to follow uncharted pathways in hostile environments.

In the discussion to follow, we will examine the sexual life-style associated with contemporary monogamous marriage as a starting point for our analysis of other ways people choose to organize their sexual lives. While none of the alternatives is as common as monogamous marriage, it is nonetheless important for us to know of their existence and how they affect the lives of the women who choose to try them. There are, of course, advantages and disadvantages to all sexual styles; we will note both insofar as space permits. While total inclusiveness is impossible, we hope to cover the major and most interesting variations in sexual life-styles as well as traditional marriage.

The Marriage Institution

Monogamous marriage is the expected relationship. Historically, it has had four main functions: (1) *economic provision* for its members, (2) *reproduction,* in a unit that maintains economic and psychological ties to specific lineages, (3) *psychological security and placement* within a society, and (4) *socialization* of children into adulthood and society as a whole. The stability of the family was predicated more on maintaining lineages and socialization of children than on the emotional needs or romantic love and self-fulfillment of husband and wife. For this and other reasons (barring disruptive factors like war and other societal upheavals), the family proved to be a remarkably stable unit. Survival needs and the need for a recognized position and status in society—plus stigmatization for those whose life-styles threatened the validity of this institution—kept people married until "death did them part."

Now, however, the construction of marriage is in flux. Romanticism and personal fulfillment have been written into our American script for marital and family stability, and as a result, a great many new emotional demands have been placed on the married couple. The effect of this in combination with other social forces has been to raise the divorce rate in the U.S. to the highest in the world among industrialized nations (Glick, 1975).

Nevertheless, it is important for us to remember that while marriage is quite fragile, it is still a status-giving, societally prized institution. Marriage is an affirmation of adult status. It infers capability—and usually willingness—to create one's own family. It assumes emotional and sexual commitment to the marriage partner, and usually vows of loyalty and . obedience are exchanged. It is thus a statement to the marital partner and a statement to the community.

When two individuals marry, they attain a specific social identity; society assesses them as a couple; they connect with other couples and build a social group; they create families and neighborhoods; and they generate an image of stability, maturity, and achievement. Someone who marries is seen as "settling down" and joining society. Someone who does not is considered irresponsible and less mature. For example, routine hiring practices of corporations generally give preference to men who are married. Since they are tied into a network of social responsibilities, it is believed that they will be dependent on and obedient to the organization. (Married women, however, do not benefit by such preference. Their marital status may work against them, since it is assumed that their husbands' jobs take precedence over their own and they may, as a result, be less dependent on and obedient to the organization.)

Marriage is supposed to be the most appropriate environment for love, commitment, and stability. If a marriage does not work out, people are likely to feel that its failure is due to the problems of the individuals involved, and *not* to problems inherent in the institution (Olson, 1972). The familiar adage that a marriage takes "work" places the responsibility for marital success with the couple; failure means that the two have not worked hard enough. The dissolution of a marriage also means, at least for many people, a sense of personal failure, a feeling of immaturity and incompetence. Success in marriage is often measured, at least by the outsider, by the number of years the relationship lasts. Length of marriage, a much easier measure to use than happiness, bestows at least some prestige on the individuals who achieve many years together. Indeed, many believe an enduring "empty-shell" marriage is better than no marriage at all. People will tolerate a great many problems and allow all kinds of violations of the marital contract before dissolving the marriage. The rising divorce rate, we might hypothesize, means that people's values about the preservation of marriage are changing. It may be in large part the result of a change in orientation from considering the family as a unit of society necessary for socialization, placement, and economic and psychological security to viewing it as a locus for personal growth, love, and *self-fulfillment*. Contemporary family texts and popular books tell us that marriage must provide for personal growth and satisfaction of the individual; this view promotes the idea that if the relationship seems boring and stagnant, the individual is entitled to end the marriage.

There are many factors involved in divorce. According to Glick (1975), some of the most influential may be:

1. Access to cheap, legally accessible divorce.
2. Acceptance of divorce among friends, family, and possible future marriage partners.
3. The affluence of society. (This includes the employment of women and their ability to support themselves once they leave marital support, and the increased feasibility of individuals supporting two households.)
4. Alimony and assistance after divorce for those who cannot support themselves.
5. Geographical mobility; a person can leave an area he or she finds uncomfortable after divorce.
6. Less power of parents over children.
7. The influence of the feminist movement in supporting options of singlehood and independence.
8. Decreased religious disapproval.
9. The relatively objective study of marriage and family life in secondary education and college.
10. The disorganizing effect of the Vietnam war on many new marriages.

Any combination of these variables may be responsible for any individual divorce.

It is important to note, however, that while the divorce rate is high, the remarriage rate is also high. The *idea* of marriage and its potential is still powerful. It is a sacred script, one we have trouble rejecting because it is so central a part of our socialization and adult expectations. Most of us resist radical restructuring of our futures and instead try to work within the institutions we have grown up with and been trained to inherit. Marriage counselors, manuals, and courts try to help individuals function within the context of the institution; they rarely advocate revolutionary change.

Marriage is the script; adult sexual conduct is expected to take place within marital boundaries. In our discussion, we will consider the frequency of sexual activity, the conditions and quality of marital sex, and its general potential in marriage.

Frequency of Sex in Marriage

Kinsey's statistics (1953)* indicate that at each point of the life cycle, married men and women have more sexual intercourse than unmarried men and women—especially as they grow older. (This might merely be an effect of cohabitation and access. Unfortunately, we do not have comparable statistics for couples who have lived together for a long time, nor do we have comparisons to just those single populations that are sexually active.) Among women, orgasmic regularity increases with the duration of the marriage, continuing up to about the twentieth year of marriage. Kinsey attributed this effect to the hypothesis that women take time to learn about their bodies and find out what pleases them. He noted that women who were orgasmic before marriage had orgasmic regularity even during the first year of marriage. This supports his thesis and undermines the myth that women reach some peak sexuality at age thirty that accounts for ease of orgasm in the next decade. Kinsey's data indicate that it is age of entry into sexual intercourse and the conditions of sexual "training" that affect ease of orgasm, not some kind of biological maturation. Difference in male and female response may be in large part attributable to differences in sexual experience (including masturbation, same-sex play, access to peer fantasy games).

---

*For a good review of this pioneering work, the reader is referred to a group of articles in Bernhardt Lieberman, ed., *Human Sexual Behavior* (New York: Wiley, 1971). Kinsey's studies had many methodological problems which make some of his findings suspect. Nevertheless, since many have been validated elsewhere and others, while inadequate, are the best guideposts we have, I have chosen to reproduce his conclusions.

On the other hand, researchers generally agree that frequency of love-making declines during marriage. Kinsey's statistics indicate that new-lyweds and people in their twenties make love two or three times or more a week; people in their thirties, close to two times a week; and in their forties and fifties, about once a week. Hunt (1974) reported a much higher frequency of this behavior.* People in their late teens and twenties had intercourse almost four times a week; in their thirties, two or three times a week; in their forties, two times a week; and in the fifties and over group, a little over once a week.

We can only speculate about this decline in coitus. Perhaps continued and unproblematic access reduces sexual excitement, and the effect of habituation is inevitable. On the other hand, decline may be caused by uncreative sex. Partners may take each other for granted and cease to be very satisfying lovers. The script for sex in marriage is not one of high passion. The husband may feel "this is only my wife and she doesn't expect me to be a tiger any more," or one or both partners may believe that marital sex is supposed to be warm and relaxed rather than a series of scenarios with games and gadgets. It may also be true that sexual self-esteem diminishes as a woman ages (since older women are not considered very attractive in this society) and this affects the desire for or access to sexual contact. Whatever the reason, the *expected* script for sex in marriage is that sexual intercourse decreases in frequency as the years pass.

The question of access is important. In marriage, as in courtship, the woman is expected to respond but not initiate. Even if the husband makes overtures infrequently, the wife cannot initiate intercourse. Her appetite is not supposed to exceed his, and if she lets him know that it does, he may view her as "castrating." In a segment of "Mary Hartman, Mary Hartman," a popular television soap opera parody, Mary is beside herself with worry because her husband is not having intercourse with her. When she tries to improve the situation, he becomes furious because she is too "pushy." She tosses and turns in bed, tickles his neck, and makes soft moaning noises, but no approach is unobtrusive enough. When all fails, she gives up, not only sexually frustrated, but feeling guilty because she has trespassed on his sexual territory.

A woman cannot be aggressive, but she is allowed to be enticing. Indeed, it is her responsibility (and not her husband's). If she fails to reinforce her partner in any way, he is entitled to lose interest in her. She may neither "let herself go" by gaining weight or becoming less attractive in some other respect, nor be unresponsive on any given occasion.

---

*It should be noted, however, that the Hunt sample was not randomly selected, and it represented a very liberal group of people. Therefore, his conclusions should be generalized only with caution. In addition, differences between Kinsey and Hunt findings may reflect measurement differences so that interpretations of real change may be unwarranted.

The social construction of what kind of sex happens in marriage seems to vary by class. Kinsey reported that activities like oral-genital sex and precoital petting all vary by class and education of the male. The college-age men he surveyed spent between five and fifteen minutes of precoital fondling, most often touching and kissing the female breast and touching the vagina. Less than one-half of the college men reported oral-genital sex, although more than one-half of the women indicated they used oral-genital caressing in their love-making. In the Hunt study there was a higher incidence of this behavior with fewer class differences; of the men and women under thirty-five, four-fifths of the married sample used oral-genital fondling as part of their sexual routine, and foreplay has been extended to a median time of fifteen minutes.

This change in behavior, however, does not mean that the sexual revolution has triumphed. In her recent study on working- and middle-class women, Rubin (1976) found that although these lower-class women engaged in oral-genital acts, they retained serious reservations about the appropriateness of what they were doing. Since these acts occurred, a more casual researcher might assume that working-class women no longer find sex "dirty"; but the in-depth interviews indicated that this was not the case. While guilt and disgust still accompany these acts, the difference is that women now engage in such acts because they feel it is *expected* of them—that they must in order to be in tune with contemporary standards.

Thus, the marital script is inadequately detailed as far as frequency and type of sexual activity are concerned. There are contradictory directives. A woman is not really sure if she should desire certain acts or not. The pubic area is tabooed in some ways (during menstruation, for example), and yet a wife is also supposed to be available on demand. She is supposed to be "sexy," yet "proper." This ambiguity affects the relationship and the quality of sex in the relationship.

Quality of Sex in Marriage

It is difficult to measure the quality of sex and individual fulfillment or dissatisfaction. Statistics indicate that the average married woman generally enjoys sex. In Hunt's study, about 60 percent of the women under forty-five stated that coitus during the preceding year had been "very pleasurable."* Responses varied widely according to age groups. Less than 50 percent of the women from forty-five to fifty-four replied very positively and only 38 percent of the group over fifty-four replied affirma-

---

Pleasurable is not a code word for orgasm. It merely connotes enjoyment whether or not orgasm occurs.

tively. However, 88 percent of the younger women, 93 percent of the forty-five to fifty-four age group, and 83 to 91 percent of the oldest group were able to answer "mostly pleasurable."

This may sound reassuring to the reader, but again, there are other data, some of them still being analyzed, that might caution us against accepting too sanguine a picture of sex in marriage (or in any long-term relationship). Masters and Johnson (1966), for instance, estimate that at least half of all marriages are sexually dysfunctional. Other researchers and clinicians have noted an increase in people seeking sexual counseling and voicing sexual complaints. It is true, however, that this rise in complaints may be due to higher expectations. It may also be due to the fact that we have only recently admitted that male dysfunction *exists* and is a common problem. We now have a script that allows us to look at the quality of sex in marriage. Sexual clinics, "textbooks," and films enable people to re-evaluate the adequacy of their sex lives by comparing their activities to those of their peers. Technically their mates may be satisfactory, but their experience may not measure up to what they think others are experiencing. In such cases, people who felt satisfied before now feel relative deprivation. They want "the world to move" for them, too.

This is complicated by the fact that sexual problems may *inherently* occur in any long-term relationship. Marriage routinizes intimacy. If the individual does not place much importance on sexuality or sexual variety, this routinization may not be very disturbing. On the other hand, since women have been told that sex in marriage will be romantic, the loss of romance may be very upsetting and taken as a reflection of personal inadequacy. Many couples turn to sexual advisers in order to reshape their sexual life so that it more nearly conforms to their earlier expectations. Achieving orgasm and sexual ecstasy becomes so important a goal that sexual activity often becomes "permeated with the qualities of work"; the act becomes bogged down with instructions, equipment and "production schedules" (Lewis and Brisset, 1967), losing its more playful aspects. Success becomes important and anxiety-producing. For example, the working-class women in Rubin's study (1976) indicated they felt inadequate because they were not as orgasmic as they were "supposed to be."

There are other pressures, not necessarily directly related to the sex act. Everyday affairs, work, and children involve a great deal of personal energy. As their relationship extends over a long period of time, marriage partners tend to see these obligations and routines as important, perhaps more important than spending a certain amount of time in bed making sex interesting for one another. In some cases one person, often the woman, has more emotional energy to spend than the partner. Women are socialized to put emotional commitments over career and personal ambition. A woman is supposed to invest herself in her husband. He, on the other hand, is supposed to invest himself in his work. In his script it is perfectly legitimate for him to direct a great part of his energy into his work and divide whatever is left over among family, friends, recreation, and sex. If his job is demanding, not much may be left over. A pattern is established whereby sex is either relegated to Saturday nights and Sunday mornings or made into a perfunctory performance that does not interfere with the ongoing business of the household. It is hard for the woman to change this pattern since she is not supposed to be the sexual initiator. If she wants change to occur, she may have to resort to indirect methods of persuasion, using performance and access as bartering commodities.

Sex also becomes a mechanism for negotiation in nonsexual areas of a couple's life. Behavior during the day can be rewarded or punished by offering or withholding sexual access or enthusiasm. Manipulation may be conscious or unconscious. A woman may not know that she does not feel sexy because she believes her husband has been unfair to her, but the end result is that sexual contact is denied. Or she may negotiate very openly, telling him, "I can't make love with you when you treat me this way." In exchange theory terms, the exchanges, sex for fairer treatment, denial of sex because of bad treatment, may bring the relationship into *balance* (i.e., each party having equal power). However, the achieved balance may not always enhance the stability of the marriage or sexual adjustment. If a woman denies sexual contact on certain grounds and her husband capitulates to her definition of the situation, sex may then be offered and the relationship will be strengthened. On the other hand, since according to the marriage script she is supposed to be accessible, he may resent being denied and, in return, deny her request for sexual contact when she desires it. In such a situation, the relationship is in danger of being damaged or terminated. However, if the exchange is predicated on a less punitive basis, we might hypothesize that the relationship will be strengthened. For example, a woman wants to show her husband commitment and love so she rubs his back for an hour after work. He wants to show her he appreciates her kindness, and he comes home early from work to make love to her. This kind of exchange reinforces positive feelings. It is only when sex is used punitively to achieve "equity" that a cycle of conflict may be generated.

Monogamous Marriage: Advantages and Disadvantages

Monogamous marriage is the normative sexual script for adult females. Most women do not debate whether it is the "right" sexual style for them. They do not know it is a debatable issue. It is only recently that marriage—and the terms of marriage—have seemed optional and therefore appropriate to discuss in terms of advantages and disadvantages.

The major advantages for women in monogamous marriage might be grouped under emotional *intensity, security, trust,* and *convenience.* The restriction of sexual activity and emotional attachment to only one partner implicit in the marriage vows can serve to enhance sexual intimacy. It also minimizes insecurities a woman might feel about the possible loss of her partner to another woman. In addition, monogamous marriage allows women to be sexually active without being labeled bad or promiscuous. A woman who is sexually monogamous and married has the moral support of society. A transgression against her virtue is righteously (and sometimes violently) corrected. If she does not challenge the boundaries of her role, she can be secure that she will be supported by public opinion. On the interpersonal level, trust is established and interaction proceeds (ideally) without invidious comparisons to other lovers. Partners are expected to relax their guard with one another and show their "real" selves. As a lifetime commitment, marriage assures a woman of a sexual and economic partner in old age. Furthermore, since each partner has only to support and please one person, energy and time are conserved.

The major disadvantages of marital monogamy fall under *sexual routinization, restricted sexual options,* and *fear of trespass.* Married couples or couples in a long-term relationship have to manage the problem of becoming accustomed to each other sexually. There is no evidence that the majority of couples are very innovative in their sexual habits, and while there is a proliferation of sex manuals, as noted above, these exhortations to creativity often just make playful sex into serious work. The excitement of a new partner is missed, and other problems may emerge if there are great differences in sexual appetites or practices between the two people. For example, if one partner enjoys oral-genital sex and the other does not, even after counseling or experimentation, a compromise must be made. Such a compromise may mean that one partner finds the relationship unsatisfactory, and this most probably will be the woman, who is expected to be passive in sexual scenarios.

These disappointments and lack of sexual intensity between the two may strain the original contract of monogamy. As insecurity develops, a slip such as an extramarital sex act may be seen as a major trespass of trust and commitment. While the act is not necessarily destructive to the marriage, it goes against promises and expectations the relationship was founded upon. Thus if a trespass does occur, it calls into question the couple's commitment to each other.

The inducements to marriage and the rules of marriage are powerful. While people can make other choices, in so doing they not only violate the expected social script on intimacy but deprive themselves of the prestige of the married status. Thus, for those who choose not to marry or who change the rules of marriage, there is both inter- and intrapersonal conflict.

The type of conflict and the choice of alternate sexual life-styles depends on how powerful the individual's own definition of marriage is. A woman may need to be married because she wants the social approval of society but be unable to follow all the rules of marriage. She may, for example, engage in extramarital sex not because she wishes to dismantle her marriage, but in order to maintain it. She may inform partners that her marital relationship is inviolable and that sex will have no impact on her family commitment. A sexual life-style that is nonmonogamous does not necessarily negate a commitment to marriage. However, if nonmonogamous behavior becomes public knowledge and is seen as a trespass of the rules of marriage, social sanctions may be brought to bear. The woman may be told that she is not mature, that she is losing the positive associations that marriage previously gave her, and she may then be forced to conform to prevailing notions of marital fidelity, find a subgroup that supports her definition of the situation, or at least try to regain her privacy and keep her behavior hidden. *Changing* the rules and definition of marriage is a much less likely outcome.

Extramarital Sexuality

In the United States, extramarital sex is thought of as "cheating," general dishonesty, and transgression of the marriage contract. Marriage norms are single standard in that they stipulate that both partners will be monogamous and that trespass will not be tolerated. In actual practice, however, the script is somewhat less absolute. In fact, many women *expect* their husbands to cheat on them—especially if they are not vigilant. There may even be some slight toleration for this activity if it is confined to "bad women" or out-of-town trips that do not threaten the marriage (Cuber, 1969). This same leeway, however, is not usually granted the female, either by herself or others. In her role as mother and keeper of the household she has less privacy in which to conduct an affair, and the double standard makes her more culpable in cases when she does have sex outside the marriage. If she is a housewife she meets fewer people and therefore has less opportunity to make an alliance. When she does meet someone, it is more likely to be a person her husband knows—all of which makes extramarital sexuality a more difficult proposition for the female.

Extramarital sexuality may be sporadic or a pattern in the marriage. It may be seen as an escape from boredom, or as a chance for personal growth (Whitehurst, 1972). Kinsey's study listed numerous explanations offered by respondents, including a need for sexual variety, social status, accommodation of a friend's request, assertion of independence from spouse, and response to a spouse's encouragement to have an affair (Kinsey, 1953: 431–436).

People usually think that the major reason for extramarital sexuality is a poor sexual relationship in the marriage. However, information from a variety of studies indicates that emotional adjustment may be more important than sexual adjustment (Udry, 1971; Neubeck and Schletzer, 1962). One might hypothesize that for women who have been socialized to accept sex only in the context of love, the lack of love (or the perceived lack of it) would be more likely to encourage infidelity than any other reason. Indeed, women who have extramarital affairs do not always have sexual intercourse in those relationships (Libby, 1973; Hunt, 1969). They may be looking for emotional, rather than sexual, solace. There are four major reasons women become involved in extramarital relationships:

1. To counteract deprivation due to spouse's absence or illness   This situation is fairly common in America today. Many women are separated from their husbands because of military duty, business trips, separate vacations, or illness. According to Cuber (1969), separations of these kinds evoke a temporary feeling of freedom from the bonds of marriage. Encounters that result are generally brief and do not constitute an ongoing, meaningful relationship which may threaten the marriage.

2. To punish the spouse   This type of extramarital involvement can be ongoing or sporadic. The woman knows she is breaking the rules of the marriage and does so to punish her mate for some perceived wrongdoing. Sometimes it makes no difference whether the husband discovers the affair or not. Hunt (1974) reports in his survey that 50 percent of husbands definitely did not know and only 10 percent suspected their wives of being involved extramaritally, but did not know for a fact.

3. To supplement a defective marriage   If a woman finds her marriage lacking in sexual or emotional qualities, she may become involved in an extramarital life-style to compensate for whatever qualities she misses. One motivation may be the desire to increase her self-esteem. Extramarital affairs can make a woman feel more desirable, more attractive, and more loved (Hunt, 1974). This kind of relationship may be long-lasting and resemble a good marriage.

4. To find a way out of marriage   Establishing an alternative relationship can give a woman the courage to leave an unsatisfying marriage. Or it can convince her that things are really bad at home and she has better options available to her.

The impact of extramarital sex on marriage depends on the conditions of the activity—whether it is open or secret, if the act can be seen as reasonable "under the circumstances," if it occurs to one or both partners, and how serious the involvement is compared to the marital commitment (Cuber, 1969). We might hypothesize, too, that the mere commission of the act will be more momentous for a woman than for a man, since it requires greater deviation from the social script. Yet even though the transgression may be greater, discovery does not necessarily mean the dissolution of the marriage.

It should be remembered, however, that despite publicity about the extent to which women participate in extramarital sex, even Hunt's study, which taps a particularly liberal group of women, demonstrated that no more than 25 percent of women in any given age bracket had ever participated in extramarital intercourse. (The male statistics are about 30 percent below age twenty-five—ranging to 45 to 50 percent by age sixty.) This does not represent any significant increase since Kinsey's 1949 data, and thus we can hypothesize that while trespasses may occur, extramarital sex has not become normative or expected. Marital fidelity still seems to be a part of the marriage contract that both partners (women more than men) try to adhere to.

Nonetheless, there are some people who do reject fidelity as a marital rule. While this group is small, it is important to know about nonmonogamous marriage as a sexual option. In beginning our discussion, it is also important to realize that nonmonogamous marriage is *not* necessarily an attempt at undermining marriage as an appropriate script. On the contrary, as we shall see, nonmonogamy is often seen as a way to preserve marriage and protect it from the problems of sexual boredom and the fear of trespass.

The Nonmonogamous Marriage: Comarital Sexuality and Swinging

We will define comarital sex as extramarital sexual relations engaged in by both partners of a marriage with each other's complete knowledge. There is a group of people who need the emotional security and the historical continuity of a lifetime relationship and yet fail to find sexual satisfaction within the confines of the traditional monogamous marriage. Some of these people—we are unsure of how many (Hunt hypothesizes 2 percent; Libby [1977] thinks it is closer to 15 percent)—consciously decide to reorganize their sexual lives.

What are the reasons someone would want to be married and not sexually monogamous? Much has been written about the possible rationales for challenging the normative order of intimate relationships, which are generally summarized as follows:

Escape from boredom   At least one marriage partner is unsatisfied with marital sexuality. This member—usually the male—exerts pressure on the marriage to expand its horizons. The dissatisfaction is not leveled at the marriage per se, but rather at a lack of sexual variety or a desire to satisfy curiosity. Both partners often feel that additional sexual stimulation from others will enrich their sexual response to each other.

Possibility for humanistic growth   Many couples feel monogamy is self-limiting and possessiveness is a petty emotion they would like to overcome. Sexual experience is seen as a way to enhance personal growth and improve personal goodness.

Sexual "fun"   Couples may feel that the monogamous structure of marriage does not allow a person to have as many experiences as might be afforded by another set of rules. The idea of an affair, group sex, three-somes is exotic and exciting. This does not mean a lack of love in the marriage. Women who opt for a comarital arrangement are challenging the connection of love and sex, not the institution of marriage. They want to incorporate the excitement of premarital courtship into the more secure framework of the committed relationship. As long as their husbands do not let society know that they are sexually nonmonogamous, they can operate with minimal risk to their reputations. They are not challenging their spouses' right to control access to their bodies, but rather acting within the rules and permissions of the marriage.

Sexual honesty   Since infidelity occurs even in marriages based on a monogamous contract, some couples attempt to bring ideology into conformance with behavior by fashioning an open marriage. By acknowledging that extramarital sex is inevitable and incorporating it into the marriage, some control is possible. Rules and regulations can be created. Furthermore, distrust will be less likely to undermine the open marriage because no subterfuge will be necessary.

Twenty-six percent of the married women in Kinsey's 1953 study had experienced extramarital intercourse by age forty. About 50 percent of the males (allowing for some cover-up) were estimated to have had extramarital sex. Sex outside the marriage is a common, not uncommon, occurrence. But even as recently as ten years ago, any marriage and family text would have condemned comarital sex or consensual adultery. Today's texts are somewhat more liberal. Open marriage is often mentioned as an option rather than an aberration, and there is a group of writers who actively support it as a life-style (O'Neill and O'Neill, 1972; Libby, 1977; Smith and Smith, 1974). This new liberalism is the result of at least three recent trends: (1) the "sexual sell," (2) the feminist movement, and (3) individualism, or the self-fulfillment model.

The Sexual Sell   As we have mentioned at other points throughout this book, we live in a culture that has not only sexualized women, clothes, and personal adornments, but also cars, vacations, and furniture—anything that passes through the advertising media. Sexuality is extolled and sold through press and visual arts mechanisms, and at the same time some control agents of society are ceasing to be active. Premarital sex with "meaning" or love is accepted as reasonable behavior by most people (Reiss, 1964). The easing (not death) of the double standard raises the possibility that women have the same kind of "drives" and desires that have previously been a male prerogative (Bell, 1966). Finally, modern styles of city living have made it possible for the individual woman to practice a "deviant" sexual style in anonymous surroundings that protect her from group ostracism or family sanctions.

The Feminist Movement   The feminist movement has given women the support of other women in their search for personal growth and change. This may mean the right to be gay or celibate, or the right to be as "promiscuous" or as "experienced" as males. New information has challenged traditional folk-knowledge and so-called scientific facts about female sexuality.

First, the idea that women can have the same sexual drive and needs as men have has been important. Writers suggest that a woman's sexual appetite can be what she wants it to be, that there are no biological limits to female sex drive (Marshall, 1971). There seems to be no evidence that female desire is any more controllable or any less "animalistic" than the male's—only that society has demanded the female shape her desires to prevailing stereotypes of appropriate female sexual expression (Schwartz, 1973).

Also important is the idea that women can change the direction of sexual bargaining in a feminist framework. Previous social constructions assigned the male the role of setting the sexual tenor of a relationship. Whether it was initiating sexual intercourse in marriage or introducing a partner to comarital sex, it was the male prerogative to direct the couple's sexuality (Palson and Palson, 1972). The feminist movement has stressed that no one person has the right to control another's sexuality. The result is that while before only men were expected to want sexual variety outside of marriage, now women also take part in the decision to engage in comarital sex. Consciousness-raising sessions for women often have as their message that female sexual responsiveness need not be traded for the financial security of a home or livelihood provided by a man and that a woman's self-concept does not have to be formulated in terms of a man's perception of her sexual desirability.

Individualism, or the Self-fulfillment Model   Fewer women are now willing to follow the directives of spouses, lovers, or family simply because it is expected of them. Feminist writers (Greer, Millett, Firestone, and others) analyze the conditions and purpose of monogamous marriage and question its utility in terms of personal fulfillment. Under this kind of social philosophy, monogamy and nonmonogamy can be expected to continue to be an issue for consideration and debate.

Swinging: One Type of Comarital Sex

Swinging is an institutionalized variant to monogamy. It is sexual intercourse outside of wedlock guided by specific rules, expectations, and values. Swingers may or may not be married, but they usually swing in couples. Singles are seen as potentially hazardous, since they seek to have an emotional attachment as well as a physical one. This, for at least one large group of swingers, breaks an important rule: swinging relationships are to be kept ''light'' and noncompetitive with the person's primary relationship—marriage is to be *protected*.

Two anthropologists, Charles Palson and Rebecca Palson, completed a participant observation of 136 swingers in 1972. They formulated a typology of swinging couples which included the couples' style, motivation, and reaction to swinging. While neither comprehensive nor exclusive, the categories they devised were provocative enough to merit reproduction here:

The eversearchers   This type of couple commonly marries young and neither person has very much sexual experience with other people. Sex in marriage is seen as too routine, and both seek sexual experience outside the marriage. Eventually, they agree to explore swinging, perhaps through a swinging publication. They find the experience rewarding and pursue other people frenetically. Later, they may become more discriminating. It remains a secret activity, and none of their friends know of their sexual life-style.

The close friends   This couple becomes involved in swinging as a logical extension of close emotional relationships with other couples. The friends they swing with have generally been friends for extended periods of time. Swinging generally starts with nudity at parties which leads to sex play. The relationships here resemble second marriages in conjunction with the first marriages and are based on concepts of sharing, openness, and commitment.

The snares   Either person in this couple may have been involved in clandestine affairs since they were married. They become interested in swinging for variety's sake. They prefer to introduce their friends to swinging by ''courting,'' becoming gradually more intimate, and then proposing the couples swinging together. They generally swing with exclusively one couple for extended periods of time. They believe swinging has saved their marriage.

The racers   Both members of this couple are highly successful and competitive. Their professional competition has curtailed nonprofessional life experiences before marriage, and so, in order to capture some of their lost adventures, they contact couples through a swinging magazine. They remain competitive, however, and jealous of each other's sexual activity. Consequently, they swing infrequently. Jealousy often forces them to break off outside liaisons in order to protect the marriage.

The successes   This couple is older, with secure jobs, a comfortable home life, children, and a good marriage. They feel they have accomplished everything, find that somewhat anticlimactic, and look for more stimulating experiences. They are "true believers" and have incorporated swinging as a life-style.

Depending on their emotional needs and/or fantasy life, people find the idea of having sex with a lot of people, often under public or semipublic conditions, exciting or repulsive. People often do find it sexually exciting to have new people desire them and to be reaffirmed as a sexual being by this reminder of their sexual marketability. On the other hand, this very same marketability may be alienating. Women can feel dehumanized or objectified by being sexually desired as just another body.

Women rarely initiate swinging. It is usually the husband's idea, and the woman accedes primarily because she feels she must in order to preserve her marriage or her husband's good will (Gilmartin and Kusisto, 1973). Nevertheless, many women do engage in and enjoy swinging if they believe it will not endanger their marriage (ibid.). Researchers find that if the first occurrence of swinging goes well, the female usually feels relief and interest. The taboo about female sexuality has been broken (no sex out of love, out of wedlock, in promiscuous conditions) and loses its power for at least a while, perhaps forever (Palson and Palson, 1972; Smith and Smith, 1974).

Swinging challenges the idea that a relationship is special because of its sexual exclusivity. It promotes nonexclusivity, and thus jealousy, but demands that possessiveness be controlled. Palson and Palson (1972) found that one ideology for the control of jealousy was *individuation*. The couple agrees that their relationship is unique and cannot be replaced by another. They admit it has flaws, but they recognize that all relationships have flaws and that it does not make sense to get rid of one set of problems for another. The emotional investment and history that the couple has is considered more important than temporary sexual excitement.

Homosexual contact between women is also integrated into the otherwise heterosexual activity of swinging participants. It is estimated that almost 100 percent of female swingers engage in some kind of same-sex behavior in the course of their swinging activities (Palson and Palson, 1972; Bartell, 1971). Interestingly, it seems to have few ramifications on sexual identity. Women generally retain their self-identification as heterosexual, rarely suffer any initial or later trauma, and feel that genital sexuality or stroking or kissing is a somewhat logical extension from the physical affection that all women are allowed in this society. Having kissed and hugged other women in greeting or when overcome with emotion, genital sexuality or stroking does not seem to depart drastically from the everyday script for same-sex expressiveness among women.

Men, on the other hand, do not allow same-sex contact in swinging situations (Bartell, 1971): the script for male sexuality is unremittingly heterosexual. Men, who mature outside a context of socially acceptable same-sex hugging and kissing, fear being perceived as unmanly and restrict the possibilities of homosexual behavior in swinging groups to women. Even this sexually liberal group is homophobic about male-male sexual contact.

On the other hand, men commonly find sexual contact between females titillating. It might be hypothesized that they find female-female sexuality exciting because they do not fear that it will eclipse their own importance to the female. Most men apparently have trouble believing that a woman, given a choice, could really reject a man for a female partner. While this does seem to be true in swingers' groups, some men have had a somewhat rude awakening when two women did in fact prefer their same-sex contact to their previous heterosexual behavior (Blumstein and Schwartz, 1974). Sometimes this has happened only for the moment of passion—other times the relationship has gone on after the first exposure. Nevertheless, these possibilities do not seem to be uppermost in the male mind. Rather, men may tend to see the female homosexual involvement as a performance for their own sexual pleasure (Bartell, 1971; Palson and Palson, 1972).

Conclusions on Nonmonogamous Sexual Options

We still do not have much data on women who have open sexual relationships. People who have comarital ideologies are often covert—outside of swingers and other organized groups, we do not know much about them. We might hypothesize, however, that at least some women would have a great deal of trouble managing open sexuality. The woman who participates in open sexuality must have an enormous degree of confidence in the strength and stability of her marriage to control jealousy and to have a firm conviction that she is not being marketed as an object or used by her partner for his own gratification. It requires that she like sexual variety, not just tolerate it. She must be ready to share her partner without being possessive or feeling that her own relationship is less special. For some these requirements are too burdensome, too dissonant, to accommodate. For others, the challenge fits important needs, psychological, physical, or both. The important decision to make open sexuality a life-style may rest on questions of self-knowledge. The ability to be somewhat introspective and honest and to communicate needs, insecurities, and permissions within the ongoing relationship is essential. Perhaps it is not lack of sexual curiosity or desire for variety and adventure that keeps the number of people engaged in comarital sexuality confined to a minority of the population, but the degree of difficulty of the other requirements and the problem of getting two people with the same outlook on life to cope with the changes that this new perspective entails.

The Single Life

A woman may live alone for periods of time or for her whole life. It may be a matter of preference or necessity. Whatever the choice, we know most women grow up expecting to get married. Little girls are steered toward home and marriage very early in life. Even without *direct* tuition, dolls, stories, and games orient the female child's fantasy patterns toward marriage and family (Lever, 1975).

Most women in this society have been told that whatever the compromise, the important outcome of dating and courtship is the acquisition of a live-in, long-term partner. According to the traditional social construction, we all need someone to grow old with (even though most women die widows), and a long-term relationship is the only way to fulfillment. Even as early as high school dating (maybe earlier for some), men are evaluated as husband material, and short-term relationships are seen as unsatisfying or perhaps as failures. If it becomes clear that this person is not a possibility for a "meaningful" relationship, that the relationship will not "go *somewhere*," the affair usually ends. Most middle-class women, even those who want careers and think of themselves as self-sufficient, do not plan on being self-sufficient alone (Macklin, 1972). They view their income as supplementary to that of their mates, and their own income success as enhancing their lives as part of a couple, not just their own individual lives (Holstrom, 1972). Singlehood is just a way station to couplehood, and it is a rare person who plans a single status for a lifetime.

Sometimes, however, the script changes later in life when economic or personal circumstances limit the options open to an individual. Women on welfare often learn that a single existence is the only kind they are allowed if they want to survive. As one welfare mother puts it, "In half the states there really can't be men around because A.F.D.C. [Aid to Families with Dependent Children] says if there is an able-bodied man around, then you can't be on welfare. If the kids are going to eat, and the man can't get a job, then he's got to go. So his kids can eat" (Tillmon, 1972). In Tillmon's analysis of welfare dependency, "You trade in *a* man for *the* man." In this case, couplehood is only promoted insofar as its structure supports the role demands our society deems appropriate. If a man cannot or will not make his family financially secure, then the state will not allow him to retain the social roles of father, lover, or member of the family. The state will take care of the children *only* if the male removes himself from the premises. In this case, women who never wanted to live the single life may have to reorganize their expectations if they wish to retain their children.

Likewise, if a woman recognizes that she is emotionally and sexually attracted to her own sex, a married life, at least in the legal sense of the term, is not open to her. (This is being contested in some states but at this time legal precedent still does not allow same-sex marriages.) While others are dating and planning futures, a young lesbian may not know how she can fit into this picture. She is probably aware that society considers women loving women as unacceptable. Her desired life-style is un-scripted. She may be afraid of her feelings and guilty about her desires. If she is not afraid, she may be ignorant about how to find other gay women. If she becomes expert at entering the gay scene, she may be unwilling to enter a relationship that would entail public exposure or conflicts with her family and friends (Abbott and Love, 1972). If she wants a family life, she may feel compelled at least to try heterosexual dating and even marriage (Hedbloom, 1973). Like heterosexual women, homosexual women are taught to want and expect marriage. Therefore, even when it runs counter to their deepest emotional and physical desires, some women will attempt to fit into the prescribed social script. For some, it is only when they are truly convinced that they cannot play the part that they reject their early socialization.

There are other categories of women who find that singlehood is the way they must live and/or the way they want to live. For example, women who have been divorced or widowed may initially be devastated by their loss. The status of the widow is generally low. She is likely to have depended on her husband as her main source of income, and there is not usually a large enough estate to provide for all her needs. The nuclear family does not provide the supports that the extended kin network provided and the widowed woman may be isolated from family as well as friends. If she is young, she may be able to return to the labor market and still be eligible for courtship; if she is older, marriage and return to full-time work is less likely (Lopata, 1973). Overall, national figures on older American women show that they are relatively uneducated and marginally employed (U.S. Census Report, 1971a).

In addition to economic and intimacy needs, the widow (and the divorcee as well) faces a sudden disorganization of social roles. The roles a woman has trained for, the daily routines of wife and companion, are suddenly no longer needed. The life ahead of her, too, seems unscripted. Lopata's study of 301 Chicago area widows indicated that these women experienced loss of a whole life-style as well as a husband and that loneliness was variously experienced as not only loss of an object of love but also the loss of a partner to do things with, divide labor with, have around the house (Lopata, 1973).

Yet as Lopata's study showed, the picture was not entirely dark. When there is no script, there is possibility for innovation. Half of her respondents stated that they now liked living alone and one-third added that they saw this as a major compensation for their loss. More than half noted that they liked having less work and a fourth prized their new independence. Only one-fifth answered the question "Would you like to remarry?" affirmatively. Sex was not stated as a major deprivation.

While divorced women face many of the same problems as the widowed, the sexual life-styles of the two have been found to differ. In a study of 632 white females conducted between 1939 and 1956, the Institute of Sex Research found that even controlling for age (since the widow sample was older) 82 percent of the divorced women experienced postmarital coitus as opposed to 43 percent of the widowed (Gebhard, 1970). Gebhard hypothesizes several reasons for these differences: (1) a higher number of the divorced women were having extramarital coitus before their marriages ended and thus had a head start on the widows, (2) the trauma of widowhood probably had an effect on delaying postmarital coitus, and (3) most women wanted coitus within the context of remarriage (as was also true for the Lopata sample). Since more divorcees than widows remarry (about one-half of all divorcees, as compared with about one-fourth of widows), Gebhard hypothesized that because the divorcees had sex sanctioned by impending marriage, this made it permissible for them to have intercourse. Widows did not find intercourse permissible to the same extent, since they did not have as many relationships committed to marriage. Gebhard felt that the widows often were not as motivated toward remarriage as the divorcees. They were more economically comfortable, and they romanticized the memory of their husbands more. We might also hypothesize that the different social constructions of *widow* and *divorcee* had something to do with the difference in sexual behavior. The imagery for widowhood is grey, isolated, and little-old-ladyish. Divorcees, however, are seen as available, slightly sexually disreputable, and maybe a little "desperate." One implies retirement from the world, the other reentry with a vengeance. One wonders how much these popular images and possible self-images affect sexual interaction.

The divorcees, widows, welfare mothers, lesbians, and unmarrieds can be divided into two categories: those who enjoy or cope with singlehood as an episodic event and try to retain couple status as much as possible and those who prefer singlehood and try to protect their independence. While we know something about the former group, we know little about the latter. Other than the stereotype of the old maid, we have no script for such a person.

Perhaps that is the reason some single women note that they are distrusted as well as pitied (Lopata, 1973). No one knows what a single woman who has no ties to the family or conventionality might do. Even if the individual has no desire to snare someone else's husband or boyfriend, those intentions may be attributed to her. Or if she is not considered dangerous, she may be seen as inconvenient. Dinner parties are often arranged in couples, and a single woman means a single man must be found. Women who want to talk about couple and/or family concerns may feel that someone with a different life-style would be uninterested or awkward to include in friendship groupings that center around these issues. If the woman has been single over a long period of time, is not living with someone, states that she is happy with the situation, and seems to be well adjusted, she is something of an enigma.

The exception to this, of course, is to be found in environments where large numbers of women like her (divorced, widowed, gay) are located. For example, in university areas there are often groups of single professional women who are known to each other because of their work and because of the fact they are a minority population in the university environment. These women meet, support each other, share positive rationales for their living situation, and create social lives for one another. While this may not be the norm, in those communities where such a subculture can be generated, singlehood is a manageable and for some preferable status within the larger social world.

Both *episodic* and *committed singlehood* offer three sexual options: (1) casual sexuality, where commitment is not necessary for intercourse, (2) relationship sexuality, which occurs within the context of a strong relationship, and (3) abstinence, long periods of having no sexual contact or intermittent periods of no sexual contact. They also offer two life-style alternatives: living alone and cohabitation. These may be different in form for homosexual women and heterosexual women, and both their separate and common dimensions will be included in our discussion.

Casual Sexuality

Two prescriptions for women, the idea of purity and the value of female sexuality as a scarce resource, are violated by casual sexuality. A woman who has intercourse outside of a relationship context is usually described as promiscuous by society, and her reputation is tarnished. A woman so labeled is considered outside the normal pool of eligible partners—because she is readily available, usually both females and males of her peer group judge her to be flawed.

Of course, the sexual leeway she is permitted depends on her social group. Women from highly religious backgrounds (Bell and Chaskes, 1970; Jackson and Potkay, 1973) or from other kinds of less supportive peer groups (Trevor, 1972; Mirande, 1968) have lower rates of premarital intercourse, and we might hypothesize that these conditions would affect other kinds of nonnormative sexual behavior as well. Liberal subcultures like college environments allow the nubile female a certain amount of sexual experimentation before marriage without undue concern. Because they are beautiful and economically advantaged, famous movie stars challenge the rules of society and still are considered desirable mates. But for the most part, women who have nonmarital or nonrelationship sexual intercourse lose status. Such women can still form a relationship should they want to, but their pool of eligibles will have been narrowed by their behavior and they will suffer in any wide public evaluation of their conduct (in a contest for an elective office, for example). There is no available construction of female sexuality that corresponds to "a man about town" or "stud."

Another problem women who prefer casual sex styles face is finding partners. For the heterosexual woman this is not difficult if she is young and comfortable with pick-up bars and "meat market" environments. If she is older, however, she cannot compete in places where people are evaluated only on their attractiveness (Lever and Schwartz, 1971), and she is forced to go to organized activities where she might meet someone of her age and background. If she is someone who has never joined church groups, singles organizations, or special interest clubs, her problem is exacerbated. If she is a woman of high status, her pool is further reduced.

Homosexual women have the same problem except that the age factor does not seem so salient. There is some indication that age does not affect female homosexual marketability in the same ways it affects the male homosexual's or the female heterosexual's attractiveness to potential partners (Saghir and Robins, 1973). Older women in the heterosexual culture are seen as having diminished sexual appeal and vitality and, often, a somewhat asexual nature. Or, if they remain overtly sexual, they are often ridiculed for being "dirty old ladies." In the female homosexual culture, however, older women are invested with some of the allure of older men in the heterosexual world. A woman's experience, job status, and maturity may make her a very desirable partner. Furthermore, older gay women, unlike older gay men, do not have a strong preference for partners who are substantially junior. Thus, age-matched couples are more likely, and expectations for enduring relationships are higher (Saghir and Robins, 1973).

Casual sexuality trespasses on the socialization of both homosexual and heterosexual women about the proper context of sexuality. Regardless of their sex object choice, most women link sex and love, and it is difficult for them to reorient themselves. In addition, to do so often requires a sense of agency. Gaining access to a variety of partners may require taking the aggressive courtship posture instead of being the passive receptor of another's attentions. For a heterosexual woman this may mean mustering the courage to enter a singles bar alone and give receptive signals. For a gay woman, it may require much more effort than mere appearance in the appropriate environment. Since all participants at a woman's bar are women, some way must be found to initiate interaction. For the woman who wants this interaction to be explicitly sexual, this can be a difficult task.

Relationship Sexuality

Single women who prefer to have sexual experience within the context of a meaningful relationship can construct it along two main dimensions: short-term or long-term affairs where the participants maintain separate residences or cohabit for various periods. These relationships may be either monogamous or nonmonogamous in nature.

The script for relationships is that they *lead* somewhere. According to this script, a meeting is supposed to start at a superficial level and then pick up momentum. Vulnerabilities, presentations of self, and intimacies are exchanged, and sexual intercourse symbolizes the degree of caring between the two interactants. As the relationship endures, more information and more experiences are shared. After a certain amount of time, the need for societal definition asserts itself and the couple is forced to confront some serious questions: What does this all mean? Where are we going? What do we mean to each other? How do we demonstrate that?

This is reinforced by the reactions of significant others. Parents ask their children if they are in love, and if they are in love, when are they going to get married. Friends start to treat the interactants as a couple and ask them about their future plans. There is no script or set of expectations for people *without* a future plan, and most people have trouble sustaining a relationship without some goal or "purpose" that they can attribute to it. This is a major dilemma for those who are committed to staying single, and especially for women who do not want to share residence with a lover. How does one establish and nurture intimacy within a present rather than a future time frame?

Some women who are committed to singlehood want to have a sustained relationship with someone, but not in joint residency. As much as they care for their lover, they feel that cohabitation would destroy the independence they prize. There is no research to enlighten us about how satisfying or unsatisfying such arrangements are, yet it seems that some women in history, both homosexual and heterosexual, have had fascinating love relationships with persons with whom they did not cohabit, or with whom they only occasionally shared residence. For example, Romaine Brooks, the artist, had an on-again, off-again love affair with Natalie Barney that changed from shared to separate domicile at different points in the relationship. Other women would live in for short times, but for most of her life, she remained single in this way and cherished her privacy. Privacy to her, as indeed to many others, did not mean loneliness. It meant solitude, time to think, time to organize her own projects. People often think privacy and loneliness are synonymous. On the contrary, being alone with oneself can be fulfilling, while being constantly with someone can be quite lonely if the relationship is not satisfying.

It is true, however, that most women, even when committed to singlehood, establish joint residence at some time in their lives. Our literature on cohabitation, however, is mostly based on studies of college students and heterosexual people whose singlehood is episodic rather than a life-style. Given the limitations of the literature, these comments on cohabitation as a sexual life-style must be seen as extremely tentative and, except where specified, relevant mostly to women who are only single between relationships.

Cohabitation

Among heterosexual populations, cohabitation with someone for all of the time or at least four nights a week is estimated to vary from 9 to 30 percent of the college population (Macklin, 1974). There is a debate as to whether it leads to marriage. One group of studies indicates that it definitely does *not* serve as a "trial marriage" (Lyness, Lipetz, and Davis, 1972; Macklin, 1972), while another thinks it is merely a stage in the serious courtship process (Johnson, 1973). There appears to be no study that looks at long-term noncollege cohabiting couples and gives findings on the durability of such relationships or evaluations of relative couple satisfaction, relationship to outside communities, and life-style differences. The 1960 census, however, lists 17,000 people who told the interviewer that they were living together, and the 1970 census lists 143,000 giving the same answer. This shows an increase of 20 percent in ten years, an impressive change, which may indicate that cohabitation is becoming more conventional and that more couples are choosing to reject or delay marriage. (The numbers are even higher than reported, because all persons living together in common law marriages were listed as married in these censuses [Clatworthy, 1975].) If so, it is a change of some magnitude, and its neglect in the literature is further evidence that our society and its observers are loath to recognize trends competing with marriage.

The advantages of cohabitation would seem to include all the interpersonal rewards of any committed relationship (love, companionship, sex, economic and psychological support). Unless the relationship is one of sheer convenience, however (i.e., a roommate), certain special problems arise that are distinct from the problems of marriage. One problem for the cohabiting couple is the existence of competing constructions. For example, there is the task of communicating to each other whether this is a premarriage arrangement with appropriate expectations or a nonmarriage relationship with either short-term or long-term commitment. Additionally, once that decision has been made, there is the task of communicating the couple's definition of the relationship to the outside world. Conveying the complexity of their desires—when neither they nor their community has a script to guide them—can be difficult.

There can be severe upset and argument when the definition of self and the definition of significant others is too far apart. For example, a woman in a committed living arrangement may consider herself successful and fulfilled in her intimate needs. She does not feel compelled to be in the relationship by law, she has her economic independence, and she is with someone who cares for her. But if her relatives see her as a sad old maid in an exploited position, or perhaps as an immoral person, she may feel rage and frustration at their definition of her world. Such differences can put barriers between friends and family, often to the general unhappiness of all concerned. Of course, if she communicates how she sees herself and this is accepted, such social ratification might conceivably strengthen family and friendship relationships and perhaps enhance the stability of the couple as well.

The situation is somewhat different for the homosexual woman. Since legal marriage is not available to her, she must make her own definitions about what is a living arrangement and what is a marriage (if she wants that construct). By young adulthood (age twenty to thirty-nine), most homosexual women have had a long-lasting relationship, and most state that they want to live with someone (Saghir and Robins, 1973). On the other hand, once achieved, these relationships have a shorter duration than heterosexual arrangements. Saghir and Robins found that only 19 percent of the gay women aged twenty to twenty-nine who had affairs had a relationship that lasted for a period of four or more years. By the age of thirty and later that had increased to 30 percent, but that is still below the expected length of heterosexual marriages. (We do not know how much more alike the figures would be if we were comparing homosexual cohabitation to heterosexual cohabitation.) During these affairs, 89 percent of the women aged twenty to twenty-nine lived with their partner, and this percentage stayed high (87 percent) for couples thirty and older. Here, too, it seems logical to assume that the lack of definition, the ambiguity of expectations, and the lack of support from the community and significant others must take its toll on duration and stability of gay cohabitation. Homosexual women have the same values in their sexual life-style as heterosexual women, but they have none of the supports and even less information about how to achieve success. (Few clergypersons or books provide advice for gay couples on how to have a good relationship.) The formation of a gay couple, its advantages and its problems, will be dealt with in more detail at another point in this chapter.

A significant aspect of cohabitation that does not evolve into marriage is that while it offers women freedom from legal definitions of marital duties, it also lacks the protections of the law. This means that cohabitants cannot take couple tax benefits, that their estates cannot legally be considered commingled, that neither partner can expect alimony or child support should it be appropriate, and that a variety of other rights and privileges are denied them. For this reason, there has been some political movement to allow gay persons to enter into legal marriage and to allow cohabiting or single women to have the same tax and other benefits as married persons. (There are some states that give a cohabiting couple de facto status as a married couple after a certain number of years. But in this case the state is not extending rights to cohabitant couples; it is merely imposing the definition of marriage upon them.)

Abstinence

There has been almost nothing written about a very real possibility in sexual behavior—the voluntary rejection of an active sexual life with partners of either sex. It is generally assumed that a woman who is not sexually active is either undesirable or "repressed" (Decter, 1972). These, however, do not have to be the only explanations of sexual abstinence. There are situations and phases in a woman's life when sexual feelings are less important than other concerns. The costs of sexual activity may sometimes outweigh the benefits. There are some good reasons why women who have functioned well as sexual beings prefer to remain inactive for a period of time. It is important to understand what those reasons are and why they might constitute a reasonable option for some women.

Hygiene and health   Sometimes we forget that sexual activity exposes areas of the body that are well suited for the transmission of bacteria, viruses, and infectious diseases. If a heterosexual woman has been sexually active with more than one partner (or active with someone who has been sexually active with more than one partner), chances are that at some time in her life she will experience sexually transmitted diseases. For example, epidemiological studies indicate that about one-third of sexually active women acquire genital herpes infection, and the majority of sexually active women have been infected with cytomegalo virus (a cause of birth defects) by the time they are thirty. (Celibate or gay women are much less likely to acquire these infections [Holmes and Weir, 1976].) Some women, after long bouts with diseases that itch, burn, and make them generally miserable, decide that sex is not worth it and take a "vacation" from it. This period may be quite brief, but it may also last for years. They may then resume their sexually active life-style, or they may prefer to have sex only under monogamous circumstances, which have a lower potential for disease transmission.

Moral and religious reservations   There are some women who feel it is important to follow religious or moral convictions that insist on abstinence until marriage. Sexual intimacy is seen as too significant to share with anyone except a life partner. In such cases, intimate behaviors are prohibited until the appropriate moment. There are also some women who, although they have been sexually active in the past, feel that those acts were unsatisfactory and part of a life-style they now repudiate. For some this may happen during religious conversion or resumption of religious beliefs. For example, some groups such as Bahai consider physical purity a prerequisite for spiritual purity. Under these conditions women renounce their past conduct and become chaste until marriage or, in some cases, for life.

Political consciousness: Feminism   The reconsideration of virginity and celibacy can also occur when women enter a new political consciousness of the relationship between men and women in this society. Some groups of radical feminists have discussed male-female relationships and found men to be oppressive and unnecessary. These women, unwilling or unable to eroticize other women, choose no sexual contact at all in preference to being sexually intimate with men, whom they neither respect nor trust. While the women who make this decision as part of a political philosophy are relatively few in number, it might be hypothesized that many individual women do this on a temporary basis after being disappointed with a relationship or a series of bad relationships.

Situational necessity   It must also be noted that some women enter phases in their lives when other tasks are more important than emotional/physical relationships. Each individual has only so much emotional and physical energy, and there are times when all of any one person's energy may be consumed by work, family or other obligations. At these times sexual entanglements may have little or no appeal for a woman, and she may be too consumed with other needs even to note the loss of sexual activity.

Because our society thinks of sexuality as a *need* (like eating and sleeping), it often does not occur to us that abstinence is a sexual option, especially when we are constantly being bombarded with books that tell us how to have more and better sex. The woman who voluntarily chooses abstinence after she passes her early twenties is faced with negative responses from peers, family, and acquaintances. Peers for the most part (unless they are part of a supportive subculture) do not perceive abstinence as a valid sexual choice. Today it is not the girl who stays out all night from the dorm who has to account for her behavior to her friends, but more often the girl who never goes out.

Likewise, families where it is considered fine for daughters to retain their virginity until marriage frequently are not so sanguine about their daughters' lack of sexual activity as they approach mature adulthood. These women, if not suspiciously regarded as homosexual or neurotic (man-hating, cold, frigid, or selfish), will then be pitied. The unanimity of this reaction is interesting since the Judeo-Christian tradition has historically praised asexuality and viewed it as a representation of spiritual purity, innate goodness, virtue, and self-control. On the other hand, as indicated above, modern theories on the use of sexual energy and the importance of sexual outlet have almost put sexuality into the same category as brushing your teeth: as an important part of hygienic ritual for both mind and body.

Asexuality, however, must not be confused with abstinence. Abstinence is no reason for society to assume a woman is repressed or undersexed. We must not forget that women may be masturbating during these periods and that masturbation produces a satisfying and intense sexual experience for many women (Masters and Johnson, 1966). In fact, some have reported that their vibrator gives them more intense orgasms than a partner, and Masters and Johnson have evidence that indicates orgasms during masturbation are at least physiologically more intense than orgasms during intercourse. Whether it is self-stimulation or a virtual shutting off of sexual feelings for a period of time, these responses are at some point a part of most women's lives. Abstinence as a life commitment is rare, but abstinence as an adjustment to a life situation seems to be relatively common.

Single Motherhood and Nonmotherhood

The option of motherhood affects both single and married women. While we are familiar with the concept of unplanned single motherhood—as a result of contraceptive failure, for example—we are not so accustomed to the notion of single motherhood as a planned decision outside the institution of marriage.

Motherhood is expected and considered normal, but only when it is in accord with society's rules. While most women are fertile and can get pregnant should they choose to do so, society attempts to regulate the terms under which pregnancy is permitted. A child should be born into an intact family—socially defined as a family with a father—if at all possible. While death and divorce may be understandable, the absence of a legal father is not. The single mother is considered immature and morally deficient, and her ability to take care of her child is called into question. If, as happens not infrequently today, she refuses to give up her child to an intact family, she is considered selfish and uninterested in the welfare of her child (Bernard, 1974). The very term *illegitimacy* indicates the degree of society's displeasure with a child born outside of marriage. The child has no "right" to be born. The mother has no "right" to give birth. There is no function for a child outside of the legal unit.

Yet some women desire motherhood, but not marriage. They see no reason why one necessarily includes the other, and they do, in fact, have several options for achieving motherhood without marriage. A woman may choose a lover to impregnate her and not tell him that he is the father of her child. She may tell a man that he is the biological father of her child but that he will have no legal relationship to that child. (The problems of unwed fatherhood are intriguing but underresearched.) Or she may adopt a child and avoid the issue of the father's relationship to his offspring.

In one study of adoptive single mothers it was found that the women were in their late thirties, usually professionals, with incomes of at least twelve thousand a year. Not all rejected the idea of marriage, but all of them felt that they could be a good mother without a husband present (Frankle, 1973). Another study, however, did find differences between these single mothers and more traditional mothers. Voluntarily single mothers were not as self-sacrificing as traditional mothers; they expressed more libertarian values about sex role stereotyping and child development than the other mothers, and they tended to be more flexible, nonauthoritarian, and permissive in their relationship with the child (Klein, 1973).

While single motherhood is becoming more common and certainly more publicized—stories on the single motherhood of Mia Farrow, Vanessa Redgrave, and other movie stars have become almost commonplace—it is still a comfortable option for only the economically and psychologically independent woman. While other women can and do have children out of wedlock, the penalties are much higher for them since economic assistance from the state is received only in exchange for their right to decide what kinds of relationships will characterize their personal lives. As mentioned above, the welfare system has very strict ideas about the conditions of motherhood and enforces those principles insofar as it is able.

The lesbian is in an especially difficult position. If she wishes to bear her own child she must have sexual intercourse as an instrumental rather than emotional act. To complicate matters even more, she is generally considered unfit for motherhood. She is likely to be refused permission to adopt and stands a good chance of having her own children taken away, if she already has a family. It is only recently that single heterosexual women were considered competent to rear a child alone; lesbian women are still not considered appropriate mothers in the eyes of society. There are a *few* cases to the contrary. In Seattle, Washington, in 1975, Sandy Schuster and Madeline Isaacson, two lesbian mothers, were awarded their children in a custody fight with their husbands and their husbands' new wives. However, such outcomes are in the distinct minority. Usually the courtroom confuses sex-object choice with the capacity to nurture, fears for the eventual sexual identification of the child, and worries about the mental health of a child in a home where both parents are of the same sex. Despite a good deal of professional commentary to the contrary, the majority of courts have refused to accord maternal rights to lesbians. Thus these women live in fear that angry or worried husbands, lovers, parents, will ask the court to take custody away from them. Agitation by civil rights organizations and gay liberationists may change this pattern of adjudication, but for the present, this is an area of great concern for women contemplating lesbian life-styles.

Childfree Sexual Life-Styles

Single women who cannot or prefer not to have children escape the stigma of "illegitimate" motherhood. At the same time, they are pitied as having missed "womanhood's greatest achievement." From very early play patterns on, women are oriented toward having children and being mothers. In the beginning it may be as subtle as having dolls, playing house, and organizing that household into a mommy, daddy, and child. As the child grows older, it may not be subtle at all. The new dolls they are selling today, for example, are not just dolls for warmth and fantasy; it could be argued that they are *training* devices. The modern doll wets and has to be changed, spits up and has to be wiped, even grows breasts and has to be prepared for adolescence! If this message is somehow missed, parents soon begin to tell their daughters about the joys of parenthood and how motherhood is a thrilling goal for any woman. There is no script for the woman who does not care for children, does not feel her talents are well expressed in maternal duties, or who would like children but finds an established career and life-style more important. Not wanting children and not expressing one's "maternal instincts" is seen as somewhat odd and selfish. The woman who has no plans to be a mother is warned that loneliness will surely haunt her in her old age should she choose present convenience over long-term rewards. Yet a *Catch 22* lurks behind this argument for motherhood, for women who devote their lives entirely to children commonly suffer severely from the "empty nest" syndrome—feelings of uselessness and even rejection—when their children leave home. And even though studies indicate that childless wives seem to be happier than women with preschool children (Bernard, 1972; Campbell, 1975), women are still told that they will suffer for choosing childlessness.

Single women are caught between scripts. They are not supposed to have children outside of marriage, but they are expected to have children in order to be fulfilled. Obviously they are pushed toward marriage as the only way to please society and society's expectations for femaleness. If they continue to resist marriage *and* motherhood, they may worry—even if they know this is the right decision for them—about their future well-being.

For this reason there has been some recent organization around the rights of women *not* to be mothers. Support groups such as the National Organization for Non-Parents (NON) try to provide new scripts for men and women which give validation to a life without children. More information about the drawbacks as well as the rewards of having children may make motherhood a less invariant part of the female script in the future.

Nonheterosexual Options

Same-Sex Relationships

The dominant sexual script for women does not include loving other women. When a woman first realizes she has romantic and sexual feelings towards her own sex, she is usually confused, upset, and guilt-ridden. Perhaps no one has explicitly told her this is possible. And since it threatens the foundations of marriage and family and everything she has been told is right for her, she immediately knows her feelings are socially unacceptable.

An individual may recognize his or her preference for same-sex relationships in early adolescence or at any point in the life cycle. In a study by Blumstein and Schwartz (1974)* on a sample of homosexual and bisex-

---

*This was an exploratory interview study of a "snowball" sample. One hundred fifty people were interviewed in Seattle, San Francisco, Berkeley, New York, and Chicago. The format was a modified Kinsey interview, which took two to three hours per person.

ual men and women, it was concluded that people who had homosexual and bisexual attractions did not necessarily form them in childhood, nor did these attractions always remain constant throughout their lives. People would change sexual preference because of situational opportunities or because of specific love relationships. Early childhood experience was often important, but it could not predict adult sexual choices. Subjects often became homosexual after satisfactory heterosexual lives or heterosexual after years of homosexual identity and/or behavior.

First crushes and sexual passions are nurtured in secrecy and fear. A young girl may not know anyone she can reveal her feelings to; an older woman may be equally isolated. It is only recently, because of gay liberation movements and in part because of the feminist movement, that young girls and women can find a support group that will help them identify their feelings, validate their desires and introduce them to women like themselves.

It is interesting to note some of the ways that adult women are most commonly introduced to homosexual contact. Some women who feel unattracted to males and attracted to women go looking for a sexual experience in a gay bar or gay people's center, where they are sure to find people who share their sexual feelings. It seems more common, however, for first sexual contact to occur with a friend—a roommate or a woman with whom there has been a close association in a nonsexual context. This seems especially true for women who have some sexual attraction to other women, but who also continue to be attracted to men. It often takes an emotional or trusting relationship to make them break same-sex taboos (Hedbloom, 1973; Martin and Lyon, 1972).

As has already been mentioned, women who have never fantasized or thought about same-sex contact are introduced to same-sex activities in swinging or in a sexual threesome (Bartell, 1971). Some women find this a critical experience and adopt gay identities. Other women discover that homosexuality is not compatible with their prior sexual identity and regard the experience as a brief homosexual moment in their otherwise heterosexual life.

Women sometimes fall in love with another woman, even though they have had no previous same-sex attractions. Perhaps since women are conditioned to prefer sex with love, once they feel love for someone, it is not difficult to translate that feeling into sexual imagery (Bengis, 1974; Blumstein and Schwartz, 1974). This is particularly true when women learn to love and respect each other rather than regarding each other as inferior creatures. While the feminist movement has not *pushed* homosexuality as some media articles have suggested (in fact, in its early stages, lesbians were actively disdained), it has allowed women to spend more time with one another in a context without stigma, to get to know and to understand gay women, and to respect and appreciate one another more.

What is it like for a previously heterosexual woman to have a homosexual encounter? Women who have been interviewed mention their surprise at touching a body like their own. They find its softness surprising, and, most of the time, they believe the style of love-making to be less "instrumental," less oriented toward the goal of orgasm. For most women, there is little vaginal penetration, perhaps the use of a finger inside the vaginal canal. Stimulation results either from touching the clitoral area or oral-genital contact. Simultaneous oral-genital contact by both women does not seem to be popular; rather, one person makes love to the other, and then the other reciprocates (Schwartz and Blumstein, 1974).

Benefits and Hazards   Nevertheless, while some lesbians and bisexuals have said that women understand each other's bodies so well that sex is better between two women than between a man and woman, it is not sex that is the binding force in these same-sex relationships. Some women prefer homosexual relationships or consider them a possibility in the future because they believe that living with another woman is easier than living with a man. In the Blumstein-Schwartz sample of women who had had both homosexual and heterosexual experience, the following reasons for a homosexual relationship were most often stated:

Same-sex relationships are more egalitarian   It is believed that a female couple can avoid power struggles and exploitative relationships. Neither person is assigned an upper hand by society; therefore, the two people can work out their own contract with little peer or social pressure concerning their private relationship.

Same-sex relationships are less role-bound   Since both women have the same gender and outward appearance, the division of labor in the home and emotional roles are assigned by preference, not duty. (While some women may ascribe gender by taking a "butch" or "femme" role, this is not necessary and is becoming increasingly unpopular in gay communities.) The couple can decide who is to work, take care of the home, tend the yard, and fix the car without feeling that the expectations for a "marital" relationship are not being met. Each person can exercise *both* the male and female parts of her personality.

Same-sex couples are more knowledgeable about each other's needs   Since both women come from a female culture, they have had similar socialization and similar experience being women in American society. They have suffered similar problems and enjoy some of the same activities. They feel they are more sensitive to each other's feelings and needs, since they have had those feelings and needs themselves.

Women are more loyal and oriented to a long-term relationship   Women have been socialized to pair-bond for a long time without feeling restless for sexual conquests. While some women do like to accumulate a lot of partners, the majority prefer to be with one person in a committed love relationship. Sexual competitions and fear of loss are muted.

These same women also listed conflicts that made same-sex relationships hazardous. Most often mentioned were:

Societal stigma—having to live a secret life   Same-sex relationships are not as public as heterosexual relationships. This may cause difficulties ranging from not being able to hold hands on the street to very important issues of family and kinship solidarity. Few gay couples can get their parents' blessings or the blessings of their extended friendship circle. Lacking social validation, the full burden of protecting the relationship rests on the somewhat isolated dyad. Being in a gay community helps, but the lack of interaction with family and other friends hurts.

Fear of partner's return to the easier straight life   Because it is easier, less penalized, in this society to be heterosexual, a partner may fear loss of a lover who has previously been heterosexual or who claims a bisexual identity. If a man comes along who offers the partner the benefits of "straight" society—economic support, family acceptance, loss of stigma—the partner may accept.

Role stress due to lack of societally assigned roles   While the lack of roles is pleasing to some couples, others find the lack of solid expectations and duties troubling. Neither woman may want to work—or both may want to. Both may want to cook, or both may not want to do housework. In such cases, couples have all the problems of heterosexual couples who have to work out new egalitarian modes of running a family.

Children   Some gay women may have children or want them. If the former, they are afraid of same-sex relationships because they may be in danger of losing their children. If the latter, they cannot have children without a male partner. Some women have considered having intercourse with a man just for the purpose of conception, but this is emotionally and legally complicated, and conception is not often guaranteed by merely one act of intercourse.

Women who think about same-sex relationships may organize them in such a way as to maximize the benefits of such relationships and minimize the costs. Sometimes a threesome will be arranged, with one male and another female. A group marriage is a possibility, with the women often relating sexually with each other as well as to the men in the relationship. Some communes offer this kind of extended family to both the females and males in the household (Berger, Hackett, and Millar, 1971). None of these variations, however, are commonly practiced, and all encounter the problems of jealousy, the difficulties of accepting a shared or secondary role in a loved one's life and of constructing roles and family relationships that satisfy everyone. At present, it is much more common for same-sex relationships to be maintained in the dyad than in an extended family grouping. The gains for the individual woman, as we have mentioned, seem to be the gains of living in a coherent female culture with someone who, perhaps, has a better chance of understanding her. The problems are most apparent in the struggle to justify and maintain one's life-style in a vacuum from one's parents, siblings, and others who might not approve or at least cannot honestly provide positive support. Perhaps one of the reasons people change back and forth from straight to gay is that same-sex relationships and heterosexual relationships offer different kinds of satisfactions, and neither can easily incorporate all the advantages of the other.

Couples and Singlehood   Homosexual women must choose whether they wish to live alone or cohabit. Some lesbians invest themselves in a long-term relationship and a close-knit circle of friends; others remain unattached and frequent gay bars and lesbian dances, looking for a variety of partners. While being a member of a couple is a goal for most gay women, it is not a goal for all. Some gay women who want to preserve their independence but avoid loneliness live in "women's houses" or with a gay roommate who is not a lover. Others have long-term lovers but do not cohabit. For most, however, the gay life is likely to be a series of different kinds of statuses. At present, the median couple duration among gay women is about three to four years (Jensen, 1974; Saghir and Robins, 1973), and the mean under two years. The reasons for the relatively brief duration of these relationships are open for conjecture and are now under study by the author. Reasons hypothesized have been lack of kin and peer support, societal stigma and oppression, lack of role congruence, and different value systems. For now it seems fair to say that people in same-sex relationships, like people in heterosexual relationships, need to have the skills to live alone as well as to live with a lover.

Bisexuality

Bisexuals, or ambisexuals,* are people who are sexually attracted to both men and women. While the amount of activity with each sex, the degree of attraction, and the degree of romantic attachment may vary from individual to individual, bisexuals all consider both sexes appropriate for erotic attachment.

---

*Since most bisexuals do not have a 50 percent attraction to males and a 50 percent attraction to females, it has been suggested that *ambisexual* is a more appropriate term. *Bisexual* is used here only because it is the more commonly understood term.

That is not to say that all people who have erotic feelings for members of both sexes (either at the same time or sequentially) label themselves bisexuals. Most people who call themselves homosexual or heterosexual feel a slight to significant degree of attraction to the less preferred sex (Kinsey, 1953). The people who call themselves bisexual are in the minority in this group, and some of these are what Blumstein and Schwartz (1975) call *ideological bisexuals*. That is, they have little or no behavior with one sex, but they still believe they are bisexual. They may be sustained in their belief because they view *all* human beings as innately bisexual or because some time in the past they have had a same-sex experience and are convinced that under the right conditions or with the right person the experience could be repeated. Finally, it is also true that there are some people who are not sure if they are heterosexual or homosexual. They may be unwilling to accept the stigma of homosexuality and prefer calling themselves bisexual, since the term connotes *some* socially acceptable sexual activity. In this discussion, however, we will not consider this last group.

From Homosexuality to Bisexuality   Female bisexuality is arrived at from two directions—a heterosexual history and a homosexual history. Women with a homosexual past have usually had some heterosexual experience (Hedbloom, 1973). While they may have rejected it as unsatisfying, they know nonetheless that they have the physical ability to perform sexually with a male. On the other hand, their experience may have been very negative indeed, and so significant as to have changed their mind about who is an appropriate sex and/or love object.

Sometimes love will justify the change from homosexuality to bisexuality. Women have been socialized to believe that love and sex justify one another, and when either occurs, the other suggests itself. This seems to be true for almost all women, regardless of their sexual identity. When a gay woman meets an exceptional man, she may change her identity—perhaps not all the way to heterosexual, since this would discount a large part of her life, but often to bisexual.

Such an identity change is not easy for homosexual women, especially those who live in a lesbian community (i.e., most of their friends are gay). Most lesbian women perceive bisexual women as being unable to come to grips with their true sexuality, "fence sitters" who try to maintain a place in both straight and gay communities. On a more personal level, lesbians often mistrust a bisexual lover because they fear she may leave them for a man in order to avoid social ostracism. Finally, lesbians feel that their political situation (stigmatization and discrimination) warrants total commitment from any woman practicing same-sex relationships.

The bisexual woman of "both worlds" is viewed as a political liability: she does not have to identify herself in a way that legitimates lesbianism;

bisexuals can appear straight when convenient and avoid the embarrassing political responsibilities of the lesbian life-style. In fact, some lesbians are afraid that bisexuality will be seen as somehow "more healthy" than homosexuality and thus further stigmatize lesbianism (Johnson, 1973; Bunch and Myron, 1975). Lesbians in feminist and lesbian organizations often believe unity is necessary among women in same-sex relationships; some believe in total separatism from men. In their view, women who do not organize with them undermine the collective good (Strom, 1976). Thus, for most, but not all, homosexual women who fall in love with a man the lack of support and trust from gay friends and lovers makes the establishment of a heterosexual relationship difficult.

From Heterosexuality to Bisexuality   The woman who goes from a heterosexual self-identification to a bisexual one also faces disapproval. Homosexuality is feared and condemned by most people, and bisexuality, despite the recent trend to say how common it is *(Viva, Playgirl, Time, Newsweek)* still involves same-sex behavior. If, however, the woman is part of a liberal community, she may find some support. Like the homosexual women we have mentioned, she may enter a same-sex relationship through a close friendship that deepens into love and eventually becomes sexual. Hedonistic sexual alliances, such as group sex or a humanistic group that endorses same-sex sexuality as a means to self-knowledge, provide another route.

Finally, some women take on a bisexual identity after disappointments in both heterosexual and lesbian life-styles. These women find out that, at least for them, relationships with both genders offer problems and advantages. They reach the conclusion that a bisexual life-style, or a life-style based on sexual relationships with whomever they love, regardless of gender, is the most congruent and comfortable choice.

What makes a person adopt a bisexual *identity* as opposed to a heterosexual or homosexual one? Research in this area is still very exploratory. A tentative list, however, includes the following (Blumstein and Schwartz, 1975):

1. Strong arousal patterns (sexual excitement) with *both* sexes, not necessarily beginning at the same time.
2. Little experience with homoerotic stigmatization (no negative construction), or ignorance, at least in early life, of the strength of the taboo.
3. Clandestine sexual experience that is predominantly positive in nature with both sexes.
4. Exposure to the ideology that bisexuality is a natural human state.
5. Involvement in a political ideology (feminist movement, sexual freedom league) that supports same-sex relationships.
6. The proper social climate, for example, an era that promotes sexual

freedom and privacy and, more generally, the right to "do your own thing." Media coverage creating a niche for bisexuals also creates an appropriate social climate.
7. Group support for a sexual life-style that creates new sexual communities.

For whatever reason, it seems that bisexuality is being given more publicity and people who thought they had to choose between two dichotomous identities are being informed that there are other choices available. During the course of the Blumstein-Schwartz study, it was noted that bisexual rap-groups were organizing and bisexuals were seeking each other out to participate in consciousness-raising sessions and provide mutual support, much as gay, black, and women's groups have done before them. How tolerant the heterosexual world will be is still open to question. While bisexuality presently seems to be somewhat less threatening then homosexuality, it is not clear whether that will be the case if it becomes more open and acknowledged. Jealousy and confusion about what the competition is like—and how to compete with another person of the same or opposite sex for a loved one—can be very real problems for the partners of bisexual people. Bisexuality may one day be more accepted than it is at present, but it seems too early to tell how prevalent such activity is and what the reaction will be if it becomes a life-style of a significant number of women.

A New Sexual Ideology

We are now in an era when we can at least read about the possibilities open to the individual who wishes to deviate from the sexual norm. There is a literature on female sexuality that suggests that the female may be as sexually capable as the male, that all she has to do is decide her needs and create her sexual style. Yet it is difficult to find someone who can see us as we see ourselves and who can evolve a *simpatico* life-style with us. While Masters and Johnson have told us that women can have many more orgasms than men, and that these orgasms get more and more physiologically intense, it may be quite another thing for a woman to find the male or female partner who will invest the time and energy in making that possible. While anthropological and sociological studies indicate that women can have the same sexual appetites as men—perhaps stronger—and that women have equal sexual rights and choices in some societies, that does not mean that these options and understandings are widely shared within our own. The double standard, as it is applied by men to women, or women to themselves, is still with us. Right now, most women still look forward to assuming the traditional female role in the monogamous nuclear family, although a fairly large group is beginning to question this construct and to seek information about alternatives.

At this point in time, however, alternatives are only somewhat attractive because we know so little about their efficacy and promise. Still, the questioning and choosing process itself offers some hope. People are thinking more about how to design their future instead of considering their lives a *fait accompli* at the age of eighteen or twenty-one. For those people who come to think that perhaps a variant sexual life-style is appropriate for them, there are subcultures, support communities, and literature to help them try out their choices. Even with support, however, people have deep fears about deviating from the patterns of their forefathers and foremothers. If their rate of success in finding satisfactory alternative life-styles is low, the obstacles they face must be taken into account. In addition, we should remember that intimate relationships (including traditional monogamous long-term marriage) are a difficult undertaking in today's world. Still, the very idea of being able to choose one's way of being intimate and sexual is exciting, and a challenge to the individual. It entails serious introspection and communication with significant others. A woman may accept, reject, and refine her personal life until she finds the style most comfortable for her. Though demanding and confusing, this opportunity does offer a woman the chance to try several scripts and several roles instead of only one.

References

Abbott, S., and B. Love (1972). Sappho Was a Right-On Woman. New York: Stein and Day.

Bartell, G.D. (1971). Group Sex. New York: New American Library.

Bell, R.R. (1966). Premarital Sex in a Changing Society. Englewood Cliffs, N.J.: Prentice-Hall.

Bell, R.R., and P. Bell (1972). Sexual Satisfaction among Married Women. Medical Aspects of Human Sexuality 6(12):136–146.

Bell, R.R., and J.V. Buerkle (1961). Mother and Daughter Attitudes to Pre-Marital Sexual Behavior. Journal of Marriage and the Family 23:390–392.

Bell, R.R., and J.B. Chaskes (1970). Premarital Sexual Experience among Coeds, 1958 and 1968. Journal of Marriage and the Family 32(1):81–84.

Bengis, I. (1974). Combat in the Erogenous Zone. New York: Knopf.

Berger, B.M., B.M. Hackett, and R.M. Millar (1971). Child Rearing Practices of the Communal Family. A Progress Report to the National Institute of Mental Health. Washington, D.C.: U.S. Government Printing Office.

Bernard, J. (1972). The Future of Marriage. New York: World Press.

———(1974). The Future of Motherhood. New York: Dial Press.

Berscheid, E., E. Walster, and G. Bohrnstedt (1973). The Happy American Body: A Survey Report. Psychology Today 7(6):119–122, 126, 128–131.

Blumstein, P., and P. Schwartz (1974). Lesbianism and Bisexuality. *In* Sexual Deviance and Sexual Deviants. E. Goode and R. Troiden, eds. New York: William Morrow.

——(1975). The Acquisition of Sexual Identity: The Bisexual Case. Unpublished.

Bunch, C., and N. Myron (1975). Lesbianism and the Woman's Movement. New York: Diana Press.

Campbell, A. (1975). The American Way of Mating. Psychology Today 8(12):37–42.

Clatworthy, N.M. (1975). Living Together. *In* Old Family/New Family. N. Glazer-Malbin, ed. New York: Van Nostrand Reinhold.

Cuber, J.F. (1969). Adultery: Reality versus Stereotype. *In* Extramarital Relations. G. Neubeck, ed. Englewood Cliffs, N.J.: Prentice-Hall.

Cumming, G. (1960). A Study of Marital Conflicts Involving an Affair by One of the Partners. University of Southern California. Unpublished M.A. thesis.

Davis, L., J. Stewardt, and S. Garvin (1975). Cytomegalovirus Infection: A Seroepidemiologic Comparison of Nuns and Women from a Venereal Disease Clinic. American Journal of Epidemiology 102(4):327–330.

Decter, M. (1972). Toward the New Chastity. Atlantic Monthly 230:172.

Ford, C.S., and F.A. Beach (1951). Patterns of Sexual Behavior. New York: Harper & Row.

Frankle, T. (1973). Single but Not Alone: Adoption Brings Family Life to Unmarried. New York Times, March 28.

Gebhard, P. (1970). Postmarital Coitus among Widows and Divorcees. *In* Divorce and After. P. Bohannan, ed. New York: Doubleday.

Gilmartin, B. (1975). The Sexual Swingers Next Door. Psychology Today 8(9):54.

Gilmartin, B., and D. Kusisto (1973). Personal and Social Characteristics of Mate-Sharing Swingers. *In* Renovating Marriage. R. Libby and R. White-hurst, eds. San Ramon, Calif.: Consensus.

Glasser, P., and E. Navarre (1974). Structural Problems of the One-Parent Family. Journal of Social Issues 21:98–109.

Glick, P.C. (1975). A Demographer Looks at American Families. Journal of Marriage and the Family 37(1):15–27.

Hedbloom, J. (1973). Dimensions of Lesbian Sexual Experience. Archives of Sexual Behavior, vol. 2, ch. 4 (December).

Holmes, K.K., and J. Wier (1976). How to Have Intercourse without Getting Screwed. Seattle, Wash.: Madrona Press.

Holstrom, L. (1972). The Two Career Family. Cambridge, Mass.: Schenkman.

Hunt, M. (1966). The World of the Formerly Married. New York: McGraw-Hill.

——(1969). The Affair. New York: New American Library.

——(1974). Sexual Behavior in the 1970's. Chicago: Playboy Press.

Jackson, E.D., and C.R. Potkay (1973). Precollege Influences on Sexual Experiences of Coeds. Journal of Sex Research 9(2):143–149.

Jensen, M.S. (1974). Role Differentiation in Female Homosexual Quasi-Marital Unions. Journal of Marriage and the Family 36(2):360–367.

Johnson, M.P. (1973). Commitment: A Conceptual Structure and Empirical Application. Sociological Quarterly 14:395–406.

Johnston, J. (1973). Lesbian Nation. New York: Simon and Schuster.

Kinsey, A.C., et al. (1953). Sexual Behavior in the Human Female. Philadelphia: Saunders.

Klein, C. (1973). Socialization of Children in Voluntary, Single Parent Homes. Paper presented at the meeting of the Society for Study of Social Problems. Unpublished.

Laws, J.L. (1971). A Feminist Review of the Marital Adjustment Literature: The Rape of the Locke. Journal of Marriage and the Family 33(3):483–516.

Lever, J. (1975). Sex Differences in the Games Children Play. Social Problems 23(4):479–489.

Lever, J., and P. Schwartz (1971). Women at Yale. Indianapolis: Bobbs-Merrill.

Lewis, L.S., and D. Brissett (1967). Sex as Work: A Study of Avocational Counselling. Social Problems 15:8–18.

Libby, R. (1973). Extramarital and Co-Marital Sex: A Review of the Literature. *In* Renovating Marriage. R. Libby and R. Whitehurst, eds. San Ramon, Calif.: Consensus.

Libby, R., and R. Whitehurst (1977). Marriage and Its Alternatives. Glenview, Ill.: Scott, Foresman.

Lopata, H. (1969). Loneliness: Forms and Components. Social Problems 17: 248–262.

———(1973). Widowhood in an American City. Cambridge, Mass.: Schenkman.

Lyness, J.C., M.E. Lipetz, and K.E. Davis (1972). Living Together: An Alternative to Marriage. Journal of Marriage and the Family 34(2).

Macklin, E.D. (1972). Heterosexual Cohabitation among Unmarried College Students. *In* Non-Traditional Family Forms in the 1970's. M. Sussman, ed. Minneapolis, Minn: National Council of Family Relations.

———(1974). Cohabitation in College: Going Very Steady. Psychology Today 8:53–59.

Martin, D., and P. Lyon (1972). Lesbian Woman. San Francisco: Glide.

Marshall, D.S. (1971). Too Much Sex in Mangaia. Psychology Today 4(9):43–44, 70, 74–75.

Masters, W., and V. Johnson (1966). Human Sexual Response. Boston: Little, Brown.

Mirande, A.M. (1968). Reference Group Theory and Adolescent Sexual Behavior. Journal of Marriage and the Family 30(4):572–577.

Nahmias, A.J., et al. (1970). Antibodies to Herpesvirus: Hominis Types 1 and 2 in Humans. American Journal of Epidemiology 91(6):539–546.

Neubeck, G., and V. Schletzer (1962). A Study of Extra-Marital Relationships. Marriage and Family Living 24:279–281.

Olson, D.H. (1972). Marriage of the Future: Revolutionary or Evolutionary Change? *In* Non-Traditional Family Forms in the 1970's. M. Sussman, ed. Minneapolis, Minn.: National Council on Family Relations.

O'Neill, N., and G. O'Neill (1972). Open Marriage. Philadelphia: J.B. Lippincott.

Palson, C., and R. Palson (1972). Swinging in Wedlock. Society 9(4).

Ramey, J.W. (1972). Emerging Patterns of Innovative Behavior in Marriage. *In* Non-Traditional Family Forms in the 1970's. M. Sussman, ed. Minneapolis, Minn.: National Council on Family Relations.

Rawls, W., et al. (1971). Genital Herpes in Two Social Groups. American Journal of Obstetrics and Gynecology 110(5):682–689.

Reiss, I.J. (1964). The Scaling of Premarital Permissiveness. Journal of Marriage and the Family, May:188–198.

———(1967). The Social Context of Pre-Marital and Sexual Permissiveness. New York: Holt, Rinehart and Winston.

Rubin, L. (1976). Worlds of Pain. New York: Basic Books.

Saghir, M., and E. Robins (1973). Male and Female Homosexuality. Baltimore: Williams and Wilkins.

Schlesinger, B. (1969). The One Parent Family. Toronto: University of Toronto Press.

Schwartz, P. (1973). Female Sexuality and Monogamy. *In* Renovating Marriage: Toward New Sexual Lifestyles. R. Libby and R. Whitehurst, eds. San Ramon, Calif.: Consensus.

Simon, W., and J. Gagnon (1970). Psychosexual Development. *In* The Sexual Scene. New Brunswick, N.J.: Trans-Action Books.

Smith, J.R., and L.G. Smith, eds. (1974). Beyond Monogamy. Baltimore: Johns Hopkins University Press.

Strom, D. (1976). Radical Lesbians. M.A. thesis, University of Washington, Seattle.

Tillmon, J. (1972). Welfare Is a Woman's Issue. Ms., Spring.

Trevor, J.J., Jr. (1972). Reference Groups and Premarital Sexual Behavior. Journal of Marriage and the Family 34(2):283–291.

Tripp, C.A. (1975). The Homosexual Matrix. New York: McGraw-Hill.

Udry, J.R. (1971). The Social Context of Marriage. Philadelphia: Lippincott.

U.S. Census (1971*a*). Social and Economic Characteristics of the Population in Metropolitan and Nonmetropolitan Areas: 1970 and 1960. Current Population Reports, Series P-23, No. 37. Washington, D.C.: U.S. Government Printing Office.

———(1971*b*). Marriage, Divorce and Remarriage by Year of Birth, June 1971. Current Population Reports, Series P-20, No. 239. Washington, D.C.: U.S. Government Printing Office.

Whitehurst, R. (1972). Changing Ground Rules and Emergent Lifestyles. Family Life Educator. Oakville, Ontario: Sheridan College Press.

Chapter Six

Women as Sexual Criminals and Victims

This chapter examines two major categories of institutional response to women's sexuality: the response to women as sexual criminals (primarily prostitutes), and to women as the victims of sexual crimes. A substantial number of women will encounter the first institutional bias; all women will at some point face the fear of or experience the second. Prostitution and juvenile promiscuity are discussed at length as classic examples of societal responses to female, in contrast to male, sexuality. Rape, the classic example of sexual crimes against women, is presented as a situation where the double standard prevails—a standard that prescribes different sets of acceptable sexual behavior for men and women.

Women and Crime

The involvement of women in criminal activity has been steadily growing since the 1950s. Their activities still include the stereotypic "women's crimes" of prostitution, shoplifting, and larceny that can be committed in the context of "normal" female behavior and that fit the traditional perception of women as sexual objects and shoppers. In fact, larceny has been defined in some legal statutes as "the deceptive use of the feminine role" because charm may be used to steal.

Prostitution and juvenile promiscuity are labeled as uniquely female crimes because they cannot, according to many state laws, be committed by males. Inherent in these crimes is the threat to society of loss of control over female sexuality rather than damage to victims or property. Women are social resources because of their reproductive capacity and because they are viewed as possessions, of either a father or a husband. As arguments against abortion evidence, many do not grant the female the same personal ownership of her body as the male. Whether for commercial or pleasure motivations, our society considers it appropriate to control her access to sexual intercourse. Public law and enforcement agencies are the guardians of home, family, legitimacy, and the moral order. Prostitution and early trespass of sexual taboos by females are therefore condemned and controlled by them.

The Prostitute

The most common crime cited for adult women is prostitution. There are prostitutes in every American city of any size, and the profession exists under a variety of guises and in numerous styles. Prostitutes work on the streets picking up passers-by and out of cars in which they circle city blocks looking for customers; or as dancers, body painters, maids, masseuses, or magazine saleswomen. They are models, strippers, stag-show dancers and waitresses, sense awareness counselors and sexual therapists, anything that puts them in contact with potential customers, especially if it provides easy opportunities for playing the sexual object and thus providing the lure. They work on call for hotels, through an answering or other referral service, and follow conventions across the country. Some women work out of airport lounges, others in migrant labor camps, and still others on retainers to large corporations with clients to entertain. In a few rural areas in the United States, notably Nevada, houses of prostitution are legal or tolerated by local officials. The possibilities for commercialized sexual exchanges are almost endless and shift to meet the customer demand and avoid the law.

The basis for the existence of prostitution is our social concept that male sexual energy requires an outlet beyond the inclinations of "good" women. The traditional view of the natural promiscuity of men still prevails and stimulates the demand for a pool of "loose" women to meet these sexual needs. The virginity cult of the Judeo-Christian tradition has always supported a spectrum of female sexual behavior with the whore at one end and the madonna at the other. Men are to avoid corrupting good women because of their importance to the social order as wives and mothers, and thus a population of loose women is necessary to protect good women from the "normal" impulses of men.

A complete social definition of prostitution is *any sexual exchange where the reward is neither sexual nor affectional.* Women prostitute themselves when they exchange access to their body for material gain (clothes, apartment, promotion, entertainment) and in so doing use their bodies as a commodity. In our society women learn the rewards of flirting at an early age. The idea is to be sexy but not cheap, a package that is attractive but not to be touched. Female attractiveness becomes a key to success in high school with peers, as cheerleader, junior prom queen, or a popular date. Beginning with learning to wink or sit on a man's lap, girls soon discover the short-term rewards of the games recommended by the proponents of "fascinating womanhood." The use of their sexuality to obtain favors and eventually to secure support is a part of the social interaction patterns females are taught. The ideal is to save enough of "it" for the right man or moment because otherwise the female devalues her most salable commodity: her sexuality.

Prostitution and the Law   The legal definition of prostitution is narrower. It reflects four main social concerns: the exchange of cash, promiscuity, relationship to sexual partner(s), and subtlety. Legally, it is the woman who engages in sex for *cash* or loiters with this intent who is a prostitute. A woman is relatively safe making exchanges for commodities other than cash which cannot be so easily recognized—an opportunity to become a model, or an evening of entertainment, for example. Gifts from sexual partners permit the assumption of affection and love, and affection is an acceptable stimulator of sexual exchange for women. In fact, it is one of the most common rationalizations for first sexual experiences. Cash, on the other hand, represents a nonemotional commercial exchange that society cannot modify to fit the acceptable limitations on the sexual activity of women.

Promiscuity—sexual exchanges with numerous men, even strangers—is an important second aspect of the legal definition. If a woman is involved with only a few men, and if she knows them well, she has little to fear from the law. She is not violating extensively the appropriate social construction of reality for women because the possibility of appropriate motivation—love—still exists. In addition, her self-identification can remain more that of party girl than prostitute. From a purely practical standpoint, avoidance of the appearance of promiscuity or indiscriminate sexual exchange makes her less obvious to the public officials whose purpose is to control such behavior. A few men/customers generally are not noticed, and if she knows them, she can be sure they are not vice squad officers or agents.

As is clear by now, the nature of *relationships to sexual partners* determines to some extent whether exchanges made fall under the definition of prostitution. Affection is definitely a mitigating factor that can make sexual activity acceptable to both the law and the society. Its absence in a sexual relationship, however, may jeopardize a woman's legal status as well as cause her social stigmatization.

A prostitute is safe violating the first three aspects of legal concern if she carefully accedes to the fourth: *subtlety*. Women arrested for prostitution are usually those who are overt in the management of their profession, the streetwalkers. Prostitutes who are subtle and conform to more traditional female behavior, call girls, for example, are rarely arrested. Streetwalkers work alone on the streets late at night: in plying their trade, they behave in a manner considered inappropriate for women. Good women do not go out unescorted at night or walk the streets alone; nor can they be identified by their flashy clothes, makeup, aggressive approaches towards male passersby, and frankly sexual verbal exchanges, as can streetwalkers. Clearly, the streetwalker offers herself as a commodity for sale and essentially forces the hand of public agencies who claim they are required by the community to enforce appropriate moral standards. The concern of society as it is reflected in the enforcement of the law is that sex for sale be invisible, or nearly so.

All forms of prostitution are illegal in the United States except in some rural counties in Nevada. FBI figures list 34,226 women arrested for prostitution in 1973 (FBI Uniform Crime Reports, 1974). The vast majority of these arrests are for open solicitation: women who are obviously engaging in sexual services for money in a promiscuous and explicit manner. Occasionally attempts are made to arrest women who work in houses or massage and sauna parlors, but arrest figures of these women are less than 5 percent of the total. Their prostitution is at least partially hidden by the other, more legitimate services they offer. Subtle prostitutes found on all social levels, like call girls and conventioneers, are rarely arrested because they cause no direct affront to the public. Their sexuality is not explicit in their behavior.

Violations of the prostitution statutes account for approximately 30 percent of most female jail populations. Convicted prostitutes serve long jail sentences compared to other misdemeanants such as shoplifters or those involved in larceny or assault. The judicial attitude represented by these sentencing patterns has no justification with reference to the traditional crime concerns of danger to person or property loss. Again, the apparent explanation is the punishment of behavior in women that is outside traditional norms and therefore a threat to social order. The importance of controlling such behavior, because of the powerful nature of the sex drive, has always provided the justification for excessive punishment. Sexual immorality has traditionally been considered a greater threat to American social order than violence or theft.

The sentencing and imprisonment statistics support this concentration on female sexual morality (FBI Uniform Crime Reports, 1974). It has been reported that 70 percent of the women who are now inmates in American prisons were initially arrested for prostitution, indicating the possible importance of these arrests as a labeling device and the significance of the resultant jail experience as an introduction to other crime. This adds up to a significant impact on the lives of the women and a great outlay of time and money by police, court, and corrections officials.

In the United States, two main types of laws control overt prostitution: (1) laws prohibiting loitering with the intent to commit an act of prostitution and (2) laws against offering and agreeing to an act of prostitution. The most common enforcement procedures involve the use of a police officer as a decoy. The officer behaves as he assumes a customer would when approached by a suspected prostitute and elicits evidence of intent. The prostitute is arrested if she mentions money and sexual service in her verbal exchange with the officer. Yet frequently these arrest techniques involve the officer in the possibility of entrapment and questionable sexual exchanges, and for this reason some jurisdictions use civilian agents who complete acts of sexual intercourse before the arrest is made. These civilians view themselves as protecting society by committing immoral acts for moral reasons. The use of female agents to solicit and arrest *customers* is rare because it requires a violation of appropriate behavior for women and an unfair use of female sexuality to entrap men. In most states customers are rarely, if ever, arrested. But a woman who has once been convicted of offering and agreeing, regardless of the circumstance, is subject to future arrests under loitering statutes as a known prostitute. (A *known prostitute* is a woman who has been convicted of an act of prostitution within the past year.) If she is seen in an area "known to be inhabited by prostitutes," she may also be arrested for loitering. The statute prohibiting loitering is frequently used by enforcement agencies to control individuals labeled as deviants.

Once arrested, prostitutes usually plead guilty because they cannot afford bail, seldom have adequate legal representation, and are aware of the bias of the judge. They are then subject to sentences ranging from 30 to 180 days in jail. Prostitutes who can afford good attorneys plead not guilty and are less likely to serve time because juries are reluctant to convict when questionable police tactics are revealed in court. There are variations in enforcement pressure from one locale to the next depending on the resources of a particular police department and the political pressure to "crack down on" or tolerate street solicitation.

Male homosexual prostitutes are arrested in many cities with the same procedures used for females. Although the percentage of male arrests is low, it has recently begun to increase in some cities because of complaints and lawsuits by equal rights advocates. The arrest of males has been traditionally negligible because of societal tolerance of male sexual activity regardless of its overtness or commercial intent. In some states where the Equal Rights Amendment has not passed only women can be found guilty of prostitution even though homosexual males provide the same service. The author was in the booking area of a jail two years ago when a transvestite was brought in and charged with prostitution. The arresting officer had assumed the offender was a female. Later, when the jail matron pointed out that the offender was a male, he was released.

Prostitution as a Problem Prostitution is defined as a problem by three basic groups: (1) law enforcement agencies, (2) public health agencies, and (3) social and moral traditionalists. Police departments view it as a problem because of the associated crime they say accompanies the street environment generated by the presence of prostitutes. Larceny, robbery, assault, and narcotics addiction are cited as crimes that breed in the environment of prostitution. Yet no causal relationship has been established and, in fact, associated crimes are not an issue where prostitution is legal. Local level public health officials, despite little evidence to support their views, suspect prostitution as the cause of rising venereal disease statistics. They desire either eradication or strict regulation with health inspections. The social and moral traditionalists are concerned about the prostitute as victim. The women, they state, are degraded, exploited, and abused by the business and the pimps behind it. In their view, the total elimination of prostitution is the only way to protect women from this life and society from this type of woman. The moralists also take a religious tack, defining promiscuity as a sin and therefore prostitution as a contributing factor in the moral decay of American society.

Feminists are often caught between two opposing views of the prostitute. Some maintain that prostitution represents the ultimate degradation of woman in that her body becomes a commerical object. Others state unequivocally that the prostitute is the only honest woman, a heroine who recognizes the sexual object reality of women in our society and makes sure she gets a fair and definite exchange for her labor.

Street solicitation is defined as a particular problem by the three reform groups noted above because of its obviousness. Others, who cannot be categorized as police, public health officials, or moralists, object to being exposed to solicitation in the street although they would tolerate the activity if it were private. They find women lounging on street corners offensive, much as they do public drunks. The important issue seems to be their desire to avoid exposure to such obvious sexual activity unless they are seeking it themselves. Businessmen feel it chases away clientele, parents want to shield their children, and passers-by do not want to be subjected to sexual suggestion by glance or comment from a prostitute. This portion of the American public would tolerate prostitution as long as it was invisible.

The clinical and academic definitions of prostitution as a problem historically stem from the concept previously discussed of female promiscuity as deviant behavior. Sexual promiscuity in exchange for money is a deviant response to the ascribed role for women according to which sex is permissible only in the context of love and marriage. Commercialized sex is a threat to a social structure that links sexual activity to the stable relationship of marriage. Unmarried women supporting themselves as prostitutes violate not only the taboos of fornication and adultery but the sexual double standard. They present a threat to married women because they offer sexual service without responsibility and to the traditional control society has exercised over female sexuality.

Prostitutes in Profile   The research available on prostitution does not discuss it in this context of male-female sex-role behavior. Instead, investigations into the causes of prostitution have concentrated on individual pathology rather than social institutions, seeking to learn why a particular woman chooses to become a prostitute instead of examining the reasons for the existence of the profession. Unfortunately, in much of the literature on prostitution conclusions are drawn from small, nonrandom samples. For example, in their book *The Lively Commerce* (1971), Winick and Kinsie allude to thousands of interviews with prostitutes which turn out to be interviews they conducted with police and probation officers who had, in turn, had the original contact with prostitutes.

The prostitute may be characterized in a variety of ways depending on the bias of the researcher and the circumstances of the population studied. Most of the research has been done by men whose view of female sexuality is frequently less objective than that of female researchers. Theodore Rubin found the early childhood experience of prostitutes deplorable because of significant material and emotional deprivation (Rubin, 1961). He interviewed women in jail. Harold Greenwald's study of call girls reported a 75 percent incidence of broken homes, but he only interviewed women who were his patients (Greenwald, 1958). Prostitutes are stereotyped by psychotherapists as lacking self-esteem, hostile toward males, unconsciously homosexual, narcissistic, rebellious against inadequate fathers, anxious, frigid, without good impulse control, morbidly dependent, and mentally defective (Glover, 1960; Caprio, 1963; Choisy, 1965; Segal, 1963; Kemp, 1936; Rubin, 1961; Deutsch, 1965). Yet prostitutes look no different from other women, they have no unusual physical characteristics, and they include the full range of intelligence (James, 1971). Other women who combine various aspects of the personality problems listed by therapists do not become prostitutes.

Surveys of prostitute populations involving larger, random samples under more carefully controlled circumstances provide less evidence of deviance from standard norms. The average age of the streetwalkers interviewed in a West Coast survey was 22.6. Of these women, 56.3 percent were black, 36.6 percent were white, and 7.0 percent were mixed between Indian, Asian, and Chicano (James, 1971). The tendency of black women to work on the streets more often than white women indicated in these findings is the result of a combination of street knowledge acquired while growing up in inner-city ghettos, economic necessity, and the racism that blocks their access to other kinds of prostitution. The mean educational achievement level was equivalent to 11.4 years of schooling, comparing favorably with basic census averages.

Picking the Profession: Motivating Factors

A summary of articles on prostitution indicates that the need for money or the *desire for material wealth* is the most common motivation for women to become prostitutes. Prostitution is viewed by many as a lucrative profession. Little training or preparation is required, the equipment is their own, and customers are everywhere. Even though most prostitutes have held jobs in other areas and, with the exception of addicts, have access to other occupations, they still indicate a preference for the financial and working conditions on the street. And while few prostitutes actually make it into the upper income brackets, the dream of success as a hooker is strong for women who see few other possibilities. Prostitutes at the top of the economic ladder can make between $50,000 and $75,000 a year. There are not many occupations easily open to women that can compare economically.

Nonetheless, the *need for money* is a more commonly cited factor than the desire for wealth. Welfare women prostitute to supplement their income, addicts to support their habits. Prostitution is the most obvious source of fast money for a woman who needs a hit of heroin or has bills to pay. Black women say it is one of the few nonmenial occupations open to them, a different kind of domestic labor. It is possible to make $100 a night working the street, good money compared to other available options as clerks, typists, or pressers in a dry-cleaning establishment. Women's salaries are very low compared to men's, and prostitution is viewed by some women as a viable equalizer.

Working conditions are also a part of the economic factor. The negatives of the profession are publicized: jail, beatings, drugs, loss of self-respect. But the positives women mention include choosing their own hours, no time clocks, wearing beautiful clothes, being desirable and salable, choosing what to do and when, travel, and easy work that is seldom boring. An attitude often expressed is that sexuality can provide money, which in turn provides freedom. As mentioned above, there are many working styles to choose from. Streetwalkers say they would never work in a brothel because of the loss of independence; they could choose neither their hours nor their customers. Women who work Nevada houses like being able to lounge around looking beautiful. All enjoy getting paid for what "they used to give away." The problem of separating emotional involvement from sexual activity is described as a separation of business and pleasure. And once women have been characterized as "loose" under noncommercial circumstances, they can justify the move toward commercialized sex as the easiest means of support.

Some research sources identify certain occupations that lead women into prostitution. Cocktail waitresses, magazine saleswomen, go-go dancers, masseuses, and models are not infrequently offered tips or sales if they will just give the customer a little more than their employers require. The cocktail waitress may be already selling her appearance in a bunny costume, and the tip being offered may equal the money she makes in one eight-hour shift. In occupations that depend on female attractiveness, female sexuality may become the more significant commodity, and there may be a slow movement from tips received for flirting to direct payment for sexual services.

The lure of adventure makes prostitution exciting to some. Women who work the streets move into an environment usually reserved for men: they are unescorted, on the street after dark, and they can take care of themselves. There is adventure in the act of strolling the streets at night in order to attract men.

Then, too, some women take pleasure in having a man desire them who is willing to pay well for access to their bodies. Prostitution enables them to be self-sufficient and control their lives. In many instances, the buyer-seller exchange places the woman in a dominant position; the customer is revealing himself to a professional, an experienced woman who has seen and been with many men, and he is therefore vulnerable to her comments about his sexuality. Her look of disdain or murmurings of pleasure can make the difference between his feelings of success or failure as a man/lover. And prostitutes who support men enjoy the sense of control their economic domination allows them.

Travel, and the sense of independence and adventure that accompany it, also add to the appeal of prostitution. Some in the profession move up and down the West or East Coast, others all over the United States. A prostitute who is intelligent and knows how to find customers and protect herself from the police can travel anywhere in the world and pay her way. Streetwalkers are not as likely to work outside the United States as call girls, but the results of one study showed that many whose home base was in Washington State had traveled to Alaska, Hawaii, the Bahamas, Puerto Rico, and Canada (James, 1971).

Some prostitutes who believe they meet many more exciting, wealthy, high-status males than straight women feel that prostitution provides *opportunities for advantageous social contacts or marriage.* In their view, it is always possible that a customer may be converted into a boyfriend, and the chance to marry well, although it rarely presents itself, is not an infrequent fantasy. This fantasy is reinforced by the common belief that men like to save (i.e., reform) women and the romantic literature which suggests that marriage to a prostitute either verifies a man's sexual prowess or proves that prostitutes make good, faithful wives once rescued. A bad woman converted to a good woman has made an informed choice, whereas a good woman has had no experience.

Research conducted by the author with streetwalkers supports these four areas of motivation but places strong emphasis on a fifth: *early life experiences* (James, 1971). Women who are raised in an environment where prostitution is a daily activity outside their front doors are more likely to see it as a possible occupation. Many prostitutes reported a relative (mother, sister, aunt) who was or had been in the business. In contrast to the models set for most young women, their models of appropriate female sexual behavior include prostitution.

Another key area of early life experience is institutionalization. Young girls who are sent to girls' homes or youth centers because they are dependents of the state, incorrigible, or runaways from home are frequent recruits for prostitution. In an initial survey of seventy-two prostitutes, 18.2 percent had been institutionalized as juveniles (James, 1971). The connections between institutions and prostitution fall into two patterns: exposure to information about prostitution from experienced inmates and recruitment by inmates who work for a pimp. Knowledge of prostitution creates curiosity, admiration of the negative status of juvenile prostitutes, and a desire for the independence that can be gained if a girl can support herself. Juvenile prostitutes seem tough and wordly to other inmates, and their ability to earn money is envied. Many juvenile runaways see prostitution as their only source of income, and money as the only way to solve their problem of dependence until they are eighteen. Having already been labeled bad by the institutionalization process, they feel they have little to lose in shifting further into the negative female image of the whore. The protective solidarity of the fast life gained by joining an existing group of prostitutes also appeals as a way of preventing reinstitutionalization. The pimp in charge will take care of them in exchange for their earnings as a prostitute. They accept the pimp as necessary to survive as a new prostitute and reconcile their dependence on him by the fact that they choose to be with him.

The *persuasiveness of pimps* is the last factor cited with any frequency in the literature. Pimps appeal to the traditional female dependence on strong male figures and the desire to be "somebody's woman." Some women begin working as prostitutes at the suggestion of their boyfriends, husbands, or a man they have only recently met. The persuasion is usually psychological, rarely, at least in recent decades, physical (James, 1973). Detailed descriptions of the interaction between pimp and prostitute produce a picture of a relationship that is little more than an exaggeration of the stereotyped male-female relationships in the larger society. Levels of love, brutality, and exploitation vary, but the basic needs are similar. A prostitute's preference for working with a pimp is discussed later in this chapter. As an individual woman's choice of companion, the pimp can be understood as not dissimilar to a husband, whether abusive or not.

No single factor explains anyone's choice of profession, whether the activity is considered deviant or normal. The *primary* reason women become prostitutes is the supply and demand equation that grows out of the sexual socialization process. Some men are socialized to view sex as a commodity that can be purchased. The male view of sexual experience has traditionally placed a higher value on quantity than on the quality of the relationship. Women who are socialized to view themselves as sexual objects may violate the ideal of the subtle sell for approved commodities and come to view their bodies as salable, accepting money for sexual access. Most prostitution does in fact pay better than other occupations open to women with limited education.

The *secondary* causes of prostitution are those that lead women— sometimes gradually, sometimes suddenly—to make the shift from subtle sexual sale to overt prostitution. Abusive family circumstances, such as incest and divorce, weaken the female's confidence that she can be a good girl and therefore undermine her sexual self-respect. Institutionalization that labels females deviant, economic stress engendered by the need to support children or an addiction, and a desire for a better standard of living are other causes of prostitution. Early reinforcement for sexual appearance and pressures for sexual activity from male friends can also be significant. Girls who are popular in high school because they are well developed or easy may wander into more overt sexual exchange.

The wider social factor of female sexuality as a commodity is based on two cultural aspects of sexuality: the first is the traditional view that men are promiscuous and the second is the consequent necessity of catering to their basic needs. Although we have no scientific research that supports these traditional attitudes about male sex drive, they are pervasive in the early literature of this century. Men patronize prostitutes because man is by nature polygamous: the "primitive sex instinct is one of variety or promiscuity" (Robinson, 1929), or "prostitution as we know it today is the result of Christian virtue, which would have man a perfect being, and of that animal instinct which drags him into the woman's arms" (Mantegazza, 1935). Such attitudes toward man's sexual nature, though more subtly expressed, are still current and manifest in the traditional view of marriage as an important social and economic institution. While men are supposedly tormented by their polygamous nature, they are nonetheless expected to avoid other men's wives in order to guard against disrupting their marriage. Thus at the same time, prostitution is viewed as a threat to both family and female role traditions, a societal evil, and as a necessity to protect good women from the "normal" impulses of men.

The Customer

The male customer is virtually ignored in both professional and media articles on prostitution because his actions are congruent with our expectations about male sexuality and he is therefore not given a criminal identity. In the most comprehensive review of intercourse with prostitutes, the Kinsey survey of sexuality in the human male, it was found that about 69 percent of the total white male sample ultimately had some experience with prostitutes (Kinsey, 1948: 597). Not more than 15 or 20 percent of these had regular intercourse with prostitutes. Young males were only infrequently represented, with the majority of customers in the thirty-seven to forty age range. Later studies have shifted the age range upward into the forties (Stein, 1974; James, 1971).

Kinsey further broke down his data on contact with prostitutes to 3,190 contacts per week in a town of 100,000 inhabitants (Kinsey, 1948: 603). Yet despite this estimated frequency of contact and estimates that the number of clients—approximately 20 percent of the male population—who have some contact with prostitutes is very substantial, articles on clients are limited. Most of the literature is limited to discussions of the basic fact that men visit prostitutes and the needs, accepted as normal, that their visits fulfill. The customer as a social problem escapes examination.

The only available book-length discussion of the customers of prostitutes is *Lovers, Friends, Slaves,* by Stein (1974). Its approach is primarily observation based on the author's training in social work, and is a pioneering effort at describing the men who visit primarily upper-class call girls. Customers are categorized to clarify the male needs serviced by prostitutes. Those categories include: opportunists, fraternizers, promoters, adventurers, lovers, friends, slaves, guardians, and juveniles (Stein 1974: 114). Opportunists were defined by Stein as men who used prostitutes' services because it was the easiest way for them to have sex with a woman when and where they wanted without risk or emotional entanglement. The fraternizer is a type of customer who wants a party with a prostitute as a diversion for him and his friends. It is seen as an appropriate form of entertainment for the night out with the boys. Promoters not only utilize prostitutes themselves but set up sexual services for friends or associates in order to increase their influence with these men. The adventurer displays an open interest in experimentation and puts value on the new sexual experiences he can have with a prostitute. Lovers see their encounters with prostitutes as romantic as well as sexual. They wish to charm them and seduce them and they need to feel loved by them. The customer classified by Stein as friend saw the prostitute in the role of confidante and comforter. For him, the prostitute's home is a place to relax and the prostitute is someone who could provide understanding and companionship. Slaves, in contrast, came to the prostitute to act out sexual fantasies of submission. Guardians are interested in patronizing a young prostitute so they can establish a paternal role, and juveniles are the opposite in that they want to relate to prostitutes who will mother them. This description of customers, by Stein, is detailed but does not cover many needs noted in our research.

As generally presented in the literature, the needs of customers are, however, surprisingly uniform. In addition to the needs implicit in the categories of clients listed by Stein, the following problems may bring a client to a prostitute: (1) sexual deprivation due to travel; (2) social needs; (3) physical handicaps; (4) special sexual needs, which might seem perverted to others; (5) impotence; (6) a need for therapy; (7) desire for sex in quantity, a variety of sexual experiences, without involvement with any one person; and (8) loneliness.

Sexual deprivation   Men who *travel* on business or are estranged from sexual partners through participating in the armed services, residence in work camps or construction projects provide business for the prostitute. The traveling salesman expresses his loneliness sexually, as does the sailor, merchant marine, migrant worker, or construction worker on the Alaska pipeline. Men have traditionally sought female companionship and sexual intercourse as a ''home away from home'' or ''woman in every port'' cure for loneliness. In contrast, women are socialized to resist similar solutions to loneliness. They face not only the reputation loss in a ''pick-up'' situation but potentially physical danger. For men, a shortage of available women in day-to-day contact, as in work camps, also sets up one side of an equation, the other of which is filled by a prostitute who provides sexual satisfaction for many men.

Social needs   Some men use prostitutes as a *social-bonding* mechanism with their friends (Stein, 1974). Going ''with the boys'' to a ''party'' or massage parlor is viewed as entertainment, something men do together. The activity is kept from wives and other noninvolved associates. Stag parties for entertainment are still being held by the fathers of this generation and some younger members of social and business clubs like the Elks, Eagles, Moose. They often appear to be father-daughter affairs, with most of the men in their forties joking with twenty-one year old topless dancers that they say remind them of their daughters. Yet, they would be appalled at the thought of their own daughters' involvement: again, the double standard and the necessity of having two classes of women.

Physical handicaps   There are men who qualify as sexually disenfranchised because they are restricted or *disabled* and turn to professional women to fulfill their needs. American society, in contrast to many other simpler cultures, limits sexual access to many populations on the basis of age, race, culture, personality, intelligence, and handicap (Marshall and Suggs, 1971). Those who do not, or feel they do not fall within the range of acceptable sexual partners, find it is safer to pay for acceptance than risk continued or possible rejection or social condemnation.

Special sexual needs   Another category is referred to by the prostitutes as *specials* or *freaks:* men whose sexual trigger falls into the section of the sexual spectrum frequently labeled perverted. People, depending on their individual experience, have special fantasies that intensify sexual pleasure. In some cases the fantasy is necessary to achieve erection and ejaculation. The range of triggers extends as far as imagination. Many are acceptable to some sexual partners such as transvestism or certain positions; most are acceptable to a prostitute who has worked more than six months. The requests that a professional gets eventually become commonplace and grist for discussion at the after-hours bar. A wife or girlfriend rarely has sufficient experience to find special requests acceptable. The man may feel ashamed of his need and conceal it from a possibly willing sexual partner in favor of the safety of reaction of the prostitute. With a professional he may not have to do more than hint at his desires for her to fill in the picture.

Therapy   Not all customers desire sexual contact. Some want a companion to take to dinner or a movie; others want someone to talk to for an hour. Women, especially experienced women, are seen as understanding, appropriate people to tell their troubles to. "Talkers" may have the woman ride out to the airport with them or sit in a hotel room while they tell her their troubles. The prostitute is the sympathetic ear in a situation where other women are too impatient or not to be trusted. The impotent man may find the prostitute solves his problems. She will not let him see his lack of erection as a failure. He has paid to be protected. Whatever role is required, she can play it—mother, sister, friend. She may dress up for him or just verbally fulfill his image needs. This is only one of the areas where the customer is, in a sense, seeking a therapist, someone to talk to. The women we interviewed often recognized their role as therapist with the joke that good whores and good "shrinks" always have more business than they know what to do with.

Quantity, variety, and noninvolvement   Variety and ability to avoid involvement are the most frequently cited needs. These needs are expressed through the *quantity* ethic, according to which the man who seduces many women gets points for potency. This value on quantity begins in adolescent bull sessions reinforced by the commercialization in the media of many women chasing one man. Seduction can be a long, drawn-out affair. The professional woman provides a shortcut. The exchange of cash on a direct basis eliminates the slower transaction of dinners, entertainment, and the development of rapport. Thus one can have hundreds of women in the time it might otherwise take to have ten; and the actual cash outlay, deleting money as time, may be the same. The quantity is guaranteed; the score is easy to predict.

The quantity ethic also relates to the desire for *variety*. If variety is the stimulant sexually, the same factors of exchange involved in quantity apply. Some men have stereotypes of sexual attractiveness—large breasts, blond hair, satin pants—that the variety of prostitutes available can fulfill. Those who prefer a dark woman in the role of sultry whore can hire black prostitutes to meet needs unacceptable and thus not satisfiable in their social circles.

Impotence   The impotent man finds the prostitute solves his problem in a variety of ways: (1) Her sexuality and its context may arouse him in a way that a "good" woman does not if he subscribes to the sex-is-dirty school. Her difference from his regular partner, given the variety ethic, may solve the problem. (2) Her knowledge of technique, use of fellatio, for example, may help him relax and achieve an erection. (3) The prostitute may view herself as a therapist and may be a successful one who takes her business seriously. She will talk with him, try to find his inhibitions, and work on solutions for the impotence. (4) She may just take his money but provide him with an excuse for his inability to achieve an erection: "Honey, you're tired, you work so hard," "You had too much to drink, you silly man," "All that tension from your job makes it difficult for you." (5) She may provide alternative routes to help him complete the illusion he needs. She may let him manipulate her to faked orgasm orally or manually, thus proving she is satisfied regardless of his condition. She will point out how important it is to her to have a man she can talk to instead of one who is always pawing her and treating her as a sex object. She may tell him that the fact that he needs to get to know a girl before he responds shows the quality of his character and please come back soon so they can develop the relationship. (6) If he insists on penetration she can provide him with a brace or a dildo. What she will be careful never to do is let him see his lack of erection as a failure. He is safe with the professional. He has paid to be protected. He will not have to face her again in case he fails. The advertising media is saturated with images of the ideal sexual partner, yet few men have access to women who meet that fantasy. Cultural stereotypes often provide a "forbidden fruit" fantasy that only the prostitute can fulfill without threat of repercussions. The cultural concept of the sensuous woman is exploited by prostitutes who seek to dress, talk, walk, and perform like the fantasy that reinforces the female whore-madonna dichotomy: the whore as the exciting sexual partner, the madonna as the wife and mother.

Other prostitutes may appeal to fantasies the customer may feel are perverse. A penchant for the very young or very old that is in conflict with the customer's place in social reality, a desire for obesity, a preference for long, flowing hair—these varieties of the female as sex object are available on the street, in the studio, or through contact by phone. Prostitutes learn very quickly to exchange customers to keep them from becoming bored and leaving on their own. On the street they will pass him to a friend or stable sister expecting a return exchange. (A stable sister is a prostitute who shares the same pimp with one or more other prostitutes.) In a phone system, the trades will be kept within a known circle of women until the customer's desire for variety takes him to another circle. Many women will try to vary their own art to keep a customer intrigued, just as many nonprofessional women vary their clothing and behavior to maintain the interest of their lifetime customer.

Variety is also an issue in the sexual service performed within the context of the exchange. Many men say they seek prostitutes for sexual variation they cannot fulfill at home or elsewhere. Labeling women good or bad in adolescence and according to sexual reputation contributes heavily to the issue of sexual variety. There are taboos against discussing or engaging in certain sexual activities with good women, i.e., wives. Homemakers are desexualized by the sexual stereotypes and, again, the media images. Home becomes an inappropriate location for sexual variety, or special activities—different positions, anal intercourse, cunnilingus, the use of oils, lotions, liquors, or tone of voice, body language, and direction of events. The professional woman provides an infinite variety of possibilities that can be granted on request or introduced through experience that contrast sharply with the limited offerings of less experienced women.

This customer category overlaps with the desire for release of sexual tension without the problems of *involvement* in a relationship with a woman. The customer does not want the trouble of an affair that his wife might find out about, or a single woman who will expect marriage or set him up by getting pregnant. He does not want to waste time entertaining a woman who may say no or the responsibility of providing her sexual gratification. A professional woman is discreet, does not expect to be entertained, always says yes, and will pretend gratification regardless of his commitment to pleasuring her. He has no responsibility for her sexual response. He pays for access to her body to achieve ejaculation, and that is what he gets without games or problems.

Loneliness   The final category, loneliness, overlaps in some areas with the desire for therapy. It refers basically to individuals who find themselves alone and want human contact. The prostitute may appear to them as the most available, the most uncomplicated, and the least likely to reject their advances.

With the exception of "freaks," or perverts, the customers whose sexual needs are discussed above are loosely defined as normal. In fact, the customers and their activities have long enjoyed a tradition of normality. Even during periods when intensive official attempts to end the business of prostitution were underway (for example, descriptions by Anderson [1974] of Chicago, 1910–1915, and by Holmes [1972] of nationwide efforts at about the same time), customers' needs were accepted as "inevitable." At most, men were chided for risking venereal disease and implored to practice self-control. The real villains, according to the reformers, were "those who made money by 'promoting' prostitution . . . , not [practitioners of] 'secret or clandestine vice' " (Anderson, 1974: 223). Since men were considered to have a basic biological need for these secret sexual outlets, it was seen as somehow immoral for women to demand money for relieving that need.

Today, men who purchase the services of prostitutes are still considered normal (nondeviant), even though their actions may be seen as unpalatable, or even immoral, according to the personal standards of the observer. Customers of prostitutes are, of course, acting outside the law; but where the law and the accepted male sex role come into conflict, the norms of sexual role playing overshadow the power of the law to label deviance. Men are expected to have a wide variety of sexual needs and to actively seek fulfillment of those needs. As part of that search, men are allowed to illegally purchase the sexual services of women with relative impunity, as arrest statistics demonstrate.

The provision of sexual services to males by women, in contrast, is clearly labeled deviant. Males break few social rules in patronizing a prostitute; females break almost all the rules of their sex role in becoming prostitutes. Streetwalkers, in particular, place themselves at the wrong end of the whore-madonna spectrum: they accept money for sex, they are promiscuous, they are not in love with the customers, they are not subtle, and they engage in "abnormal," or deviant, sex acts—acts which "respectable" women are expected to find unthinkable. The location of the streetwalker's place of business also labels her as deviant. Men may walk the streets freely wherever and whenever they wish; yet just by being downtown late at night without a male escort a woman is suspect.

Most importantly, however, the independent, promiscuous, overt sexuality of the prostitute challenges the traditional assumption that female sexuality is entirely dependent on—and awakened only by—male sexuality. As Davis (1937: 755) states, "Women are either part of the family system, or they are prostitutes, members of a caste set apart." Unregulated sexuality is accepted from males; from females, whose sexual stability is the sine qua non of our family concept, however, extramarital or premarital sex threatens the basic structures of society. So threatening is the idea of female sexual independence that we have laws defining juvenile women who engage in sexual intercourse without official permission as deviants "in danger of falling into habits of vice."

The Pimp

There are other men in the prostitute's life besides police and customers. Friends and acquaintances within the fast life, as involvement in prostitution is called, are important to the life-style. Streetwalkers usually do not work alone. With exceptions, all streetwalkers have a man somewhere in the background. In other prostitution styles, such as the call-girl system, a man is less important to business survival than on the street, but he may still be an important part of the prostitute's life. He may be called a pimp, but prostitutes dislike the term and usually refer to him as "my man." The *man* may function as a pimp; he may be a boyfriend or husband, or a combination of pimp and boyfriend. In cases of lesbian prostitutes, this role is filled by a woman who treats her women in much the same fashion as the man would. The lesbian pimp usually works with very young girls, often runaways from home or juvenile institutions. They are afraid to work for a man and find a female is more supportive of their situation as new girls in the business.

A pimp is someone who acts as an agent for others and essentially recruits them for a percentage of the money they make. In past decades the pimp took an active role in finding customers for prostitutes, but this is no longer the usual style. The pimp does not perform a direct service himself; he has others do it for him while he receives, manages, and controls the proceeds. Pimps are now referred to as *players, midnight executives,* and *fast-steppers.* (See James, 1972, for an ethnosemantic analysis of the domain of pimp.)

The ideal pimp fills many roles in his relationship with the prostitute; he is husband, boyfriend, father, lover, agent, and protector. As husband he may pay the bills, take care of the car, and father her children. His role as boyfriend includes taking her to parties and providing other entertainment. These two both overlap in his role of lover. As father he may discipline her for inappropriate behavior and make all her decisions. The agent and protector provides bail money and the services of an attorney, when necessary, and protection from others on the street through his reputation as a strong man whose women are not to be "hassled." How well he fills any one of these roles depends on how "good a pimp" he is and his relationship with the woman. Although individual cases vary depending on particular circumstances, prostitutes give basic reasons for having a man: respect, business, and love.

A Source of respect   Regardless of how people may wish to qualify the statement, women in our society feel they need a male companion if their position is to be respected. Women alone, if they are not elderly or widowed, are viewed as "needing a man." Unmarried daughters are harassed, women without men frequently feel their life is incomplete, and friends are forever trying to make a couple out of two singles. The same feelings of need for a male associate are pervasive among women who lead the fast life. In fact, sex-role behavior is conservative among prostitutes, and a woman needs a man or she is regarded as an "outlaw," someone who is abnormal by the subculture's values. If her man is in prison or has recently been killed, she is allowed a period of grace, but few other excuses for being without a man are acceptable.

A woman needs a man, not only because woman alone is incomplete, but for basic protection from harassment by other men. A prostitute without a pimp is considered fair game by other pimps, who will attempt to "catch" her. She is looked down on by her colleagues and is more open to abuse from others on the street. A pimp's name is significant as a "keep away" sign, not unlike the wedding ring in more traditional cultures; a woman on the street without a man "behind her" risks assault or robbery. His reputation provides respect and therefore protection. He does not in fact appear on the street, but instead socializes with other pimps in bars or private homes. Protection from customers is left to the prostitute and her coworkers, since the pimp is not around when she is working.

A woman's status among her peers in "the life" is directly related to the status of her pimp. Just as the banker's wife is accorded more status than the truck driver's, a prostitute's reputation in large part depends on her pimp's. If he is well dressed, handsome, drives a prestige automobile, and handles himself well, she will be highly respected; on the other hand, if he is less than stylish and unsuccessful in playing his role, her stature will be diminished. The woman is defined by the man for whom she works, and a really top pimp finds women asking and paying to be associated with him rather than waiting for him to recruit them.

A business manager   A second major factor in the prostitute-pimp relationship is business. Many prostitutes feel that they need a man to take care of business details that women traditionally have not felt capable of handling. They need a man to tell them when and how to work, to keep them in line, to give them confidence, and to take care of them. Ideally, the pimp takes over on all accounts. He handles the money, pays the bills, makes the investments, and gives her an allowance. He provides a place to live, food, clothing, transportation, entertainment, medical care, and arrangements for children. He is expected to take care of bail when she is arrested, provide a lawyer, and give her financial and moral support if she has to serve a sentence. The pimp takes care of her property and sees that her children are taken care of during the times she is working or serving a sentence. As one pimp put it, "I provide the mind and she provides the body. After all, that's the difference between a man and a woman." One of the older women interviewed put it this way:

> I gave him all of the money and, like I say, all my business was taken care of. I didn't have to worry about it. If I went to jail I'd be right out, if I needed an attorney he'd pay for it, and he sent money to my kids, and he was always buying me something. We had our little misunderstandings but nothing really serious. We did a lot of things together. We were in New York, he sent me to business school, and he went to a school of acting; we had a lot of fun. We traveled together, we even bought a house, but after the Feds were bothering me so much we had to give it up.*

Someone to come home to   The third important consideration in establishing an association with a pimp is affection. As prostitutes point out, everyone needs someone to come home to, and for them, it has to be someone in "the life." The prostitute needs a man who understands the profession and accepts her, and the pimp provides her with varying degrees of affection. Whatever his role, whether that of a wonderful lover or a controlling father, he supports her with talk of how special their relationship is and how they can make it together. To love and be loved was often stated as being the motivation to stay with a pimp (James, 1973).

The reasons offered by both pimps and prostitutes for this kind of relationship do not differ greatly from the reasons most men and women have for marrying. Respect, business, and love—though perhaps not in that order—are major motivating factors. In reality, detailed description of the interaction between pimp and prostitute produces a picture of a relationship that is little more than an exaggeration of the male-female relationships in the larger society. Levels of love, respect, and economic exchange vary, but the needs are the same.

Misinformation surrounds the pimp-prostitute relationship. This situation is in part due to past behavior of pimps, sensationalist journalism, and a protectionist policy toward women. Some pimps have been brutal in the past and exploitive, but the interaction is changing. Prostitutes are demanding better treatment or working alone; pimps are discovering that they can be more successful using psychological coercion. The women work harder for the maintenance of a positive relationship with their man, and the police are less likely to become involved if there is no violence. However difficult it may be to accept, many women choose to prostitute and prefer to give their money to a pimp. Understanding of the pimp-

---

*Excerpted from the author's research notes.

prostitute relationship should be based on the recognition of these dynamics.

The security of a particular pimp-prostitute relationship is, however, often bleak. The pressures inherent in their life-style, arrest, incarceration, and the jealousy that is felt by women who share the same man contribute to strained relationships. The ability of a single prostitute to maintain her relationship with her pimp is based on acceptance of the ethics of the life-style. Streetwalkers label themselves as outside the straight world and a part of the fast life. In "the life" the rules are different. A man, as long as he meets his obligations to each woman, may have more than one woman partner. Each woman may believe she will eventually be the one he chooses to be with when they have "made it together" and no longer need to be involved in prostitution. Some women are only interested in a short-term relationship because of their desire for the protection derived from association with a pimp. They pose no threat to the long-term woman because they make no demands for a position as "main lady." The set-up of a pimp and his women is referred to as a *stable*. The duration of a stable is often only a few months as one or more of the women move to another man.

A particular prostitute may stay with a pimp five, six, even ten years, but she rarely settles down with him and lives out her dream of marriage and security with him. Most pimps, when they leave the profession, also leave their women. When they settle down it is with women who have not been prostitutes, and often in this situation the pimp becomes a conservative husband and father. Yet the prostitutes ignore such examples of the end result of most prostitute-pimp relationships and choose to believe that for them it will be different. The dreams of the fast life are very potent and quite like the dreams of marriage that absorb many female teenagers when they first fall in love. The problems are not seen as clearly as the cultural stereotype presented in brides' or homemakers' magazines.

Surprisingly enough, more prostitutes leave the profession successfully than do the pimps whom they support. Few pimps leave the life before they are destroyed by it through violence, imprisonment, or drug addiction (Milner and Milner, 1972). Prostitutes, if they have avoided alcoholism or drug addiction, drift out of the life as they get older. They take other jobs, go on welfare, and in some cases marry someone who has little knowledge of their past. Pimps, unless they are very successful in another status career, such as entertainment, rarely survive past forty. Most of them find it impossible to compromise and reenter what they describe as the "square world." Only positions of fast-life status, such as writer, producer, bar owner, entertainer, or actor are viewed as viable alternatives. As one interviewed pimp pointed out, "It's a hard life taking care of women and keeping them together with everyone on your back."

Except in the People's Republic of China, attempts at ending prostitution have been total failures. Russia and Cuba claim to have eliminated prostitution with programs similar to those in China, but there is evidence to the contrary. Journalists report the easy availability of prostitutes in both Moscow and Havana despite severe fines for customers and prison sentences for prostitutes. China's success seems to be based on the complete equality of the sexes in domestic, economic, and political spheres combined with the discipline and commitment required by "pure" Communist ideology. The supply of prostitutes has been eliminated by offering women equal economic opportunities and sentencing prostitutes to intensive five-year terms of reorientation. The demand has been eliminated through emphasis on discipline and heavy prison sentences for customers.

Other countries have accepted the existence of prostitution and made various legal arrangements. Countries in the Middle East, the Far East, the Caribbean, and South America regulate it by requiring brothels to be licensed and by subjecting prostitutes to health inspections. France, Britain, Italy, Japan, Germany, and a total of 100 members of the United Nations have eliminated the crime of prostitution and have abandoned attempts to regulate it (United Nations, 1951). The criminal laws in those countries seek instead to control public solicitation and to discourage the pimps and procurers who live off the earnings of prostitutes.

The country most open in its treatment of prostitution is West Germany, where prostitutes are considered a social necessity. The West German government actively supports the building of pimp-free prostitution hostels where prostitutes can live and work in comfortable rooms with ready access to shopping centers, bowling and tennis, and mandatory medical inspection. Sweden has a special employment stipulation whereby a woman can work as a prostitute only if she has another full-time job in a "legitimate" field. The emphasis is on making sure the woman has an alternative and a job to go to when she is too old to prostitute.

Decriminalizing a Victimless Crime

In the United States a number of groups are working toward changes in the prostitution and other sex laws: The National Organization for Women, American Civil Liberties Union, sections of the American Bar Association, and the National Council on Crime and Delinquency. The main thrust of their efforts is decriminalization and acceptance of prostitution as a victimless crime, or a crime without a complainant—a crime where the so-called victim does not file a complaint. (Other victimless crimes are vagrancy, gambling, pornography, homosexuality, and public drunkenness.) The only person who files a complaint against a prostitute is the police officer who, in passing as a customer, has been solicited by her.

Neither the customer, who actively seeks a service, nor the prostitute, who willingly sells, is a true victim. Those who refer to the prostitute as a victim do so in a nonlegal sense: they see her as a victim of her immoral life-style, and not of a crime.

In the movement to change the prostitution statutes, decriminalization is viewed as the least abusive choice. Unlike legalization, it would remove prostitution from the criminal code entirely and thus eliminate entirely a need for legal definitions and involvement. Ideally, all sexual behavior in private between consenting adults would be outside the purview of the law. Options for controls within any given community would relate only to obviousness of the sexual activities, possible disease problems, business and zoning regulations, and age of consent.

Taxation and health and age requirements can be approached in a number of ways. The individual prostitute might be issued a small business license along with a health card. The license would be similar to that of a masseuse; the place of business would have to conform with tax and zoning requirements; she would be required to report her income to the Internal Revenue Service, be of age, and obtain a health card and keep it current. Violations would mean the revocation of the license and would be handled by a nonpolice administrative agency. Advertisements would be limited to discreet classified ads. Houses of prostitution would not be licensed.

Regulations such as the above would, of course, still limit personal freedom in a purely private area. The nonlicensed prostitute could still be prosecuted although hers would be a civil citation, not a criminal one. The "consenting adults" approach must be balanced by the reality of public expediency. Decriminalization, with some restrictions, is regarded as a provisional solution only while efforts are made to change the more fundamental causes of prostitution.

In summary, prostitution is a social and cultural phenomenon that results from the double-standard bind. The range of accepted sexual behavior for males in our society is considerably wider than that for middle-class women. Thus lower-class women, and particularly those who have been set apart by the label *deviant*, must serve as substitutes for the middle-class women so firmly restricted by their class proscriptions. Prostitution allows men temporary freedom from sexual restraints and the opportunity to move briefly into the deviant subculture.

The more highly restricted female sex role contains almost none of the sexual motivations and behaviors allowed the male; nor does it permit a woman to serve as a professional sexual accompanist for those men who would rent her services. The prostitute is a *deviant woman;* her customer is a *normal man*.

The puritanical overtones of the middle-class double standard make prostitution essential if the accepted male sex role is to be fully acted out. As a result, the male need for purchased female sexual service is, and long has been, viewed as inevitable and therefore not to be punished. The women who provide this service, however, are in violation of their full role and dangerously at odds with the conventions of society. They are therefore jailed, stigmatized, and exiled from "decent" society.

Unless the demand for prostitution, as well as the supply, is recognized prostitution cannot be understood, much less eliminated. Men must be able to view sex as something other than a purchasable commodity. Women must be able to find value within themselves apart from the attractiveness of their bodies. The sexual socialization process of males and females is the key to the existence of prostitution. The stigmatization of women as whores is the result of a promiscuity standard that does not exist for males.

Juvenile Promiscuity

The sexual labeling of young females is based on the same set of sexual expectations that are applied to the prostitute. Specialists in the area of juvenile delinquency have traditionally described the female delinquent as a sexual delinquent (Vedder and Sommerville, 1975). Sexual acts by juvenile females violate behavioral expectations for young women but are rarely against the law for adults. Yet they are treated by juvenile courts as criminal acts. The sexually uncontrolled adolescent girl is more threatening than her adult counterpart because of her youth and its equation with innocence and the responsibility of society, particularly males, to protect the chastity of virgins. In contrast, juvenile males are virtually never reported for inappropriate sexual activity unless it is also an adult offense such as rape or molestation. Males who are sexually active are viewed as exercising the male prerogative to be wild and uncontrolled while they are young and have no family responsibilities. They are encouraged to "sow wild oats," to be "one of the boys," and to prove their manhood. Females must prove their femininity in the opposite direction, through passivity.

The difference in treatment is well documented. Girls who are referred to juvenile authorities for any activity from shoplifting to running away are almost automatically given gynecological examinations to determine virginity, pregnancy, or infection with a venereal disease (Chesney-Lind, 1973). These examinations may be used to prove the allegation of sexual promiscuity as well as to protect the health of the female. The state of the hymen—the fact that it is not intact—may be used by the court as evidence for institutionalization. Boys are rarely, if ever, examined. While young women are placed "under the protection of the courts" and incarcerated in juvenile institutions for extended periods of time on the basis of their "moral state," young men are rarely incarcerated unless they have committed a criminal act that would also be an adult violation. Such discrepancies in treatment are justified by the importance of protecting females and controlling their sexual behavior.

This double standard is also applied to age. Juvenile males obtain adult status and release at age eighteen. If designated as incorrigible, promiscuous, dependent, or simply a person in need of supervision, a female can be held until age twenty-one. These practices are believed by some to help the female juvenile by providing support and protection until she is of marriageable age or able to be independent from her family and the state. Examination of the workings of the juvenile court process, however, provides evidence that the court is in fact exceptionally harsh with juvenile females, especially in the areas concerned with sexual behavior.

A review of the delinquency labels applied to girls points out the sexual interpretations added to any unacceptable behavior. *Incorrigible* is a frequently used juvenile criminal category, the definition of which is dependent on parental concepts of acceptable female role behavior. In their desire for their daughters to be popular and attractive, families encourage them to be sex objects while expecting them to avoid sexuality: Teenage girls are to be admired but not touched. It is all right and approved for girls to attract boys, but staying out late, "running around," or suspected sexual involvement may result in their being reported to the authorities. Crossing the fine line that separates the good girl from the bad girl can bring rigid or nonsupportive parents to file a report of incorrigibility. A designation by the courts of incorrigibility is frequently a result of behavior that indicates violations of sexual restrictions. Often, juvenile females who smoke, violate liquor laws, skip school, or come home late are reported by their mothers to juvenile authorities as impossible to handle. In contrast, juvenile males are reported most often by school authorities or police officers for clearly criminal activities such as burglary and auto theft. Many parents and the juvenile courts support a double standard which allots females a much narrower range of acceptable behavior.

Promiscuity is another classic label applied to juvenile females but not to their male counterparts. Pregnant young women, especially if they desire an abortion, may be referred to the juvenile court and can be classified as delinquents. Families that suspect their daughters are involved in sexual activity can refer them to the court for examination or commit them to juvenile institutions for safekeeping. In an article on the labels applied to juvenile female delinquents, Strouse (1972) reports many such cases. One was a recent case in Connecticut where a sixteen year old girl was sent to the State Farm for Women because her parents and the court agreed that she was in "manifest danger of falling into habits of vice." The general supervision law under which she was committed was challenged and upheld on the assertion that her commitment was not a punishment but a "protective safeguard."

In jurisdictions where promiscuity is no longer an acceptable charge, incorrigibility or other labels are applied. According to Gold (1971: 2), "An unstated fear or dislike of sexual promiscuity and illegitimate births by young women and girls is behind the unequal treatment implicit in the New York Family Court Act." This act created the PINS (Person in Need of Supervision) label for a juvenile who is in trouble but has not committed a crime. An examination of a list of 1,500 metropolitan juvenile court cases by Reiss (1960) demonstrated that the judges involved refused to treat any form of sexual behavior on the part of boys, however bizarre, as warranting more than probationary status. In all cases of sexual activity involving an adolescent couple, however, they regarded girls as the "cause" of sexual deviation of boys and refused to hear the complaints of the girls and their families. Regardless of whether juvenile court officials are male or female, their decisions usually reflect the same double standard of sexual behavior that defines the female as the seductive element in any sexual interaction and precipitates many young girls' arrest.

Juvenile prostitution also has a wide definition in most juvenile courts. Parents or authorities may suspect the girl is involved in prostitution without direct proof or may prefer to avoid the label of prostitution when proof is available. When a clear charge of prostitution is made, a long sentence in a juvenile institution usually results, because prostitution is viewed as an extremely deviant activity for young women. In contrast, again, acts of vandalism, drinking, and car theft among teenage boys are viewed as acts typical of a behavioral "stage" or a demonstration of their masculinity through delinquent behavior.

Prostitution provides unique opportunities for juvenile women. As noted above, it enables them to support themselves at a much younger age than legal employment. They can earn enough to achieve independence from parents, travel enough to avoid pickups as runaways or probation violators, and feel they are adults because customers seek them out as women. The excitement, adventure, and income is heady stuff for an adolescent child-woman. If parents are unresponsive, if school is boring, and if juvenile authorities are oppressive, the fast life offers an escape. Already labeled as promiscuous the juvenile feels there is little to lose and potential recognition for her "cool" and "fast" life to be gained. The money means independence, the most common factor these young women need: freedom from the controls placed on them by their families, school, or the juvenile court.

Women as Victims

Crimes committed against women frequently involve the same institutional definitions of female sexuality that are significant in promiscuity and prostitution, a double standard that punishes women who cross the whore-madonna line, whether by choice or force. Rape and other sexual abuses of both child and adult females appear to be increasing, and public information on their circumstances is expanding. The police, hospitals, and courts deal with the victims of these crimes, and their attitudes and practices are now being questioned and investigated. Once an incident is reported, these institutions process both the victim and, with the exception of hospitals, the offender. The reputation of police departments in particular has been so poor in this area that many woman never report their assault for fear the resultant investigation will be more abusive than the crime of which they were a victim. The individual victim may even come to accept the judgment of others that she asked to be raped, that she was somehow guilty of precipitating the assault. In the last five years new research studies have been published describing how victims of sexual crime are handled. One central message emerges from all of them: society's views of the crimes and of the victim amount to an indictment of female sexuality (Burgess and Holstrom, 1974; Brownmiller, 1975).

Rape

Brownmiller's book *Against Our Will: Men, Women and Rape* provides a historical analysis of rape in our civilization and how much it reveals about current male-female relationships (1975). She concludes that "the threat, use and cultural acceptance of sexual force is a pervasive process of intimidation that affects all women," whether they become actual victims of violence or not (1975: 15).

The rate of forcible rape in the United States supports the contention that sexual assault is a major problem for women: according to recent statistics a forcible rape occurs every ten minutes. The volume of forcible rape offenders increased in 1973 by 12.7 percent over 1972, and 117 percent over 1960. This represented the greatest percentage increase among the crimes of violence for adult male offenders in 1973 (FBI Uniform Crime Reports, 1974). The actual number of rapes that occur appears to be much greater than these data indicate because it is estimated that only one in four rapes is ever reported. In 1972, 44 percent of all reported rapes took place in only fifty-seven cities (National League of Cities, 1974), with

Denver, the rape capital, New York, and San Francisco leading the list. In a single city, Seattle, where intensive rape research and projects encouraging reporting are under way, the frequency of rape charges has increased 420 percent from 1966 to 1974 (Seattle Police Department, 1975). The increased reporting of rapes may not be an accurate reflection of increased attacks; it may be a response to public consciousness raising that has resulted in increased willingness to report rape. Regardless, the number of women involved on a constant day-to-day basis makes rape one of the crimes women fear most.

In large part, the new awareness of the problem of rape has been generated by organizations identified with the feminist movement. Their analysis of the treatment of victims by police, medical personnel, and criminal justice systems has led to increased consciousness, rape relief programs, police training, and legislative changes in the legal requirements for prosecution. Programs that have grown out of this new awareness provide assistance in six main areas: (1) understanding the crime of forcible rape and eliminating the myths that impair the enforcement of the law; (2) education for women in self-protection, knowledge of rape practices, and survival if assaulted; (3) rape relief centers where women can report rape if they prefer not to go to the police and where they can receive aid and counseling; (4) police sensitivity training and the use of policewomen in responding to rape reports and conducting investigations; (5) the development of model legal codes and prosecution procedures to aid in conviction of offenders while protecting victims; and (6) research into the possible causative factors of rape built into our definitions of male and female sexuality.

The implementation of knowledge derived from these programs and a realistic understanding of rape is complicated by definitions of good and bad sexual conduct for women. One commonly expressed societal view is that women ask for rape because they dress seductively and act promiscuously. Hitchhiking, drinking in bars alone, and accepting dates from strangers are all viewed as "asking for it" by some jurors and many criminal justice personnel. Seductive clothing such as short skirts, halter tops, or no-bra outfits are all seen as come-ons which leave the victimization in question. "A victim's 'moral character' may be admissible as a defense in some statutes. Again, the assumption is that an unchaste female, or a female with such a reputation, is more likely than not to consent to sexual intercourse in any given instance" (Amir, 1971: 23). Research on actual rape circumstances indicates that up to 70 percent of all rapes occur between complete strangers where knowledge of past sexual experience is unknown and 38 percent occur within a woman's home or apartment where the offender has not previously observed the woman's clothing habits (personal communication, Donna Schram, 1973).

A second common attitude is that "a good woman cannot be raped."

Yet the background studies of rape victims indicate the full spectrum in terms of age, sexual experience, social class, religious beliefs, education, marital status, and personal habits. The theory that women can stop rape has also produced contradictions. Police officials advise women to be passive, to avoid resistance which might possibly increase injury. Juries, however, rarely convict the rapist without clear evidence of resistance. Statistics on the assaults and homicides accompanying rape put the victim in a very difficult position. If she fights, she may be seriously injured; if she does not resist, she may not be accepted as a victim.

The myths and misunderstandings that surround the crime of rape are supported by the same double standard that was discussed in the context of prostitution and juvenile promiscuity. Women are expected to control sexual access to their bodies; men are not expected to control their sexual desires. A woman who mixes her sexual messages by violating traditional behavioral boundaries for women "gets what she deserves." These societal attitudes lead to abusive treatment by police, insensitivity on the part of medical personnel, abuse and defamation in court, and suspicion by husband, family, and friends. The classic question, "Tell me now, didn't you sort of enjoy it?" is still being asked.

While efforts to clarify these societal definitions and produce change in the handling of rape cases continue, emphasis is now also being placed on the education of women in the avoidance of possible rape situations. Major studies of rape situations provide knowledge of the modus operandi of reported rape offenders. The most frequent victims of rape are single, relatively young women, and the most common place of attack is within their own residences (National League of Cities, 1974). The offender either breaks in or uses a ruse to get the woman to open her door. In Denver, Philadelphia, and New York, the majority of rape offenses occurred in the downtown city center area, where there is the highest concentration of young, single women. In more than half the cases examined—67 percent in Denver, 63 percent in Seattle, 55 percent in Kansas City, and 52 percent in Philadelphia—the victim and the offender were total strangers. These studies also report time of day, day of the week, and month of the year, pinpointing weekends between 8 P.M. and 2 A.M. as the most potentially dangerous time.

Knowledge of rape circumstances leads to standard advice to women which many women's groups feel is unfair and difficult to follow: Do not go out alone; do not open your door to strangers; never pick up or accept rides from strangers; and never put yourself in a position, even with an acquaintance, where you will be unable to defend yourself (Storaska, 1975). If you are assaulted, resist initially if there is any chance of someone coming to your assistance or of escape, then submit with minimal verbal comment and call the police as soon as you are sure the attacker is gone. Given the reality of rape, this advice is good but its implicit limitations on women's freedom are profound. Few males would accept advice not to go out alone at night. How can a woman protect herself even with an acquaintance, given the physical strength differences between men and women? Why are these restrictions directed at women rather than men, who are potentially the aggressors? Again, the double standard of control over male and female sexuality is apparent.

Investigations of rape provide additional examples of the effect of societal attitudes on rape convictions. The Denver study reported by the NLC provides a breakdown of the usual police problems in attempting to clear rape cases (National League of Cities, 1974). Of the 915 offenses reported during the two years of this study, only 16 percent were cleared by the arrest of the suspect. The reasons given for not being able to arrest or charge in the cases where the suspect was identified were as follows: in 43.2 percent of the cases the victim refused to prosecute or was unavailable; in 24.9 percent lack of evidence was an obstacle—either the victim did not resist enough or was labeled as "asking for it"; in 10.6 percent of the cases the suspect had been arrested previously by another jurisdiction; and in 17.5 percent the district attorney refused to file the case, usually because the victim's sexual reputation could be attacked. Forty-nine percent of the total cases were inactive. The reasons stated were lack of suspect identification, failure of the victim to cooperate, or lack of sufficient information. These statistics are similar to those available through other rape arrest analyses.

The absence of severe physical injury and victim reputation are often major obstacles to the prosecution of rapists. A victim who has not been seriously injured may be viewed as not having attempted to defend herself—as having, in a sense, cooperated in the assault. In addition, victims refuse to report or prosecute because they want to avoid publicity that will identify them as "violated" women. They are afraid of the reactions of parents or spouse and also fear retaliation from their attacker, an eventuality against which they are generally unable to protect themselves. Their socialization into nonaggressive behavior and their concern with sexual reputation often negates their ability to fight the assault, legally or socially. Finally, as mentioned above, a victim who leads a sexually active life may be considered "unrapeable"; her testimony is suspect because she "had nothing to lose."

Studies of police investigation of rape have all concurred in their reports of these problems of insensitivity to the victim and inadequate response to the crime, i.e., disbelief in the occurrence of rape, insufficient staffing, and lack of knowledge or concern for the evidence required for prosecution. Public pressure for reform has resulted in the use of policewomen and separate counseling agencies that act as advocates for the victim throughout the police investigation, as well as the institution of improved training and education in forensic procedures.

The attention rape has received as a result of criticism of the institutional responses to rape victims has also led to renewed comments on possible causes. Research has tended to focus on the tension built into our definitions of male and female sexuality: the aggressiveness expected of the male, the push to "score" implicit in the fearsome term *sissy* in combination with society's insistence that the female be attractive, desirable, and popular, but *not* "easy." Accusations of female seductiveness and male inability to resist recall similar arguments for prostitution that justify arresting women and not men. This tension creates many circumstances that could be called pseudorape when the male senses that no means yes and the female means to convey that message. This further confuses the reality of rape when no stated by the victim means no. The victim is caught by her socialized involvement in traditional sexual gamesmanship and the possibility of misinterpretation.

The rapists who have been studied are those who were caught and convicted. They generally fall into the lower end of the occupational- and social-class scales (Amir, 1971), fit almost equally into married and single categories, and show few other distinguishing characteristics. Young, for the most part in their early twenties, they usually have previous convictions for other crimes. Indeed rape is often committed as an adjunct to another crime such as burglary or robbery, and offenders tend to characterize it as victim-precipitated—the result of seductive or reckless behavior on the part of the victim. Viewed in this way, rape is an ever-present possibility if a woman is not careful. Explanations for its occurrence are thus diverted away from the offender and back to the victim.

Psychoanalytic explanations for rape are as confusing and diverse as those for prostitution. Rape is sometimes defined as a act of political vengeance and also as a neurotic revenge for a deprived childhood, a seductive mother, or a rejecting wife. In many cases it is viewed neither as criminal behavior nor a result of identifiable personality disturbances. In this sense, again, rape is a traditional right of a man if a woman violates her assigned role position.

Revision of criminal codes is now being undertaken in many states to underline the criminal nature of rape and to make conviction more likely and thus a more effective deterrent to offenders. Statutes that require a corroborating witness (never required in robbery) for prosecution are being reviewed and replaced because they demonstrate an antivictim bias. Bills are pending that disallow evidence of a rape victim's past sexual conduct "other than with the defendant." In California such information is already prohibited. In New York, Connecticut, and Ohio, requirements of corroboration by medical evidence of sperm or assault have been dropped. These amendments suggest the beginnings of a shift in institutional response that will make it more difficult in the future to write off the rape victim as in some way the provocateur or inventor of her own attack.

Sexual Abuse of Children

Rape is only one of the crimes involving female sexuality, and according to many researchers, it is not as common as incest and molestation of children. Sexual intercourse with a person within prohibited degrees of blood relationship, usually including mother, father, aunt, uncle, brother, sister, and grandparents, constitutes the crime of incest. Some state statutes also include stepparents and half-brothers and sisters. Incest appears under many charges and is more common than is publicly acknowledged. If sexual intercourse is denied but sexual activity with a child transpires, the charge is often child molestation regardless of the familial relationship. Carnal knowledge, indecent liberties, statutory rape, child abuse, and child neglect are other charges that may be made in the case of sexual abuse. Female children are the victims of these offenses ten to one over male children and their cases are apparently given more attention because of the implications of their victimization on their emotional stability and future sexual reputation (De Francis, 1971).

Incest   There are no known societies, with the exception of the ancient royal lineage of the Egyptians, Incas, and Hawaiians, where it is or was permissible for father and daughter, mother and son, or brother and sister to have sexual intercourse or marry: incest is one of the few universal cultural taboos cited by anthropologists. The reasons behind these restrictions are varied, but an important element involving female sexuality is the reduction of the competition between mother and daughter that Freud termed the Electra syndrome. The vast majority of reported incest involves father-daughter or stepfather-daughter relationships which reveal, in fact, the competitive situation. Social restrictions against incest in our society are also based on the importance of maintaining the nuclear family, fear of genetic defect, and the abhorrence society has of adults who exploit the dependence and sexual immaturity of children.

Because of the hidden nature of these crimes the actual extent of incest is unknown. Estimates indicate, however, at least 4 percent of the population has been involved as a victim or offender (Kinsey, 1953; McDonald, 1971). Researchers report that most cases go unrecorded because of the desire of parents to protect their image and the offender, who is usually the wage earner, a lack of sympathy for the child, or actual collusion by the mother in the sexual activities (De Francis, 1971). As more knowledge about sexuality and the effects of incest is communicated and more awareness of children's and women's rights is developed this situation may change.

Concern in other areas of physical abuse of children has also led to increased reporting of sexual abuse. The movement for children's rights is an apparent outgrowth of the movement for women's rights. Some agencies of society are now beginning to take a stand for protection of children from sexual violence, just as the review of rape laws has begun to redefine women's victimization.

One important factor affecting the increased number of incest cases reported is the breakdown of many marriages and the resulting increase in strained family relationships. Fathers and daughters in separated homes do not develop natural familiarity because they do not live together. The breakdown in marital and consequently sexual relationships between a father and mother may also place increased pressure on the daughter to become a wife surrogate. A direct result of the dissolution of a marriage is often remarriage, which in turn exposes the child to a stepfather who may not feel as strong a compunction to observe incest taboos as a natural father. Even when the mother does not remarry there is still the problem of exposure of the children to her male friends or sexual partners.

Research into adult and juvenile crime has also contributed to increased awareness of incest and other forms of sexual abuse. Female runaways, juvenile prostitutes, and young girls turned in to youth centers as promiscuous or incorrigible are often found to be the victims of sexual abuse within their homes (De Francis, 1971). Corresponding research with adult female offenders, especially prostitutes and addicts, indicates the same significance of sexual abuse as a destructive influence on personal development (James, 1973). The resultant impairment of the female child's sexual self-respect appears to have far-reaching implications for her adjustment as a woman. In a society that has only two labels for women, respectable or not respectable, and treats them accordingly, the violated child finds it difficult to avoid negative self-labeling. Clearly she is no longer a "good" girl, and like the rape victim, she may be accused of seductive behavior. Regardless of age, the female is supposed to resist the male, who may be unable to resist.

The most common incest relationships reported are father-daughter, followed by stepfather-daughter, uncle-niece, grandfather-granddaughter, brother-sister, and, infrequently, mother-son. The average age of the female victim is thirteen; the age range in most studies is between seven and nineteen, although infant cases have been reported. The age range of the offender is late thirties to early forties. The two age concentrations are significant: for the victim it is adolescence, just when she is beginning to develop sexually, and for the offender it falls at the time of the male "forties crisis," the period during which doubts of sexual prowess may occur. Incest usually happens within the child's or the offender's home and continues over a period of years. Threats to the child or the passive submission of the child to the situation prevent a report of the offense.

The discovery of such long-term sexual abuse usually results from a combination of factors. In the father-daughter relationship, the mother may discover the activity and refuse to collude despite possible loss of the man and his economic support. She may want to get even with the offender or protect the child. More commonly, the daughter resists her father's jealous efforts to restrict her activities with boys her own age as she becomes older and more independent. She may run away, report him for beating her, or become difficult to manage. The incest activity may come out when the juvenile authorities become involved in her associated behaviors. In some cases an older daughter seeks to protect a younger sister when she sees her father making advances, or she is jealous. And when a victim becomes pregnant, the offender may subsequently be identified as the responsible party.

The problems of incest, aside from the nature of the taboo, lie in the institutional responses to the female child and the lack of assistance available to her. The male, when discovered, usually blames the seductive girl, and her mother frequently joins in. Once again, it is the female who is responsible for stopping sexual advances of an uncontrolled male: women, even children, are expected to control sexual access, while men, even adults, are expected to have little or no control over their sexual needs. The problems of corroboration of the crime are similar to those of rape. The usual legal response because of the difficulties of prosecution is to refer the case to juvenile authorities. Charges are not pressed against the offender, and the victim is institutionalized. The child is left with the burden of guilt for her sexuality because she is often removed from the home and placed in a foster home or institution, ostensibly for her own protection, while the offender remains with the family. Punished and rejected in this fashion, she views herself as the offender.

Child Molestation The molestation of children—sexual activity with them not involving intercourse—presents issues similar to those of incest. The incidence of various types of molestation, like that of incest, is estimated to be many times larger than reported. The reasons are the same: in two-thirds of the known cases the offender is a family member or close friend. Contrary to the common myth, molestation is not a single event occurring most frequently between strangers in parks. It usually involves relatives or family friends in the victim's or offender's home, and in almost half the cases examined in one study the offenses were repeated against the child more than once (De Francis, 1971).

The response of the social institutions of the criminal justice system to reported molestation is often described as more abusive than the molestation itself. The child is rarely protected through lengthy police investigations, questionings, and court proceedings, and may be accused of lying or attempting to attract attention if the incident involves a close family member. In many cases, the child protective division of social and health institutions is unable to show an understanding of the emotional impact of the crime and the problems it may create for the child. It is in fact easier to treat incidents of child molestation as a fantasy of the child rather than a reality. As with other sexual crimes, depending on tradition and treating the female victim as an offender is the less difficult course. When the male is accused and prosecuted he is also treated harshly but viewed as sick, not seductive.

Conclusion

The existence of prostitution is based on the American cultural view of sex as a purchasable commodity. The media provide the affirmation of a sexually saturated society where many products are bought and sold with the promise of sexual satisfaction. Our discussion of customers outlined the needs that create the demand. Our discussion of prostitutes pointed out the possible reasons that women provide the supply. An end to prostitution is dependent not on legal reform but on the end of the sexual socialization process that produces the supply and demand for the profession.

The causes of rape and sexual abuse of children are more difficult to ascertain. Putting aside the motivations of the offender we are left with the abusiveness of the institutionalized response to the victim. A case has been made that both rapists' motivations and institutional responses are products of the myths and tensions built into the double standard of sexual behavior. The current emphasis during male adolescence on "scoring," regardless of the intimacy of the relationship with the woman, depersonalizes sex and offers quantity and not quality as the ego enhancer. The double standard sets a whore-madonna spectrum on which a woman's sexual reputation is measured and further depersonalizes sex by limiting it to "loose" women. The argument becomes circular. Good girls and women do not get sexually assaulted. Girls and women who are sexually assaulted are no longer good. They are, in fact, precipitators of their assault by retrospective reputation. Throughout history most societies have noted that a population of such loose women is necessary to meet male sexual appetites while protecting good women who are or will become wives and mothers.

Prostitution also provides the population to meet male desires for promiscuity. The male defines his masculinity through these paid encounters. The female defines her feminity as a good woman by refusing to be paid, or gives it up by accepting the label *whore*. The male customer buys an illusion of sexual success combined with physical release. Access to females is commensurate with success. To be a ladies' man is a compliment whether he purchases the companion overtly or subtly through favors less obvious than cash, or forces himself on women. Behind the exchange is a socialized male-female need: the male need to feel he is an attractive, competent lover by whatever means; the female need to be desired as a sex object and receive some economic support as a result.

The sexual definitions of male and female role behavior set up the tension. Prostitution can provide ideal situations for fulfilling these role expectations. It is the business of fantasy. As Stein has pointed out in her book *Lovers, Friends, Slaves:*

> The ability to switch roles quickly is the core of the call girl's work. Men don't come to her hoping to find a relationship with a real woman, but with a three-dimensional responsive embodiment of a fantasy woman. They pay her for the opportunity to satisfy their desires with a partner, undiluted by intrusion of an unpaid partner's own desires and personality. (Stein, 1974: 119)

In a house, apartment, or regular phone business, the illusion may be built up over a number of visits. Marie, the working woman, calls John, the trick, tells him she misses him and asks him to come over. What she is really missing is the rent money; she has had a slow week. John turns up because a man should not refuse a woman's request to see him; Marie needs him, and Marie makes him feel good. He knows Marie thinks he is a wonderful lover with a good body because she has told him so. He knows he pleases Marie sexually because of the orgasm she has so quickly and easily with him. All is clearly articulated; there is no silent affirmation of pleasure, no room for doubt. In his mind the thirty dollars he leaves her is not relevant to the exchange. The money may nag a little, but basically he is just helping her out because she is a working woman. The commodity that John has purchased is the illusion of his desirability and his potency, which, as for most women, becomes more important than the sexual release.

The same illusions, or commodities, are present in rape. The rapist often forces the victim to say she enjoys him and affirm his sexual prowess. He describes the rape as a conquest. And society supports the illusion that women enjoy being ravished and that men who "take what they want" are in some senses to be admired. So, too, the incestuous father will state his right to his daughter's body and his sensitivity as a sexual teacher. In the same family the mother will point out the daughter's seductiveness and the fact that "she's always been that way." The society, the family, and the institutional structure created by them accept the double standard and respond accordingly.

The issues presented here of women's involvement with the criminal justice system as offenders and victims are now the subject of intensive review by those interested in civil rights and social change. Prostitution and sexual assault are central issues in the legal reform supported by the feminist movement. Further knowledge of the circumstances of these crimes and understanding of their causes is needed to protect both men and women from abuse. The importance of rational and sensitive response to women, whether as delinquents, prostitutes, or victims of sexual assault, is at last being discussed. The cost of continued judgments based on stereotypes rather than realities is clearly too high.

References

Amir, M. (1971). Forcible Rape. Chicago: University of Chicago Press.

Anderson, E. (1974). Prostitution and Social Justice: Chicago 1910–1915. Social Service Review 203 (June).

Brownmiller, S. (1975). Against Our Will: Men, Women and Rape. New York: Simon and Schuster.

Burgess, A.W., and L.L. Holstrom (1974). Rape Trauma Syndrome. American Journal of Psychiatry 131:981–986.

Caprio, F. (1963). The Sexually Adequate Female. New York: Citadel.

Chesney-Lind, M. (1973). Judicial Enforcement of the Female Sex Role: The Family Court and the Female Delinquent. Issues in Criminology 2:51–69.

Choisy, M. (1965). Psychoanalysis of the Prostitute. New York: Pyramid Books.

Davis, K. (1937). The Sociology of Prostitution. American Sociological Review 2:744–755.

De Francis, V. (1971). Protecting the Child Victim of Sex Crimes Committed by Adults: Final Report. The American Human Association, Children's Division. Denver, Colo.

Deutsch, H. (1965). Neuroses and Character Types. New York: International Universities Press.

FBI Uniform Crime Reports (1974). Crime in the United States. Washington, D.C.: U.S. Government Printing Office.

Glover, E.G. (1960). Roots of Crime. London: Imago.

Gold, S. (1971). Equal Protection for Juvenile Girls in Need of Supervision in New York State. New York Law Review Forum 57:2.

Greenwald, H. (1958). The Call Girl. New York: Ballantine Books.

Holmes, K.A. (1972). Reflections by Gaslight: Prostitution in Another Age. Issues in Criminology 7:83.

James, J. (1971). A Formal Analysis of Prostitution. Final Report to the Division of Research. Part 1: Basic Statistical Analysis; Part 2: Descriptive Report; Part 3: Formal Semantic Analysis. Department of Social and Health Services, 1–468, Olympia, Wash.

————(1972). Two Domains of the Streetwalker Argot. Anthropological Linguistics 14(5):172–181.

————(1973). The Prostitute-Pimp Relationship. Medical Aspects of Human Sexuality. November:147–160.

————(1976). Ongoing research. Funded by NIDA #DA 0091801, Female Criminal Involvement and Narcotics Addiction.

Kemp, T. (1936). Prostitution: An Investigation of Its Causes, Especially with Regard to Hereditary Factors. Copenhagen: Levin and Munskgaard.

Kinsey, A.C., W. Pomeroy, and E.C. Martin (1948). Sexual Behavior in the Human Male. Philadelphia: Saunders.

Kinsey, A.C., et al. (1953). Sexual Behavior in the Human Female. Philadelphia: Saunders.

Mantegazza, P. (1935). Sexual Relations of Mankind. New York: Eugenics.

Marshall, D.S., and R.C. Suggs, eds. (1971). Human Sexual Behavior. Englewood Cliffs, N.J.: Prentice-Hall.

McDonald, J.M. (1971). Rape Offenders and Their Victims. Springfield, Ill.: Charles C Thomas.

Milner, C., and R. Milner (1972). Black Players: The Secret World of Black Pimps. Boston: Little, Brown.

National League of Cities (1974). National Conference on Rape. Washington, D.C.: National League of Cities.

Reiss, I.J. (1960). Sex Offenses: The Marginal Status of the Adolescent. Law and Contemporary Problems 25(2):309–333.

Robinson, W.J. (1929). The Oldest Profession in the World. New York: Eugenics.

Rubin, T. (1961). In the Life. New York: Macmillan.

Seattle Police Department (1975). Annual Report: 1974. Seattle, Wash.: City of Seattle.

Segal, M. (1963). Impulsive Sexuality: Some Clinical and Theoretical Observations. International Journal of Psychoanalysis 44:407–417.

Stein, M. (1974). Lovers, Friends, Slaves. New York: G. P. Putnam's Sons.

Storaska, F. (1965). How to Say No to a Rapist—and Survive. New York: Random House.

Strouse, J. (1972). To Be Minor and Female: The Legal Rights of Women under 21. Ms. December.

United Nations (1951). International Convention for the Suppression of the White Slave Traffic. New York: United Nations.

Vedder, C.B., and D.B. Sommerville (1975). The Delinquent Girl. Springfield, Ill.: Charles C Thomas.

Winick, C., and P. Kinsie (1971). The Lively Commerce: Prostitution in the United States. New York: Quadrangle Books.

Chapter Seven

Conclusion

Throughout this book we have tried to identify the social scripts which shape sexual identity and sexual behavior. We have seen that female sexuality, in its many particulars, is no brute fact of biology. Rather, its status as fact is imparted by social constructions. The "facts of life" that most people learn capture only a part of the reality which we have dealt with.

Sexual Scripts

Sexual scripts constitute the available repertoire of socially recognized acts and statuses, and roles and the rules governing them. These learned scripts become the net which the individual casts over her experience in order to capture its meaning. Thus scripts operate both at a social and at a personal level. They are embedded in social institutions and at the same time internalized by individuals. The dominant scripts receive our first attention because of their primacy and potency among people's sexual options. They carry the force of socialization. When the individual woman challenges, modifies, or rejects the sexual programming of her society, it is against the background of the dominant script. For us to ignore this scripting in seeking change is as pointless as for persons seeking economic revolution to ignore the structure and constraints of capitalism.

The scripts we have found in our survey are mainly scripts men have provided for female sexuality. Contradicting these are sexual scripts now being defined by women for women. These new scripts have to contend with the power of the traditional scripts. We have found that this power operates in two ways: through the power of naming, and through the power of sanction.

The Power of Naming

Berger and Luckmann's (1966) analysis has given us the basis for understanding the power of naming. That which is named is "real" and can be talked about. Experiences can be shared in terms of that which is named. Others can be taught to name their experience in a like way. That which is not named is not "real"; moreover, preemptive naming of some items precludes the claims of others to reality. Thus the preemptive discussion of the vaginal orgasm precluded the discussion of any other.

The selectivity of focus and language in the work of American sex researchers has repeatedly drawn our comments in the book. Some aspects of female sexuality are not given names and hence cannot be talked about; implicitly, they are treated as if they did not exist. This is the case with bodily states and products like vaginal secretions and also with feelings, like the relief and euphoria many women feel when their menstrual period starts. Other aspects of female sexuality are given names which reveal a male orientation: for example, *frigidity, foreplay, promiscuity.* Some aspects of female sexuality suffer benign neglect at the hands of the professionals: Klaich's (1974) collection of historic celebrations of love between women reveals that this sexual life-style has existed throughout the centuries, yet it sometimes appears that we have discovered it only in this generation.

Another example of the power of preemptive naming is the tendency of men to define female sexuality in terms of biology, ignoring feeling-states in terms of which women might define their own sexuality. Research cited by Parlee shows that biologically oriented scripts are given more weight than biological events. Schachter and Singer (1962) demonstrated that subjects adopted a socially-provided definition of the situation as the label for their own physiological state. Men's as well as women's self-reports reflected a biological script for "premenstrual blues" though the nonverbal reality did not conform. Here it is apparent that the script and not the biology is the determining factor.

A biological approach to sexuality also supports the Big Lie, a way of labeling children as asexual. To the extent that sexuality is described mainly in terms of hormone levels, the prepubertal person can be defined as outside the realm of the sexual. In this case, what children learn, see and feel about sex is defined out of existence.

These examples of naming fit in with the dominant heterosexual/procreative script. Those who are incapable of reproducing are defined as asexual. This holds for the postmenopausal woman as well as the prepubertal child. In our view, any "loss of femininity" in the postmenopausal woman is more likely to result from sexual rejection than from lowered estrogen levels.

The Power of Sanctions

The enforcement of sexual scripts relies on sanctions which can take the form of material constraints or social disapproval. Sanctions can consist of verbal labels; this may be as simple as the Good Girl/Bad Girl polarity or as complex as the Freudian projection of male mutilation concern onto the female. Scientists writing on such topics as menstruation seem to reveal a concern with pollution. Much of the professional writing on female sexuality appears to share a negative tone, reflecting male projections more than women's feelings about themselves.

Future Change?

Sexual scripts exist, and they are powerful. However, they are not necessarily immutable. Berger and Luckmann have described the process by which such social constructions, or scripts, become institutionalized. New sexual scripts continue to emerge from this process, as our examination of the feminist influence reveals. As situations are typified and so recognized by enough people, they become part of the sexual script. It is only within the last fifteen years that contraception has become normal behavior for unmarried women. The resulting freedom from unwanted pregnancy, in its turn, opens up additional dimensions of sexuality for many women.

The need to change the sexual scripts for women is a central concern of our book. Although there is certainly resistance, a number of societal and behavioral trends point to future change. Experience with multiple partners expands the feedback opportunities women have about their sexuality. This can help sexual identity develop and crystallize and foster reflection which in turn contributes to choice. Increasingly, fertility is becoming a contingent rather than a necessary experience for women. The development of celibacy as a principled choice signals women's reclamation of their sexual autonomy, and autonomy is essential for sexual agency. Women are insisting on control over their own sexual experiences, particularly orgasm, and rejecting the vaginal orgasm, the simultaneous orgasm, and even the "multiorgasmic" scripts. As women develop sexual agency, it becomes easier to resist the male initiation script and to substitute the idea that sexuality is an inherent and continuous aspect of women rather than something bestowed or episodically switched on by a man. The weakening of connections between sex and marriage and marriage and fertility also weakens the dominant script.

Another impetus for change comes from the women's self-help movement with regard to health. Perhaps one by-product of the women's health movement will be the development of a vocabulary for the realities which are yet unnamed. An audience has already been created for such unheard-of activities as cervical self-examination, and women are learning to use the speculum, an instrument which was once part of the physician's esoterica. The politics of the women's health movement is important for women's sexuality: instead of being done to, women are doing it themselves.

Feminist constructions of female sexuality have a number of distinctive elements, among them a concern with bringing the self back into sex. Feminist attacks on male-oriented pornography can be seen as a rejection of the sexual alienation imposed on women by this material. Celibacy may have a related meaning, for by the choice of celibacy a woman places herself and her feelings, rather than a man, at the center of her universe.

Many of the elements of female sexuality emphasized by feminists combine in the idea of sexual agent. The sexually agentic woman has the capacity to design her own sexual life. This way of functioning is antithetical to the male initiation script, which assigns the woman the role of object. The sexually agentic woman does not allow anyone else to define her sexuality, whether she is menopausal or nubile, gay or straight. She may initiate and she may select; she does not acquiesce.

The feminist influence can be seen in an emphasis on quality of sexual relationship and an insistence that quantity does not make quality. The idea that bigger is better is challenged, along with an overemphasis on intromission and coitus. A new focus on quality of relationships will lead to new research on the processes of investment and deinvestment in sexual relationships.

Feminists have taken up naming, and in so doing challenge men's names for aspects of female sexuality. Via traditional scripts, men have defined what "counts" as sexuality. Feminists are reclaiming the unnamed and the disregarded. By speaking the unspeakable and creating a community of shared meaning, they secede from the dominant scripts.

Sexual Pluralism

Although our idea of sexual scripts is very close to Berger and Luckmann's social construction, there are differences. Our view, more than theirs, emphasizes change in the individual and pluralism among coexisting sexual scripts. Our examination of the available sexual scripts supports the idea of sexual pluralism. We do find a degree of competition among sexual scripts. Each one is defined in such a way as to deny the reality of the others. Positive evaluations are tied to enactment of the dominant script, and negative evaluations or labels to other options. This array of sanctions reinforces the boundaries of the dominant script: for women, being heterosexual/monogamous/married—permanently. We have noted, too, that other sexual options appear unscripted from the vantage point of the dominant script, even though some—for example, the gay life—are largely scripted. Perhaps more to the point, *transitions* from the dominant script to variant scripts are unscripted. The function of sexual socialization, and of the sanctions surrounding the dominant script, is to keep individuals within it.

Nevertheless, the existence of pluralism implies options. The existence of options, of course, does not automatically produce awareness of options. It is this awareness which is the prerequisite for choice. We differ from Berger and Luckmann in contending that the "problem" of identity is endemic to sexual life today and that choice among sexual options is an important phenomenon.

Veevers's (1974) research on voluntarily childless couples shows that where no alternative script exists, people do not really make a choice. In the case of voluntary childlessness, couples eventually acknowledge their atypical life-style but do not recall making a choice.

We may speculate that in the future, sexual life histories will reflect choice. In a pluralistic society, individuals will be exposed to alternative scripts rather than being shielded from them. At present there appear to be options at virtually every developmental stage in the model of sexual identity presented in Chapter 2. As the hold of the dominant script over individuals' lives is weakened, changes and transitions in sexual identity will become more frequent and more accessible to study.

Sexual identity will be an even more important focus of research in the future than it has been. Extraordinary transformations of identity must be studied, in addition to the normal developmental transitions built into the script. Choices, reflecting options, are an aspect of sexual histories which have been neglected in the past. Basic questions concerning gender identity and sexual object choice remain unresearched to this day. Our examination of sexual scripts suggests why these blind spots persist in professional sex research. The presently dominant script builds discontinuities into sexual histories by disregarding or negating some aspects of the individual's experience—for example, same-sex experimentation.

The study of sexual histories will also shed light on the question of trade-offs in various sexual life-styles. Following our emphasis on fluidity, change and choice, future research will seek to explore individuals' experience with a variety of sexual life-styles. The complex trade-offs between risk and security, variety and fidelity, excitement and dullness may vary systematically across life-styles. Future research may be more truly comparative in focus and discard the framework of dominant and deviant scripts.

Private and Public Constructions of Reality

Throughout the book we have emphasized that the relationship between social constructions and personal reality is imperfect. It is a dialectical process, rather than a mirroring process. The role of choice in female sexual life-styles and sexual identity depends in part upon the individual's questioning response to the dominant script which forms the background for her own experience. The lack of fit between personal experience and sexual script means that almost all sexual histories contain lost data: experiences which do not fit the script and are not integrated into the scripted sexual identity. These experiences can be the organizing point for transformations of sexual identity.

The dialectical relationship between private and public constructions of reality is illustrated by the contemporary phenomenon of cohabitation. Individuals who opt for this sexual life-style are struggling to define it for themselves. Cohabitation is not, as some have assumed, a trial marriage or way-station in the courtship script. It is not restricted to adolescents, and it may be a permanent rather than a transitional choice. Cohabitation illustrates an aspect of sexual scripting which is often overlooked: the systematic interrelations between sexual institutions and other social institutions. Cohabitants may have distinctive economic, social, and employment patterns, as compared with singles and married couples.

In studying human sexuality, the degree of social scripting is often underestimated. Thus researchers overlook the ways in which sexuality, as an institutionalized human activity, is tied in with other social institutions. Cohabiting couples, for example, had difficulty in the past with civil institutions because of their nonmarital status. Banks would refuse mortgages to nonmarried partners, and landlords looked askance at cohabiting couples. Zoning regulations in many localities make it difficult to establish communal households. Our ways of thinking about—and providing for—women's fertility are still largely tied to the nuclear family and to marriage as a means of economic subsistence. Religious institutions have had rigid rules about sexuality and have enforced them with sanctions such as excommunication. A variety of sexual practices are outlawed in many states, and individuals can be prosecuted for their sexual behavior. The courts are currently pondering whether lesbian mothers can be fit parents. These institutional constraints on sexual behavior and sexual life-styles should not be overlooked. Particularly as we look toward change in sexual scripts for women, we should be aware that it is not enough to change what happens between consenting adults.

Future Research: An Agenda

The highlights of each of our chapters may provide an agenda for future research. Following the introduction in Chapter 1, the primary concern of Chapter 2 is the construction of sexual identity through critical periods in the life cycle. Each point in the cycle is scripted with the underlying expectation that a woman is not sexual before nubility, is only moderately sexual during marriage, and loses her sexuality after her reproductive years are over. Nonprocreative sex acts are ignored or tabooed. This observation supports Paige's (in press) description of "sexual pollution taboos." Menstruation, postpartum, and menopause are seen as nonerotic incidents in a woman's life. These are infertile times, and sex during these periods would have to be recreational. As recreational sex has become more acceptable, such taboos have become less operational. But it is important for us to remember that the sexuality of a woman is still associated with her fecundity.

Chapter 2 points out the dynamic rather than static nature of sexuality. In reviewing the stages Laws describes, one gets an overall sense that there is an extraordinary amount of "lost" data on childhood. Childhood sexuality and private sexuality (masturbation, fantasy) are not studied. Same-sex experimentation is assumed to be nonexistent. Sexuality that does not fit into the marriage script is left unresearched.

The stage of "nubility" and puberty is one of particular poignance. Marketability in the marriage exchange is important, and in this period a woman begins to learn what her chances are. She becomes extremely aware of her selling points and her deficiencies. There is little research on the impact of these discoveries, but we assume they have great meaning to the individual. The research on body image is sparse and more is needed. Women believe socialite Babe Paley's dictum that "the most important thing in the world is to be slim, beautiful, and rich," and yet most fail to meet these standards. How much does this have to do with problems of low self-esteem and negotiations of courtship? More research is needed.

As the female becomes involved in sexual interaction, it becomes apparent that her sexual adequacy is to be judged by her acceptance and experience with men. A woman who has not had intercourse is seen as virginal—i.e., pure, although she may have had extensive masturbatory and petting experience. Nonetheless we use male standards of sexual initiation, in this case, intromission of the penis in the vagina, to define a woman's sexuality. This theme continues in our use of the word *foreplay*. Foreplay assumes coitus is the essential event. But there is no foreplay to lesbians. If women had the power to script sexual interaction, foreplay might be called the main event, and intercourse a nice specialty in sexual enjoyment.

Laws shows how each sexual act is tied into marriage. Yet she points out that the family itself is desexualized. The incest taboo exists because there *is* some sexual undercurrent to parent-child relationships, but we do not want to study those issues.

Likewise we see that the older woman is underscripted and understudied. Her sexuality is only a joke. If a woman is wedded to the script that men initiate, chances are her sexual contact will decrease with age. Changing scripts may allow older women to initiate sexual activity and lead lives that are more sexually satisfying. We do not know much about the sexually agentic woman at any point in the life cycle, and we must know more.

Overall, Laws leaves us with several major points to think about: First, sexual identity formation and sexual object choice are central problems. The formation of sexual identity is a problem for everyone, and we know little about that process. Second, there are discontinuities in sexual histories, and we have not studied these discontinuities. Researchers have been guided by scripts rather than raw data. Third, at all points women learn to interpret their sexuality with reference to men. A woman is dependent on her first lover for information about herself. Men control the definition of the situation, and this *power of naming* controls the social construction of female sexuality.

In Chapter 3 Parlee questions how female sexuality has been researched—and underresearched—this time in regard to body processes. In her discussion of menstruation she uncovers the systematic bias in both empirical and conceptual organization of the topic. For example, there is no study on feelings of joy during the menstrual cycle; studies are geared toward premenstrual and menstrual depression and mood swings. Menstruation is not viewed as a happy event.

Parlee argues that the social context of pregnancy, birth, and postparturition has been ignored. We do not know what is happening in women's lives during these events and cannot say how the physiological affects the social and vice versa. The observation here that pregnancy is viewed as stigma suggests a number of interesting questions. A pregnant woman changes the context of the environment she is in. We do not know how people are reacting or what they are thinking, but a pregnant woman is given special status. We should do research on aspects of female sexuality as stigma. How does knowing a woman is menstruating affect interaction? How does knowing a woman is pregnant affect sexual arousal?

There is not enough psychological research on changes during pregnancy. The present research treats pregnancy as a linear effect, as if the first trimester is like the second trimester is like the last. Over the course of the pregnancy, there are bodily changes, and reactions to the pregnant woman change. As the reactions change, she responds to those reactions. Research needs to reflect this degree of sophistication. It is only to the nonpregnant person that the first three months seem like the last three months.

There are other major gaps. We do not know much about critical periods of interaction of the mother and father with the child after birth. Might it be the pollution taboos that stifle research?

Parlee reminds us that menopause is an unscripted area of behavior. A woman who is past being a mother is not supposed to be sexual: we do not give her an identity. Any role crisis precipitated by this nonstatus is usually lumped under the term *mid-life crisis* and blamed on hormones. Biological perspectives have monopolized these research topics.

Parlee's important points are these: The analysis of woman's body is mainly organized around negative stereotyping. There is a great deal of selectivity in what is studied and what questions are asked. Again, we are confronted with the politics of naming. The micro-events of a woman's life are not seen as important, and therefore they are treated as if they do not exist. This does not really fit the social data we have, but the research on biological functioning does not confront this contradiction. Parlee pinpoints many specific research issues and failings.

In Chapter 4, Laws analyzes the common elements of sexual transactions, beginning with courtship. The most important idea about courtship scripts is their framework of "going somewhere" as opposed to "going nowhere" (Libby, 1976). Dating is organized toward marriage or exploitation, and there is not too much in between. If the relationship is "going nowhere," the male may still want sexual access because that has value for him outside an affectional relationship. The female does not want to give sexual access in a "nowhere" relationship since it does not help her gain the man for marriage and it may damage her marriage market value under the double standard. Dating takes place in a scarcity economy. The risk of being classified as a "bad woman" is to be avoided. A woman wants to be rare and valued. The script discourages her from being sexually agentic—from having a lot of sexual experience during courtship. She must be sexy enough to attract but not so easy as to lose her "good girl" status.

This tightrope becomes harder to walk these days because sex is more expected, yet sexual access in and of itself does not define the relationship. It is a dilemma for the female: she must judge how much to give and how much not to give. No script gives her good directions for this central problem of contemporary courtship and contemporary adolescence. There is an important research issue here. We know young adolescents are sexually active. What are their scripts for what they are doing and why they are doing it? We have not asked these questions, and we do not know their answers.

We need to know more about the way women organize emotions during courtship and how it differs from men. Hochschild (1975) has hypothesized that women regard emotions as an investment to be nurtured as a growth stock and men do not. How does this structure relationships? If women place a different emphasis on emotional stock, they treat relationships differently, whether investing (courtship-marriage) or deinvesting (breaking up–divorce). We need some empirical research here.

There is not much research on how people make the transition between dating values and marriage values. No one has studied the effects on the first year of marriage from various courtship backgrounds.

Laws shows how the double standard permeates different types of sexual transactions. Transactions are always organized by the right of the male to define the situation. Men keep the advantage in a number of ways. One is the fact that men share sexual information, whereas women protect their reputation by keeping quiet about their experience. They deny each other alternative sources of information.

It is important to view American courtship as a very special institution. It begins early and may be renewed at different points in the life cycle because of death or divorce. It has highly scripted behaviors and yet we do not know much about the costs of various scripts (e.g., going steady) or about the transaction costs of unscripted behavior. We need to explore the long-term effects of dating training on intimate relationships.

In Chapter 5 Schwartz describes and discusses sexual life-styles. A sexual life-style comes into being because the choice of a style of sexual interaction necessarily organizes other parts of one's life. Marriage is analyzed as the major script for women. When a woman chooses an alternative life-style she has to consciously reject marriage; she cannot ignore it. No woman escapes having to deal with the fact that society expects her to marry. Furthermore, if a woman has enough information to reject marriage, she still may lack the information she needs in order to make an intelligent alternate choice. She is denied other scripts.

The script for marriage, however, has changed. Women can now support themselves outside marriage and therefore can divorce more easily. Since marriage is no longer essential for economic survival, more stress may be placed on sentiment. When the major motif is sentiment, the marriage may be more likely to break up. As a result, we may see a new script for marriage, one of open-ended term contracts rather than vows to stay together "until death do us part."

Within marriage we are once again confronted with the fact that women are not allowed to be the sexual initiator. This may have an effect on the frequency and quality of sex in marriage. Since direct action is illegitimate, women may have to resort to more subtle manipulations of their husband. This gives rise to stereotypes common to oppressed peoples, such as "sneaky" or "scheming."

Women are expected to be available to their husband and "good in bed." They are caught in a sexual revolution that has not yet brought about the extinction of the double standard. For some wives, this means they have to be good and bad at the same time.

In extramarital relationships, risk may be reduced for women because of the presence of a husband. This is particularly true in consensual adultery, but it may also be true in "cheating" as long as the husband does not find out. Even in the latter case, the wife may still be protected by others in order to protect her husband from a loss of face and her family from possible disorganization. If she is discreet, society is interested in helping her keep up appearances.

One type of comarital sex is swinging. Swinging is an innovative way to protect marriage and include sexual variety. It is important because it illustrates that merely breaking the rule of monogamy will not weaken the dominance of the marriage script.

As we review various forms of sexual options, the problems of managing these life-styles without scripts becomes obvious. For example, cohabitation may superficially look like marriage, but it is quite different. There are competing constructions of what it really means—both to public audiences and to the cohabiting couple. They may feel they are to be treated as a unit, or they may not. There is no script to guide them. Most of the research that has been done on cohabitation does not provide useful scripts because almost all of it describes the living arrangements of college students who have developed a very special kind of cohabitation. It is a *premarital* form of living together. We need to know more about people who have lived their lives together without the benefits or disadvantages of legal sanctions.

Likewise, there is no good research on sexual abstinence, planned single motherhood, and voluntary childlessness. These areas are almost entirely unscripted or involve contradictory scripts. The single woman is not supposed to have children.

The lesbian life-style is of course absent from the dominant female script. Once a woman does find her way into a gay subculture, there are scripts provided there. Bisexuals, however, have no support group and no script to organize their life-style. There is a straight script, and there is a gay script; but there is nothing between the two. The very idea of intermediate sexual status is a troubling one to most people. People like to categorize themselves and others. Bisexuals disorient the normal taxonomy.

This chapter emphasizes the relative lack of information about any life-styles but marriage and the negative images of single life-styles for women. Quality and quantity of sex are different issues in all kinds of relationships for women, but this is a female, more than a male, concern. Quality for men may more often be fused with the concept of quantity. However, unless they are able to initiate sexual interaction, many women will have difficulty attaining the quality desired in their sex life.

We appear to have no research on sexual abstinence. One of the reasons may be that women who are practicing it as a principled life-style are not talking about it. Celibacy may be an assertion of privacy in one's sexual life. One of the prerequisites for sexual agency is autonomy. Celibacy is one way of reclaiming autonomy—by not being sexually available to anyone. It is a rejection of alienation. The extent to which this may be seen as an option by many women—for long or short periods of time—is yet to be seen.

In Chapter 6, James discusses institutional responses to female sexuality and women as criminals and victims. In discussing prostitution James offers a definition broader than the commonly accepted one. As James defines it, "any sexual exchange where the reward is neither sexual nor affectional is prostitution." The parallels to marriage and other kinds of relationships are obvious.

James notes that prostitution is only prosecuted when it is not subtle. If a woman protects the legitimacy of societal scripts by not flaunting her trespass of them, she may be allowed to continue prostituting herself. It seems that it is the appearance, not the reality, which is most important. Indeed, the paradox is that, since men are supposed to have uncontrollable sexual appetites, there must be some women to accommodate these men. The marriage relationship is not sufficient: there must be some group outside of wives who are available. On the other hand, this group must not be so large as to create a great number of unattached females who might come to possess a degree of sexual agency. Thus prostitution must be limited enough to protect the script of female sexuality but not so much so that prostitutes are no longer available to men. Prostitution does not transgress the sexual scripts of men. It is not surprising, then, that the customer is not prosecuted.

Many women become prostitutes for the sake of money and adventure. It is interesting that prostitution is one of the best options society can offer women who want to earn big money and live their own life. Prostitutes, however, are not exempt from the female script. They incorporate traditional role relationships with men via their connection with a pimp. Prostitutes still want a man to handle their business relationships, to give them love, and to "understand" them. They want respect for their work, and only someone in the "life" can do that for them. Thus they buy into a protection racket, because they need the pimp to protect them from other pimps and people who might want a slice of their profits. This is not unlike women who go steady or marry because at least then they do not have to contend with the same kind of sexual assault from as many men. Men are likely to respect each other's territory and property. So any man—even a scrap of a man—is necessary for respect.

In discussing juvenile delinquency, James notes that sex becomes an issue in labeling young girls as "incorrigible." This does not happen to young boys. The latter are never incarcerated *before* commission of a crime because of "sexual waywardness."

Women are discussed as victims. Rape is another Catch-22. A good woman cannot be raped; if she is, she is not a good woman. Women are blamed for being sexual. In order to protect themselves from accusations of complicity, they are expected to stay in at night, not talk to strangers, and refuse to hitchhike. A long list of such restrictions soon becomes a canon of social control. The victims are held accountable for the victimization.

Rape is also described within the normal script for male socialization. Men are taught to avoid being "sissy." Things female are devalued. One must avoid placement in female categories. What better way of showing contempt for the female sex role and female sexuality than rape?

The victim is also punished in cases of child abuse and incest. The child in such cases is frequently taken out of the family. This "preserves" the family. There is no research on the impact of this expulsion on the child, but it seems reasonable to assume that the child feels punished.

James shows the continuities between prostitution and other male-female relationships and the negative feelings about female sexuality which are directly related to rape, blaming a child for incest or molestation, and the incarceration of female adolescents.

A Challenge to the Reader

Many readers will reject the scripts we have anatomized in these pages. Though these scripts are embedded in the social institutions of our time and define reality for large groups of people, individuals may feel that they can repudiate them and live happily ever after. The strength of sexual scripts can best be tested by trying to counter or change them. As a first step, we invite the reader to invert some of the major sexual scripts in imagination.

For example: Women judges define sexual crimes. Young boys are sentenced to correctional facilities for heavy petting. Men convicted of sexist behavior at professional meetings are fined and a misdemeanor entered on their record. Repeated offenses make a man ineligible to hold elective office, vote, or own property. Men who are found guilty of taking a woman's no for a yes are remanded to compulsory psychiatric evaluation.

Men who tempt women, of whatever age, are incarcerated as incorrigible sexual delinquents. Rapists, the most loathed criminal category, rarely make it to trial but are often found mysteriously hanged or stabbed to death in their cells.

Or: The female peer group monitors and tests the sexual performance of eligible males. Their strengths and weaknesses as lovers and companions are evaluated and recommendations made as to their potential for further training. Women are the arbiters of both beauty and sexual competence, and there is no appeal. Bad performance or bad behavior is sanctioned, either directly by the women, or through social pressure from their men. Because of the high regard women have for each other, they delight in selecting special gifts (males) and bestowing them on their friends. Due to the pressure of their many responsibilities, women cannot afford the time to discover and woo males with promise. Often the screening and selection must be done by their friends or agents. The man who is beautiful and adept can often establish himself comfortably before his charms fade. Of course, with the decline in marriage, a permanent arrangement is becoming increasingly rare.

And: Older women, by virtue of their power and experience, command the greatest selection of men. Although they are sometimes abrupt and even selfish in arranging their own pleasure, it is an honor (and often economically advantageous) to be seen with one of them. A man so selected moves among a better class of people, and even though the association may be temporary, valuable contacts may result. One in a million makes an advantageous or a happy marriage via this route.

Inevitably, some women exploit this all too natural situation. The female pimp, though she tends to be a pillar of the community and active in philanthropic causes, does sell male flesh. The men in her stable are pathetically dependent on her for self-esteem as well as protection and, of course, business. She exploits their only talent, but the burden of managing their finances and even the simplest decisions falls on her. Although this profession raises a few eyebrows, the pimp's work is not pure profit. She has heavy responsibilities and cares for her charges, no doubt, better than they could fend for themselves.

Of course many of our women, with somewhat nobler values, invest in the institution of marriage. Often these women are capable of sincere and altruistic love, as can be seen by the way they check their own passions and gently lead their partners into greater sexuality. Many young men enter marriage with undeveloped ideas about sexuality and must be trained away from the immature habits of thrusting and ejaculation. It is usually up to the wife to determine when and how often marital sex is to occur, as well as the forms it is to take. She must initiate and guide the whole encounter, and often she must be extraordinarily sensitive in order to determine when her partner is receptive. Some men are virtually lacking in sexual feeling and must be coaxed into love-making by their partner. The wives of such men are not to be envied, and their natural sexual drive oftentimes must find a more vigorous outlet outside of marriage. Sometimes the only help for such marriages is for the husband to seek professional aid in overcoming his frigidity.

The sexual exploitation of men has become a commonplace of advertising. The display of male allure helps sell many products unrelated to sex. A lucrative subspecialty consists of aids to men which will increase their resemblance to the models and movie stars and help them inspire the same reaction in their partners. It is sad, but true, that the enhancement of male beauty benefits us all by enhancing our sexual lives.

References

Berger, P., and T. Luckmann (1966). The Social Construction of Reality. Garden City, N.Y.: Doubleday.

Hochschild, A. (1975). Attending to, Codifying, and Managing Feelings: Sex Differences in Love. Paper presented at the annual meeting of the American Sociological Association.

Klaich, D. (1974). Woman and Woman: Attitudes toward Lesbianism. New York: Morrow.

Libby, R. (1976). Social Scripts for Sexual Relationships. *In* Sexuality Today and Tomorrow: Contemporary Issues in Human Sexuality. S. Gordon and R. Libby, eds. N. Scituate, Mass.: Duxbury Press.

Paige, K. (in press). Sexual Pollution: Reproductive Sex Taboos in American Society. Journal of Social Issues.

Schachter, S., and J.E. Singer (1962). Cognitive, Social and Physiological Determinants of Emotional State. Psychological Review 69:379–399.

Veevers, J. (1974). Voluntarily Childless Wives: An Exploratory Study. *In* Pronatalism: The Myth of Mom and Apple Pie. E. Peck and J. Senderowitz, eds. New York: Crowell.

Index